PEACEMAKING CREATIVELY THROUGH THE ARTS:

A Handbook of Educational Activities and Experiences for Children

Phyllis Vos Wezeman

Illustrated by Judith Harris Chase.

PEACEMAKING CREATIVELY THROUGH THE ARTS:
A Handbook of Educational Activities
and Experiences for Children

by Phyllis Vos Wezeman

Copyright © 1990
EDUCATIONAL MINISTRIES, INC.

ISBN 1-877871-01-X

EDUCATIONAL MINISTRIES, INC.
2861-C Saturn Street
Brea, CA 92621

Dedication

To David R. Woollcombe
...and the people of the Peace Child Foundation.

For most of my life I felt that peacemaking was someone else's responsibility. It was the task of the President, the Congress, and the Department of State. Most of the grass-roots peacemaking activities I witnessed seemed to be protests or demonstrations, and I did not feel comfortable participating in them.

When confronted, in 1985, with the challenge of producing a play, Peace Child, for The United Religious Community and the Family and Children's Center, I said, "No." Knowing how much work would be involved in such a project, coupled with the fact that I was not a peacemaker, seemed sufficient cause for such a decision. However, through a series of unexpected and almost unexplainable events, I undertook the task. It was a life-changing experience. Through the course of preparing and presenting this play, I came to realize that peacemaking was my role and my responsibility.

The conclusion of the play began the start of a search to find positive, creative ways in which to empower children to become peacemakers. This handbook is a result of that endeavor.

Thank you, David, for writing Peace Child, and for the important part you, Rosey, and the people and programs of the Foundation play in my life.

Special Thanks To:

The people who have served on the United Religious Community's "Peace Is Possible" Committee for Inspiration, Insight and Ideas for this project:

Karen Anderson	Margaret Kenney
Mary Beth Byrne	Melva Martin
Paul Chilcote	Carol McKiel
Lois Clark	Pauline Mudas
Jacqueline Dickey	Martha Payne
Larry Dwyer	Tom Petersen
Sondra Engel	Sara Webb Phillips
Anita Fishman	Art Quigley
Bruce Haapalainen	Alberta Ross
Jean Harris	Judy Shalkowski
Roberta Hill	Joan Sniadecki
Jeff Iacobazzi	Richard Spleth
Loretta Jancoski	Ted Stanley
Angie Jerney	Lynette Sumpter
Tom Jones	Janice Sutter
Kathy Keener-Han	John Tryon
Leroy Kennel	Colleen Wiessner

To the United Religious Community staff for dedication and direction:

Dr. James Fisko
Maggie Mitchell Dyskiewicz
Jodie Bilinski
Rose Bond
Lynne Czosnowski
Mary Linley
Sharon Morgan
Fran Rinehart
Rosemary Wells
Yolanda Wilder

To Dr. Charles DuVall for the simple word "Go" which prompted a volume.

To Judith Harris Chase for the excellent illustrations.

To Educational Ministries, Inc. for permission to adapt six "Peacemaking Creatively..." articles I originally wrote for Church Educator, September 1989 through March 1990.

To my husband, Ken, for not only typing a mammoth manuscript, but for enabling and encouraging.

To my children, Stephanie, David and Paul, for commitment and care.

Table Of Contents

CHAPTER ONE

OVERVIEW

The Problem

We live in an unpeaceful time. People of all ages, and especially children, are surrounded by violence on several levels. Many come from homes where abuse, physical, sexual or emotional, is a common occurrence.[1] Some live in neighborhoods where conflict is the rule rather than the exception. Nearly all live in communities where unrest is the theme of much of the news reporting. On a national level, there is war and the threat of war, both conventional and nuclear.[2] In the international sphere, there are reports, accompanied by pictures, of riots and fighting in many parts of the world. In short, we are surrounded by destruction and the threat of violence.

All of us must cope with the brutality of the age. If we are to be truly human, however, we must do more than cope. We must do all we can to change our homes, our neighborhoods, our communities, our nation and our world. We must work to make the world less violent and our homes less destructive to the human spirit. Our goal, however, should be to attain peace that is more than the absence of war and violence. This kind of peace is connoted by the Hebrew word Shalom. This is a view of peace as wholeness and well-being. This concept is characterized by Lorne Peachey when he writes, "The peace, then, to which we [aspire] is more than a passive concept: the absence of conflict or war. It is rather learning the values of reconciliation and problem-solving, of justice and love, of establishing proper relationships without as well as a sense of well-being within."[3] This work cannot begin with adults, for by the time one reaches adulthood most of our personality characteristics and our life-long attitudes are formed. As Gandhi said, "If we are to reach real peace in this world, and if we are to carry on a real war against war, we shall have to begin with the children."[4]

The Potential

Children need to explore and experience a variety of peacemaking themes and concepts in a positive and creative manner. Joanna Rogers Macy, in Despair and Personal Power in the Nuclear Age, writes, "It is, therefore, not sufficient to discuss the present crisis on the informational level alone, or seek to arouse the public to action by delivering ever more terrifying facts and figures. Information by itself can increase resistance, deepening the sense of apathy and powerlessness. We need to help each other process this information on an affective level, if we are to digest it on the cognitive level."[5] The arts are a useful means toward achieving this goal. Artistic media can help children to imagine a world at peace. The arts can help children go beyond imagining the world at peace as well. As Duane Sweeney writes, "...students [are] stimulated to begin acquiring the knowledge and skills they will need to play a part in shaping the future they envision.... They [are] encouraged to create fresh solutions and express their own ideas."[6] Thus, by unleashing the creative imagination, children can find hope for the future. Through artistic expression children can also participate in finding solutions to the difficult problems they face as they seek peace in all aspects of life.

The Possibilities

This resource is a handbook of creative activities and exercises to enable children to explore and experience nine peacemaking themes:

- Peace with Self
- Peace in the Family
- Peace in the Congregation
- Peace in the School
- Peace in the Neighborhood
- Peace in the Community
- Peace in the State
- Peace in the Nation
- Peace in the World

Each section contains an introduction to the theme and one or more activities using each of the following art forms:

- Architecture
- Art
- Banners/Textiles
- Cartoons
- Clown/Mime
- Creative Writing
- Culinary Arts
- Dance
- Drama
- Games

- Music
- Photography
- Puppetry
- Storytelling

An overview of each art form and its application to peace education is provided in this chapter.

An extensive annotated bibliography, containing a listing of reference and activity resources, as well as books to further expand each art form, is included.

The Purpose

A purpose, or goal statement, is included at the beginning of each of the over two hundred activities. While these statements are specific to each particular exercise, the purpose of all of the activities may be summarized in the following phrases:

- To heighten positive self-esteem in children.

- To give substance to the concept of peace.

- To portray peacemaking in active rather than passive ways.

- To inspire and excite children about peacemaking.

- To enhance young people's ability to think creatively and to apply it to peacemaking situations.

- To identify processes and skills of peacemaking.

- To explore concepts of peace.

- To promote non-violent conflict resolution.

- To teach methods of attaining peace within all spheres of life.

- To use the Bible's teachings, and Jesus' example, as a guide for life.

The Participants

Although the activities are intended for use with children in grades one through six, they may be easily adapted for use with any age group. They also provide the opportunity for working with multiple age groups. "Older children can help the younger ones with the tasks. Younger children can share their excitement and sense of wonder with the older ones. Older children can increase their understanding of the concepts by explaining them to the younger ones, which helps the younger ones, too. Young people who may feel 'too old' to participate in the activities may benefit from helping to direct a younger group in their completion." [7]

While the activities are particularly geared for use by religious educators, teachers in public, private and parochial settings will find them an excellent way to educate children about peace in positive, creative ways. They may also be used in families as well as church and community youth clubs.

Procedure

The activities are designed to involve the student as an active participant in learning rather than a passive recipient of information. The more the student is engaged in the process, the more powerful will be the effect upon his or her life.

The exercises should be adapted to meet the learning abilities of the students. They have been designed as guides rather than lesson plans so that they can be used in many contexts.

The materials used in the experiences are readily available or easily obtainable. The amount of time necessary for completion of each procedure has not been indicated as it will depend upon the way in which the activity is used. Some require advance preparation. This is clearly indicated in the directions.

This book can be used in more than one way. The themes may be explored in sequence as a peace curriculum or the activities for a particular art form, such as music, may be utilized to enhance existing lesson plans. Alternatively, exercises may be selected to supplement other learning materials.

14

Overview of the Arts

ARCHITECTURE

Architecture is an important, but often over-looked, medium to use as a method for introducing children to and involving them in peacemaking activities. Topics to consider range from energy sources to ethnic heritages, landscaping to land use, and neighborhood renewal to national monuments.

Explore architecture to build new awareness of both short term and long term peacemaking possibilities. A suggested design for an activity using this art form is provided for each theme.

ART

Two activities involving the medium of art are included for each theme. The specific methods suggested emphasize craft, drawing, painting and paper techniques. Additional experiences including art are spread liberally throughout the book. For example, a creative writing exercise suggests having children draw or paint their feelings, the banner and textile section contains complete instructions which incorporate batik into a project, and several of the storytelling activities offer art related suggestions to reinforce comprehension or to provide closure.

The activities and exercises offered under the theme "art" are only a starting point. Any art technique, such as pottery or print-making, papier-maché or plaster molding, can have a peace application added to it. Resources on the native and national arts of many countries are available in libraries. Works of world-renowned artists, in all media, may be found in museums.

Art projects offer an excellent way to help children develop peace awareness, but more importantly, they provide an opportunity for children to explore and express their feelings. Art does more than educate people for peace, it releases the creative potential that is needed to make peace possible.

ART: DRAW YOUR DREAM OF PEACE

To a child, a world at peace might seem like an unattainable goal. The threat of nuclear war and the annihilation of all people plague some children's thinking.[8]

One way for a young person to contribute to a world at peace is to imagine what such a place would be like. Once conceptualized, the child can then begin to work towards that goal. The art activity "Draw Your Dream of Peace" provides an opportunity for children to visualize concepts of peace.

The illustrations provided for each theme are based on drawings from a community art exhibit sponsored by Martin's Super Markets and the United Religious Community (U.R.C.) in South Bend, Indiana. Children drew their dreams of peace on entry forms printed on brown paper grocery bags which were available in twelve stores. More than nineteen hundred entries were received. They were displayed in the markets as well as at several community events. A slide-tape show, illustrating various peace concepts, and traveling exhibits were produced.

The drawing samples, adapted with the permission of the U.R.C., and the discussion suggestions provide a starting point for helping children not only illustrate their own dreams of peace, but also for identifying ways the dreams can become reality.

BANNERS/TEXTILES

Banner and textile projects, with and without words, can proclaim messages pertaining to themes ranging from peace with self through peace in the world.

Banners may be constructed from almost any fabric, even paper. The type of material is often determined by whether the piece will be used inside or outside. Color, a critical factor in the impact a banner will make, should be a consideration in selecting the material. The design can be sewn on by hand or machine, or glued in place.

The space in which a banner will hang determines the size of the piece. In a small space, use a banner that will not look crowded. In a large space, make sure it is large enough to be seen. Hang the banner on a dowel or curtain rod, broom handle or wire.

Suggested places to display banners are:

CONGREGATIONS
- Sanctuary
- Classrooms
- Social Hall
- Entrance/foyer/narthex

SCHOOLS
- Classrooms
- Gym
- Hallways

PUBLIC BUILDINGS
- Offices
- Empty store front windows

COMMUNITIES
- Banner poles on street
- Community parades
- Hunger walks

HOME
- Inside
- Outside
  - by family
  - by neighborhood

The banner and textile suggestions for the nine themes range from items that can be made by individuals or groups and include many techniques, such as patchwork and weaving. Fabric based activities are also included.

CARTOONS

Funnies. Comics. Cartoons. Regardless of what they are called, these drawings and depictions, illustrations and images, sketches and symbolizations provide an opportunity to help children consider an issue or communicate an idea. The activities included in the nine themes involve exploring existing cartoons or designing new ones. Use these entertaining, yet educational, messages in ways that will contribute to comic relief while causing careful reflection.

CLOWN/MIME

"Throughout history the clown has presented the truth of life in exaggerated, fantastic ways. The clown tears people from the ignorance of their human condition, pulls them into the spectrum of fantasy and thrusts them in front of a mirror of life." [9] Clown and mime are wonderful media to use to communicate peace and justice concerns. Through involvement with these fresh, fun approaches, people can begin to comprehend and respond to serious, complicated issues.

A clown or mime activity is included for each theme. Some are simple exercises while others are serious skits. Ideas are provided for Quick Clowns, Kindness Klowns and Community Clowns. Techniques and tips, how-to's and hints, and make-up and mannerism methods are given in the various activities.

CREATIVE WRITING

Writing activities and projects can be used to help students discover and develop creative, yet concrete, ways to address themes of peace and justice. The techniques and topics to consider are unlimited. The expression of ideas and emotions should be emphasized rather than the mastery of mechanics. The concentration should be on content instead of form. Assistance may be offered in spelling, punctuation and grammar if a child requests it or if a final editing is necessary.

Creative writing activities may be adapted to the age and abilities of the students. Include younger children in projects by having them dictate their ideas to an older pupil or to an adult, or by providing tape recorders into which they may speak their sentences and stories.

Positive, creative, experiential activities are suggested for the nine themes of this book. The ideas are intended to enable teachers, pastors, leaders and parents to help children expand and express their peacemaking potential. The ideas may be combined to develop one lesson or they may be used individually in a variety of ways.

CREATIVE WRITING: POETRY

"Words that stir the imagination, that speak to the senses, that move us deeply and strongly — such words are part of the secret of good poetry."[10] Not only does this sentence from a children's literature textbook describe a characteristic of poetry, it also provides reasons why poetry is an effective peacemaking tool. The imagination of children must be stirred so they can commit to and work powerfully for peace. The rhyme and rhythm, and the variety of styles of poetry, make this a particularly attractive art form to use with youth. Young people enjoy hearing the compositions of others and also writing their own work.

Ideas and activities to help children explore peacemaking, creatively, through poetry, are provided for the nine themes of this book.

CULINARY

Focusing on food is an experiential and educational way to help children explore concepts ranging from peace with self through peace in the world. Issues such as hunger awareness, stewardship of God's gifts, multi-cultural understanding and cooperation can be addressed in taste pleasing and thought provoking ways.

The activities suggested for the nine themes are intended to help young people become more aware of the customs and cultures of people around the world. They are also designed to challenge the participants to realize that choosing foods which are good for them and that require less energy to grow, process and prepare will result in stewardship of the world's limited resources and, therefore, more food for all people.

The story of the Feeding of the Five Thousand, John 6:1-13, illustrates not only Jesus' use of food as a teaching tool, but also the importance he places on sharing with and caring for others.

Additional information on hunger would supplement the ideas suggested and may be obtained from many of the resources and organizations listed in the bibliography.

DANCE

"Dance has the power to renew - to enliven - to draw a people together. Dancing people are people who can shake off the failures and disappointments of life, feel the Spirit quicken within them, and face the future with hope."[11] Dance, therefore, is a powerful medium to use in peace education. Symbolic expression of the human body sometimes reaches the hearts and souls of people more effectively than spoken or sung messages.

A traditional form of worship in the early Christian Church, dance can be used in conjunction with readings, songs and prayers to raise the level of spiritual awareness about peace issues. Used in education, it can help children explore and experience a variety of themes and concepts.

Dance is available to everyone. Inexperienced and trained dancers can share equally in creating movements and pieces that range from simple to elaborate, from concrete to abstract. A learning activity using dance is provided for each theme.

DRAMA

Drama is a powerful method to use to educate about peace. Lauren Friesen's article "Teaching Peace Through Drama" suggests reasons why this is true. "As the plot unfolds, the audience responds with understanding or confusion. As the characters develop before their eyes, viewers begin to recognize themselves, their families, neighbors, or forgotten friends. In the scenery, the spectators see their own houses, apartments, villages, or cities. The difficulties of characters and the changes in plot bring out many emotions, attitudes and personal struggles within the audience. Any sensitive viewer must consider the complexity of human relationships, the value of human dignity and the peaceful or violent consequences of human actions. The story on stage does not present an escape from reality, but rather an unfolding of events which are common and true to humanity."[12]

Producing drama is in itself a peacemaking project. Whether it is simple or elaborate, a group cooperates together to write a script, rehearse lines, build scenery, hang lights, produce costumes, design make-up, and much more. There are many parts which make up the whole.

In the nine themes, different methods for using drama are offered. They range from acting out stories of peacemakers through various techniques to preparing and presenting short scenes and situations on peace concerns and concepts. Information on plays students may produce, or adults may perform for pupils, is also suggested for each section.

GAMES

"In playing games, we can recapture some of the fun of learning. Injustice and inhumanity themselves are not fun, they are extremely sobering, but discovering the reasons for them need not be. So often people feel uncomfortable and guilty when they look at these issues; they don't want to have to think about them. But if they can enjoy themselves while learning about serious issues, they are more likely to think about them more positively and more often." [13]

People of all ages and abilities can enjoy and learn from games. They are a good way to mix people, and in the process, to strengthen friendships and relationships.

The current emphasis in games is on cooperation rather than competition. When people work together, instead of against each other, the elements of advantage and the fear of being eliminated are removed. Each player tends to feel good about himself or herself and these feelings are shared with other players.

The games suggested for the nine themes can be led by people with no prior experience or particular expertise. They do not require expensive equipment or time consuming preparation. All encourage cooperation between the participants.

MUSIC

Learn a song from the continent of Africa. Try an instrument from a country in Europe. Attend a concert of music from Australia. Listen to a record with the lively rhythms of South America. Play a tape of a children's choir in Asia. Write new words to a folk song popular in North America. These are just some of the ways in which music can be used to help children explore and experience peacemaking.

Music is used extensively in the worship, education and outreach ministries of a congregation. It is an art form and teaching tool which is familiar to both the educator and the pupil. Since it is a participatory learning activity, it is a good method to use to help a student discover his or her unique role as a peacemaker.

For each of the nine peacemaking themes, three ideas for using music are provided. One involves an activity incorporating music, and the other two offer many ways to use songs. A suggestion is given for adapting a familiar song to a peace message by writing new words. A list of songs with peace and justice themes is also furnished.

PHOTOGRAPHY

Taking pictures, showing films, making videos, viewing filmstrips, clipping newspaper or magazine photos... all are methods involving photography which are intended to educate, entertain, enlighten and enrich. They are methods which enable learners to explore and experience a variety of peacemaking activities and approaches.

Nine suggestions for peacemaking creatively through photography are included in this handbook. These are only a start. Develop others to meet specific curriculum needs and classroom circumstances.

PHOTOGRAPHY; MEDIA

According to Pat Gerard in the One World Week handbook, One World On Your Doorstep, "visual aids, or media, are among the most used — and abused — tools. Film, video and slides can have an immediate, powerful effect, but they will only be truly effective if proper thought is given to the context in which they are seen." [14]

There are many things to remember when showing a film. Be sure the equipment is in proper working order and that it is being operated by someone who knows how to use it and how to correct problems if something goes wrong. Preview the film before showing it. Check that everyone can both see and hear the show when it starts.

There are three basic types of media: shorts, which last up to ten minutes, medium-length, running twenty to fifty minutes, and feature films. How a film is used depends, in part, on how long it takes to show it. Shorts are useful for introducing a discussion, beginning a meeting, or as a component of a church service. Medium-length includes many films and slide/tape sets produced by agencies. Before showing one, give people a brief introduction and ask them to write down what they expect to see and feel. Following the show use these answers as part of a discussion. [15] Feature films will take up much of the program for an evening and may also be included in day-long and week-end events.

Films are available from libraries, colleges, school systems, resource centers, denominations, organizations and distributors. One film is suggested for each of the nine themes that follow. The films listed which are available from Church World Service may be obtained free of charge. Only return postage is required.

PUPPETRY

Puppetry is the art of bringing an inanimate object to "life" and communicating a message with it. This ancient medium has been used around the world to entertain, to educate and to enlighten. In Southeast Asia, shadow puppets are the tools that dramatize religious epics. In Europe, priests introduced the marionette to help people visualize Bible stories. In Africa, carved figures are devices to transmit oral history.

The ideas for the nine themes focus on puppets which can be quickly and easily constructed from low-cost or no-cost readily available items. Stress stewardship of the earth by using re-cyclable materials as much as possible. The six basic types of puppets, hand, rod, marionette, shadow, finger and body, are represented in the examples.

Two puppetry organizations emphasize and can provide material on the use of this art form as a peacemaking tool. They are:

Puppeteers of America
5 Cricklewood Path
Pasadena, CA 91107

UNIMA U.S.A.
Browning Road
Hyde Park, NY 12538

STORYTELLING

The art of storytelling has been used throughout the world for centuries. By means of this inviting, involving method, values and traditions have been passed from generation to generation.

Jesus taught in parables as a way to help people understand complex and controversial issues.

"Stories can help children develop values that encourage sensitivity to environmental and peace concerns. These stories can inform, inspire, plant hope and encourage peace." [16]

Several storytelling methods are suggested in this handbook. These include ways to help children tell their own peacemaking stories, ideas for introducing young people to peacemaking themes and concepts through this medium, suggestions for sharing this art form, as well as a few stories to tell.

STORYTELLING: CHILDREN'S BOOKS

Introducing children and youth of all ages to peace and justice concepts can be aided by the use of a very accessible and attainable tool: books. The subject matter contained in this medium scans the themes of peace with self through peace in the world.

In the introduction to the excellent resource, Building A Foundation for Peace: A Bibliography of

Peace Books for Children and Young Adults, the compiler explains ways in which peace and justice related books can be used with children of various ages. "Education is a building process starting early in life and hopefully continuing to the end of life. Books can be categorized according to reader age: Lower Elementary, Upper Elementary, Middle School and High School. The lower elementary books provide footings upon which to build as the child enters school. Most of these books promote self-esteem and love for other people. Many of the upper elementary books expand upon this concern for others and add in role models. The middle school books begin introducing a global perspective, and they also promote social action. The high school books provide a more technical perspective of the dilemmas of the nuclear age and provide direction for peace efforts. The majority of the books in this last group are very suitable for adults who are willing to examine their beliefs and convictions." [17]

Books may be read to children by adults, offered as electives, or assigned for reports. They may be obtained from libraries, resource centers, bookstores and publishers. A selection of peace books set up in a special place in the classroom or home should encourage children to explore them at their own pace.

It is, of course, recommended that teachers and parents read the books before they are made available to the children. This enables adults to be prepared to answer questions that might arise and to deal with feelings that may surface.

Five books, suitable for children in grades one through six, are suggested as resources for each of the peace themes in this volume. This is only a starting point, as numerous other titles and topics are available. Many of the books noted may also fit more than one category.

Folktales from a variety of countries are suggested as a way to help children reflect on nine peace themes. The Young Peacemakers Project Book provides a series of questions to use with children once a folktale is read or told. They include:

"What was the story about?

In what country did the story take place?

What things did you learn from the story?

What did you learn about the country?

How did the story make you feel?

Was it funny, sad, or happy? Did the story tell about life and death? What did it have to say?

Did it tell about being rich or poor, justice and injustice, or love, magic, and nature?" [18]

Folktales may be found in collections of literature from the specific country. A modern day version is provided with the activity for "Storytelling: Folktales," however, others may be located by looking up the title in the card catalog or computer listing at a library.

An excellent resource to use in conjunction with folktales is Fact, Fantasy and Folklore: Expanding Language Arts and Critical Thinking Skills. [19]

STORYTELLING: FOLKTALES

Folktales provide the oral and written traditions of people around the world. Many of these stories emphasize concepts such as cooperation, sharing and problem solving which can be used to address issues of peace.

[1]Brenner, Avis. Helping Children Cope with Stress. Lexington, MA: Lexington Books, 1984.

[2]Macy, Joanna Rogers. Despair and Personal Power in the Nuclear Age. Baltimore: New Society Publishers, 1983, 48-50.

[3]Peachey, J. Lorne. How to Teach Peace to Children. Scottdale, PA: Herald Press, 1981, 9.

[4]Gandhi, Mahatma. Quoted in Park, Mary Joan. Peacemaking for Little Friends: Tips, Lessons & Resources for Parents & Teachers. Saint Paul, MN: Little Friends For Peace, 1985, i.

[5]Macy, Joanna Rogers. Despair and Personal Power in the Nuclear Age. Baltimore: New Society Publishers, 1983, xiii.

[6]Sweeney, Duane. "Peace Child: A Play for Children." The Peace Catalog. Duane Sweeney, ed. Seattle: Press for Peace, 1984, 133.

[7]Fry-Miller, Kathleen, and Judith Myers-Walls. Young Peacemakers Project Book. Elgin, IL: Brethren Press, 1988, 4.

[8]Macy, Joanna Rogers. Despair and Personal Power in the Nuclear Age. Baltimore: New Society Publishers, 1983, 48.

[9]Robertson, Everett, ed. The Ministry of Clowning. Nashville: Broadman Press, 1983, 7.

[10]Sutherland, Zena, and May Hill Arbuthnot. "Poetry." Children and Books. 7th ed. Glenview, IL: Scott, Foresman, 1986, 275-276.

[11]Ortegal, Adelaide. A Dancing People. West Lafayette, IN: The Center for Contemporary Celebration, 1976, 1.

[12]Friesen, Lauren. "Teaching Peace Through Drama." Working for Peace: A Handbook of Practical Psychology and Other Tools. Wollman, Neil, ed. San Luis Obispo, CA: Impact Publishers, 1985, 236.

[13]Gerrard, Pat, and Tany Alexander. One World on Your Doorstep: Planners' Handbook for One World Week and Other Events. London: One World Week, 1986, 17.

[14]Gerrard, Pat, and Tany Alexander. One World On Your Doorstep: Planner's Guide for One World Week and Other Events. London: One World Week, 1986, 47, 49.

[15]Taylor, Neil, and Robin Richardson. Seeing and Perceiving: Films in a World of Change. Ipswich, Suffolk: Concord Films Council, 1977, 37.

[16]Mc Cracken, Barbara. "Teaching Peace, Teaching Justice: An Educator's Guide." National Catholic Reporter. 23 Sept. 1988, 1.

[17]Blaufuss, Deloris, comp. Building A Foundation For Peace: A Bibliography for Children and Young Adults. 2nd ed. Burlington, IA: Saint Luke United Church of Christ Peace Fellowship, 1986, introduction.

[18]Fry-Miller, Kathleen, and Judith Myers-Walls. Young Peacemakers Project Book. Elgin, IL: Brethren Press, 1988, 62.

[19]Lipson, Greta B., and Baxter Morrison. Fact, Fantasy and Folklore: Expanding Language Arts and Critical Thinking Skills. Carthage, IL: Good Apple, 1977.

CHAPTER TWO

PEACE WITH SELF

Introduction

"No peace in the world
        without peace in the nation;
No peace in the nation
        without peace in the town;
No peace in the town
        without peace in the home;
No peace in the home
        without peace in the heart." [20]

This paraphrase of poem number fifty-four from the Tao Te Ching captures the essence of all peacemaking: peace with self.

The activities and experiences in the section, "Peace With Self," focus on helping children develop a positive self-concept. Self-concept has been defined by different authors in different ways. The Young Peacemakers Project Book offers this explanation:

> *"Self-image is the objective picture people have of themselves. It includes whether people consider themselves short or tall, chubby or thin, athletic or non-athletic. It is simply a description of oneself without evaluation. Self-esteem is the evaluation a person gives to the self-image, such as too tall, too heavy or not athletic enough. Much of one's self-concept is based on the feeling of being unique and special, but not odd or weird. Self-esteem is supported by reinforcing positive evaluations of the diversity among people." [21]*

"Psychologists tell us that unless a person can value him or her self, that person cannot value someone else." [22] "The sense of feeling loved and capable lies at the root of trusting human relationships." [23]

The activities in the chapter "Peace With Self" are intended to teach and encourage a positive sense of self-worth in children, so that "peace may begin as a seed in the heart, take root in the community, grow in the nation, and flourish in the world." [24]

Architecture

PURPOSE:

To help students realize that energy conservation requires individual responsibility.

PREPARATION:

Materials
- Information on alternative energy sources
- Posterboard
- Scissors
- Glue
- Markers
- Paper
- Pencils
- Colored Pencils

Advance Preparation
- Obtain literature and materials on alternative energy sources

PROCEDURE:

Compared to people in many parts of the world, Americans tend to lead a wasteful lifestyle. This involves using more than their share of non-renewable resources and frequently polluting the environment in the process. Architecture can be one area in which a lifestyle of consumption can be changed to a lifestyle of conservation.

Help the pupils become aware of alternative construction techniques and energy sources such as solar heating and cooling, earth homes and natural landscaping. People in rural areas may also explore the use of wind driven electrical generators.

Form small groups and have each team pick a different topic on which to do research and a report. Guide the groups in choosing from the materials and developing displays to share with other people.

Once the displays are completed, pass out paper, pencils and colored pencils and give the learners an opportunity to design and draw their dream homes incorporating many of these energy- saving options. Add them to the displays.

Art

PURPOSE:

To use fingerprints as a method of emphasizing the value and uniqueness of each individual.

PREPARATION:

Materials
- Posterboard
- Paper, various colors
- Scissors
- Pens or markers
- Ink pads
- Tree branch
- Coffee can
- Rocks
- Tissue paper or fabric
- Ribbon or yarn
- Paper punch
- Tape or string
- Paper towels, dampened

Advance Preparation
- Cut leaf patterns from posterboard

PROCEDURE:

Help each child feel special by talking about the uniqueness of fingerprints. Make sure the children realize that before they were born, God made a special design on their fingers. Their design is different from everyone else's.

Make a fingerprint tree with the children. During the process, emphasize the value and uniqueness of each person. Tell them that just because leaves are not the same color or an identical shape, doesn't mean they can't belong on the same tree. Many different leaves go into making a tree beautiful. Stress that many different people contribute to making the world beautiful.

Provide leaf patterns, colored paper and scissors. Instruct the pupils to draw a leaf on their paper and to cut it out. The leaves may also be drawn free-hand. Make ink pads available and have each person press his or her thumb into the ink and then onto the leaf. Pass out damp paper towels for finger cleaning. Distribute pens or markers and have the children add their names to their leaves.

Set a tree branch into a coffee can pre-filled with rocks. Decorate the can with tissue paper or fabric which has been secured in place with ribbon or yarn. Attach the leaves to the branch and display the tree.

Talk with the children about ways in which the uniqueness of individuals contributes to a beautiful world.

Art

PURPOSE:

To help children discover and use their creative abilities.

PREPARATION:

Materials
- Food coloring, various colors
- Straws
- Scissors
- Paper, white

Advance Preparation
- Cut straws in half

PROCEDURE:

Involve the children in an art activity, breath painting,[25] to help them explore and express their creative abilities. Design the experience in a way that will aid them in understanding that their gifts and talents have great peacemaking potential and power.

Talk with the students about times they feel peaceful and things that help them feel peaceful. Comments may include walking in the woods, riding a bike, studying hard and feeling ready to take a test, or petting a kitten. Ask them to imagine the colors and shapes they associate with some of these occasions and occurrences. Give them an opportunity to share them on paper.

Demonstrate the process for breath painting. Place a sheet of white paper on a table. Use a straw and blow a few drops of food coloring across a page. Bursts may be created by holding the straw close to the paper and blowing a "t" sound through it.

Place bottles of food coloring and straws within sharing distance of the students. Give each person three sheets of paper. Invite them to paint a shade of peace on one, a shape of peace on another and a symbol of peace on the third.

Gather the children in a circle and tell them to place their pictures in front of them. Ask them to share information and insights about the project and their personal peacemaking potential.

Art:
Draw Your
Dream Of Peace

PURPOSE:

To have children draw a picture of an experience that helps them feel peaceful.

PREPARATION:

Materials
- "PEACE WITH SELF" coloring sheets
- Crayons or Markers
- Paper

Advance Preparation
- Duplicate coloring sheets

PROCEDURE:

Distribute the coloring sheets and ask the children to describe the picture. Talk about things that help them feel peaceful.

Provide crayons or markers and invite them to color their picture. When the pupils are finished, tell them to turn their papers over and to draw pictures of themselves doing something which gives them inner peace.

Art: Draw Your Dream Of Peace

On another piece of paper draw a picture of yourself doing something which helps you feel peaceful.

Banners/Textiles

PURPOSE:

To help children see hands as both tools for and symbols of peace.

PREPARATION:

Materials
- Felt squares, one per person
- Felt or fabric pieces, large
- Dowel rods, 12", one per person
- Scissors
- Pencils
- Markers, permanent
- Glue
- Yarn

PROCEDURE:

Use this banner making activity to demonstrate that peace is possible on a personal level.

Place fabric pieces, scissors, pencils, markers and glue within sharing distance of the students. Direct each child to choose a large felt or fabric scrap and to trace his or her hand onto it. Tell the boys and girls to cut out the tracings.

Have each person use a permanent marker and write his or her name in the center of the shape. Instruct them to write, in order, the letters of the word "peace" on the tops of the thumb and fingers. Ask the children to think of words, beginning with each of these letters, which describe how they can be peacemakers. More specifically, help the learners identify ways and words to illustrate how their hands can be used as peacemaking tools. These words may be written on the thumb and fingers, or just recited and remembered.

Pass out a felt square to each person and ask the pupils to glue their hand shapes to it. Demonstrate how to cut several small vertical slits near the top of the felt square for the rod and help the young people do this step. Pass out rods and offer help in sliding them through the material. Cut lengths of yarn to serve as hangers and give one to each child to tie to the sides of his or her rod.

Gather the group in a circle, join hands, and pray that each person may be used in a powerful way as a peacemaker.

Cartoons

PURPOSE:

To afford children the opportunity to design a personal peace graphic.

PREPARATION:

Materials
- Paper
- Pencils
- Markers
- Newspapers
- Magazines
- Items with peace designs, such as buttons, posters, tee-shirts, bumper stickers

PROCEDURE:

In the chapter "The Arts In Peacemaking," author Ingrid Rogers writes of inserting cartoons or peace symbols into her correspondence.[26] Invite each student to design a personal peace graphic to use on the outside of envelopes, the bottom of letters, or the inside of cards. Tell them to think of what they make as part of their signature for peace. The drawing may even incorporate a name. Indicate that the graphics may be comical or serious.

Explore themes for these quick cartoons by looking at logos and designs in newspapers and magazines, and at ideas on buttons, posters, tee-shirts and bumper stickers.

Distribute paper, pencils and markers and provide an opportunity for the learners to draw one or more designs and to decide on the one they like best. Create a bulletin board collage of all of the graphics.

Clown/Mime

PURPOSE:

To help children describe emotions.

PREPARATION

Materials
- Index cards
- Marker
- Box

PROCEDURE:

Feelings are as much a part of a child as fingers and toes, yet they are often much less obvious and need more clarification. Part of the process of becoming a peacemaker is learning to identify and express feelings. For children, this requires practice and participation.

Ask each child, in turn, to name a feeling. As the feeling, such as "happy," "sad," "angry," "confused" or "surprised," is named, write it on an index card and place it in the box. Suggest various feelings if the children run out of ideas.

Gather the pupils in a circle. Ask one person at a time to pick a card from the box and to pantomime the feeling written on it through facial expressions and body language. There should be no talking. Invite the remaining learners to guess the feeling. Continue until everyone has had a turn. Ask the children to name, describe or mime feelings that are specifically associated with a sense of peace with self. These could be "calm," "secure," "happy," "content" and "assured." Suggest that when the students feel peaceful they try to identify the feeling they are experiencing at the time.

Creative Writing

PURPOSE:

To begin a journal project with children as a way to help them explore peace with self.

PREPARATION:

Materials
- Notebooks, three ring with pockets
- Notebook paper
- Markers, permanent
- Pens or pencils

PROCEDURE:

Start children on a journal project as a way of helping them explore peace with self. The Peacemaking for Little Friends curriculum calls this a "Just Me" notebook.[27] Explain the project and inspire the group to use their personal peace pages as a way to communicate thoughts and feelings and to explore problems and possible solutions. Make the children aware that although writing is a good way to do this, art work is also encouraged.

Distribute notebooks which have pockets and three ring clips, and permanent markers. If the group is notified in advance, it may be possible to have each person bring his or her own supplies. Provide time for the boys and girls to decorate the covers with words and symbols representing themselves. This could include drawings and designs about their hobbies, family, school, pet, favorite places, special foods and so forth. Tell each person to write his or her name on the cover.

Pass out notebook paper and pens or pencils. Ask each participant to reflect on a peaceful event which happened recently or a peaceful thought from the last few days. Tell them to write something about it on the piece of paper.

Invite the children to record one personal expression or experience of peace each day.

Creative Writing: Poetry

PURPOSE:

To help children develop a valuable peacemaking skill, the ability to express thoughts and feelings, through involvement in a free verse writing activity.

PREPARATION:

Materials
- Chalkboard or newsprint
- Chalk or marker
- Paper
- Pencils or markers
- Magazines
- Scissors
- Glue

PROCEDURE:

Ask the children to name words that express emotions. Answers may include "happy," "sad," "surprised," "frightened," "joyful" and "confused." As the students suggest the words, write them on a chalkboard or on a piece of newsprint. Provide an opportunity for the learners to describe some of these feelings in short first person sentences. For example, "I feel happy when I pet my puppy," or "I am excited when I get a letter." Guide the conversation to a discussion about feelings associated with peace. Ask the children which words on the list describe personal peace. These could be "calm," "content," "secure" or "creative." As new words are suggested, add them to the list. Tell the pupils that they will have an opportunity to create a short free verse poem to describe a personal feeling of peace. Remind them that free verse is a style of poetry without a pattern of rhyme and rhythm.

Distribute a piece of paper and a pencil or marker to each person. Provide magazines, scissors and glue to share. Instruct the group to write the words "Peace is Feeling..." on the top of their papers. Tell them to look through the magazines to find words to complete this statement. Direct them to cut out these words and to glue them onto their papers. Offer one or two examples such as:

Peace is Feeling... happy when I fly my kite.
Peace is Feeling... creative when I write a poem.

After the poems are written, pair the children and let them take turns sharing their pieces with each other.

Culinary Arts

PURPOSE:

To have the students compare the number of calories they consume in a day with what is available to children in other parts of the world.

PREPARATION:

Materials
- Statistics
- Posterboard
- Markers
- Tape
- Newsprint or butcher paper
- Calorie charts
- Scissors

Advance Preparation
- Find calorie statistics for various countries.
- Cut paper for body tracings.

PROCEDURE:

Living more simply so others may simply live is more than just a phrase. It is an individual choice. Engage the class in an activity which will help them compare the food they eat and the total number of calories they consume to what is available to people in other parts of the world. In advance, obtain statistics from a denominational or world hunger relief organization on the number of calories people in various parts of the world consume per day. This information is also available in the reference section of the library. World Resources states that a person needs approximately 2,370 calories per day. In the United States the average per person daily calorie intake is 3,682. In Bangladesh it is 1,804.[28] Make a poster or chart containing this information and hang it in the room. Also exhibit calorie charts.

32

Pair the students and have each person make a life-size body tracing on newsprint or butcher paper. It would be helpful to have lengths of paper cut in advance. Pass out two pieces to each set of partners. Instruct the children to place the paper on the floor, to have one person lie down on a piece and to have the other person use a marker to trace his or her partner's outline onto the sheet. When the first drawing is completed, have the pupils switch roles and make the second drawing. As the children finish, tell them to get scissors and to cut out their tracings.

Provide markers and ask the students to draw their faces, as well as any other simple decorations, on the figures. Tell the children to draw pictures on the papers of everything they have eaten in the last day. This includes meals as well as snacks. Hand out pieces of tape and have the learners hang the pictures in the room.

Show the children how to use the calorie charts to calculate the total number of calories they consumed. Demonstrate how to compare these figures to the intake in various countries.

Discuss ways in which the children may eat more simply and more sensibly and how this can contribute to food for others.

Dance

PURPOSE:

To use dance as a medium to illustrate that peace flows from self to others.

PREPARATION:

Materials
- "Peace is Flowing" music[29]
- Accompaniment, optional

PROCEDURE:

Use dance to help the children understand that the peace of God extends to others through their attitudes and actions. Add simple movements to the song "Peace Is Flowing" and guide the young people in a meaningful and meditative prayer.

Suggested movements[30] are:

1. **Peace**
(Fold arms across chest.)

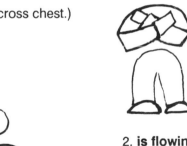

2. **is flowing like**
(Stretch arms out in front of body.)

3. **a river**
(Lower arms at sides.)

4. Flowing out to you (Lean to the right, stretching out right arm to a neighbor in giving posture.)

10. Let it flow through me. Let it flow through me. (Get up quickly, and skip in a clockwise direction, clapping in rhythm.)

5. and me (Return to "peace" position.)

11. Let the mighty love of God flow out through me. (Join hands and move in center, raising arms to a point, and then lowering them again.)

6. Spreading out into (Stretch arms out in a cruciform shape and turn to face out of circle.)

12. Let it flow through me. Let it flow through me. (Skip round, holding hands, and change direction at second stanza.)

7. the desert (Slowly sink onto knees.)

13. Let the mighty love of God flow out through me. (Repeat as movement 11.)

8. Setting all the captives (Cover head with arms.)

If verses two and three are used, change movement one to:

1. Love (verse two) (Hold hands to heart.)

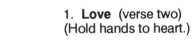

9. free! (Stretch up with quick motion.)

1. Joy (verse three) (Clap hands.)

Continue the remaining movements as for the peace verse.

Drama

PURPOSE:

To affirm individual peacemaking values by writing original plays.

PREPARATION:

Materials
- Paper
- Pencils

PROCEDURE:

Involve the children in a dramatic activity that will affirm their peacemaking values. Ask each person to think of an issue that is personally important to him or her. Topics may range from being against drugs to being for human rights.

Provide the boys and girls with an opportunity to write an original play on the topic. If several students choose the same subject, they may wish to work together.

Begin the project by offering simple guidelines for developing the theme. Suggest that the children decide what characters are needed, how many scenes there will be, and that they outline what will happen in each scene. When these tasks have been accomplished, have them write the dialogue.

Pass out paper and pencils and allow time for the pupils to work on their plays. Offer assistance and encouragement where needed.

Arrange to present some or all of the dramas for other classes or groups.

Drama: Plays

PURPOSE:

To act out the life and work of one man whose desire for peace spread to many people.

PREPARATION:

Materials
- Appleseed: A Play of Peace [31]

PROCEDURE:

In this play, the story of John Chapman, better known as Johnny Appleseed, is presented by ten actors in a flexible space. The dialogue, much of which is in verse, presents the apple as a symbol of peace, and re-traces Johnny's travels throughout the country making peace with Indians, animals and nature. His quest to protect the innocent and to undo violence and destruction is emphasized. The insensitivities Johnny Appleseed encounters with the early settlers finds its counterpart in today's society.

Games

PURPOSE:

To enhance children's self-esteem by using their names in an introductory activity.

PREPARATION:

Materials
- Bean bags
- Blackboard
- Chalk
- Construction paper, white
- Scissors
- Markers
- Pins or tape

Advance Preparation
- Cut a dove shaped name tag for each student and write his or her name on it.

PROCEDURE:

Self-esteem is enhanced by calling a person by his or her name. Help the children learn each other's names by using this easy, engaging exercise.

For younger children, call one person's name and toss a bean bag to him or her. That person then calls a name and tosses the bean bag to another student. Play continues in this manner until everyone has had a turn, or until the names are learned.

For older children, have one person begin by stating his or her name and adding a phrase to indicate something that he or she likes. This could be a hobby, color, place, food or Bible story. The next person repeats this information and adds his or her own name and statement. As play continues and as the list grows longer, encourage and enable the pupils to cooperate to remember the information. When everyone has had a turn, repeat the process, only this time ask everyone to state a way that they are peacemakers.

Accommodate the visual learners in the group by having the children, in turn, write their names on the chalkboard.

At an appropriate point, if desired, pin or tape a dove- shaped name tag to each person's clothing.

Music

PURPOSE:

To explore the feelings various types of music evoke in individuals.

PREPARATION:

Materials

PROCEDURE:

Invite the children to listen to different kinds of music. Play records and tapes which range from calypso to classical, rag to rock, and pop to polka.

Explore with the students how the music makes them feel.[32] Does fast, peppy music help them feel happy? Does slow, solemn music make them sad? What type makes them feel calm and peaceful? Encourage the children to share their feelings with the group. Assure them that it is all right for everyone to have different responses and reactions.

In addition to verbalizing the emotions during or after hearing a composition, provide an opportunity for the learners to write a poem or to draw a picture to help make the experience more concrete. Distribute paper and pens or markers and provide time for the pupils to complete their projects. This may be done with or without music playing in the background.

Music: Song Adaptation

PURPOSE:

To use a familiar song to help children identify personal actions that promote peace.

PREPARATION:

Materials
- Music, "If You're Happy and You Know It"
- Accompaniment, optional

PROCEDURE:

Sing the familiar song "If You're Happy and You Know It" with the children. Change the words of the song to "If You're a Peacemaker and You Know It." Sing new action phrases such as "Shake a hand," "Show a smile," and "Hug a friend." For the last verse, try all three motions together.

Invite each student to name an additional way in which others may see that he or she is a peacemaker. Sing about them, too.

Music: Song Suggestions

PURPOSE:

To sing songs through which children can discover their personal role as peacemakers.

PREPARATION:

Materials
- Music
- Accompaniment, optional

PROCEDURE:

Sing songs which suggest a message of peace with self. Some are:

"Breathe on Me, Breath of God," [33]

"It's Up to You and Me," [34]

"Let There be Peace on Earth," [35]

"The Peace of Mind That Christ Can Bring." [36]

Photography

Display the framed portraits in a prominent place. If a bulletin board is created, add the words "Peacemakers Are Special People." Give the children ample time to view the gallery.

PURPOSE:

To use a picture of each child in a way that will heighten self-esteem.

PREPARATION:

Materials
- Camera
- Film
- Scissors
- Glue
- Rings, metal or wooden
- Magnetic strips
- String or ribbon

PROCEDURE:

Use a picture of each child in a way that will help him or her feel special. Choose a craft, such as refrigerator magnets, to make with the snapshots.

Introduce the project by telling the children that peacemakers are very special people and that they will be seeing several of them today.

Take a picture of each student with a Polaroid camera. Photographs may also be taken and developed in advance so that they are ready to use at the time of the project. Distribute the photographs to the respective children.

Hand a metal canning jar ring or small wooden curtain ring to each participant to use as a frame. Pass out scissors and show the pupils how to cut the pictures to fit the frames. If the snapshots are small, cut background material to the required size and attach the picture to it. Provide glue to share and tell the learners to stick each photo inside its frame. Attach a magnetic strip to the back side, or tie a string or ribbon from the top of it for hanging.

Photography: Media

PURPOSE:

To help children visualize, through the use of media, the concept of peace with self.

PREPARATION:

Materials
- Film, I Wonder Why [37]
- Projector
- Screen
- Extension cord

PROCEDURE:

Illustrate the concept of peace with self by showing the film, I Wonder Why. When a young black girl reflects on the experiences and emotions which are important to her, she includes many things common to all people. She then raises the question, "I wonder why some people don't like me?" This five minute film is a good tool for discussing personal peace and also for addressing the issue of prejudice.

Puppetry

PURPOSE:

To heighten self-esteem in children by making "me" marionettes.

PREPARATION:

Materials
- Paper lunch bags, 5 per person
- Paper grocery bags, 1 per person
- Newspapers
- Markers
- Staplers
- String
- Needles, large eyes
- Scissors
- Wood strips, 1" x 4" x 3/8", one per person
- Wood strips, 1" x 14" x 3/8", one per person
- Glue or nails
- Hammer, optional

Advance Preparation
- Make a control stick for each person by gluing or nailing a four inch wood strip to a fourteen inch wood strip. The piece should resemble the letter "T."

PROCEDURE:

A positive self-concept is a powerful peacemaking tool. Promote the development of self-esteem by involving the children in a puppetry activity to make "me" marionettes.

Have markers available and pass out one lunch bag to each participant. Tell the pupils to draw their own faces on the bags. Distribute four more lunch bags to each learner and instruct the children to open the five bags and to set the sacks in front of them. Provide sheets of newspaper and show the boys and girls how to crumble one piece at a time and to use it to stuff each bag half full. Help the children fold over the tops of the bags and staple them shut.

Give each student the large grocery bag. This is the body of the puppet. The small, stuffed bags form the head, arms and legs. Guide the youngsters in stapling the small bags to the appropriate places on the large bag. If desired, allow the students to color the puppet at this point. While the children are coloring, move around the room and thread lengths of string through the arms and the head of the puppet. It may be helpful, especially if young children are involved in the project, to join the control bar to the strings at this stage of the activity. Attach the arm strings to the ends of the longer stick and the head control string to the shorter stick.

While working on each individual's puppet, use the time to emphasize the unique and special qualities of each boy and girl. Nurture the self-concept of the students and let them know that they have the potential to be powerful peacemakers.

Show the children how to operate the marionettes and hold a peacemakers' parade through the room.

39

Storytelling

PURPOSE:

To use storytelling as a method to help children identify themselves as peacemakers.

PROCEDURE:

Involve children in an exercise to help them express their ideas on and their involvement in peacemaking. Pair the students, or form small groups, and have them share stories of an experience that promoted peace with an older person, a differently abled individual, someone from another race, or a person from a different religion. Encourage them to relate the encounter in terms of what it taught them about being a peacemaker.

For an alternative or additional activity, have the partners complete sentences that relate peacemaking to the use of all of the senses. These could be:

Peace to me is the sound of _____.
Peace to me is the smell of _____.
Peace to me is the sight of _____.
Peace to me is the taste of _____.
Peace to me is the touch of _____.

Invite volunteers to share examples with the group.

Storytelling: Children's Books

PURPOSE:

To read books to boys and girls which express the theme peace with self.

PREPARATION:

Materials
- Book(s)

PROCEDURE:

Share a book with children which focuses on the theme of peace with self. Some suggestions are:

Evan's Corner.[38] The story of a small boy who discovers that a peacemaker cannot stay in his own room, but must help others in the world as well.

Feelings.[39] A book to help children explore the various feelings all people experience.

Hugs and Shrugs: The Continuing Saga of a Tiny Owl Named Squib.[40] The story of Squib, the owl, who feels that something is missing in his life and sets out to find it. He discovers that what is missing is found inside, inner peace, not outside in the world.

I Feel.[41] Many emotions are covered, pictures are included, and children are encouraged to talk about how they feel.

Why Am I Different?[42] An illustrated book covering the many ways in which children are different. Discussion suggestions are included.

Storytelling: Folktales

PURPOSE:

To use the folktale, Anansi the Spider,[43] to help children identify personal skills and strengths that can be used as peacemaking tools.

PREPARATION:

Materials
- Folktale, Anansi the Spider

PROCEDURE:

Share one or more of the African tales of Anansi the Spider. These stories can help children discover that their own gifts and abilities are powerful tools for peacemaking. Anansi's methods of facing challenging situations by using critical and divergent thinking and problem solving skills provides a model for young people to employ to overcome everyday obstacles.

Use these tales as spring-boards for discussing ways in which people's imagination and creativity can aid in accomplishing peace. Be sure the pupils realize that if they can imagine, or envision, something, they can work to attain it.

[20]Quoted in Obold, Ruth. Prepare for Peace: A Peace Study for Children. Part III: Grades 7-8. Newton, KS: Faith and Life Press, 1986, 8.

[21]Fry-Miller, Kathleen, and Judith Myers-Walls. Young Peacemakers Project Book. Elgin, IL: Brethren Press, 1988, 32.

[22]Dixon, Dorothy Arnett. Teaching Children to Care: 80 Circle Time Activities for Primary Grades. Mystic, CT: Twenty- Third Publications, 1981, #I.1.

[23]Ward, Elaine M. All About Teaching Peace. Brea, CA: Educational Ministries, Inc., 1989, 7.

[24]Strain, Marie M., ed. Ideas for Celebration of Peace. Concord, MA: National Peace Day Celebrations, 1985, 34.

[25]Dixon, Dorothy Arnett. Teaching Children to Care: 80 Circle Time Activities for Primary Grades. Mystic, CT: Twenty- Third Publications, 1981, #28.

[26]Rogers, Ingrid. "The Arts in Peacemaking." Working for Peace: A Handbook of Practical Psychology and Other Tools. Neil Wollman, ed. San Luis Obispo, CA: Impact Publishers, 1985, 230.

[27]Park, Mary Joan. Peacemaking For Little Friends: Tips, Lessons and Resources for Parents and Teachers. Saint Paul: Little Friends for Peace, 1985, 16.

[28] World Resource Institute and International Institute for Environment and Development. World Resources. New York: Basic Books, Inc., 1988-89, 250.

[29]The music to "Peace Is Flowing" can be found in: Office on Global Education for Church World Service [McFadden, Sandra L., Phyllis Vos Wezeman, Tom Hampson, and Loretta Whalen]. Make a World of Difference: Creative Activities for Global Learning. Baltimore: Office on Global Education, National Council of Churches, 1989, 154.

[30]Wilkinson, Anne. It's Not Fair: A Handbook on World Development for Youth Groups. London: Christian Aid, 1985, 64. Adapted with permission.

[31]Graczyk, Ed. Appleseed: A Play of Peace. New Orleans: Anchorage Press, 1971. Available from Anchorage Press, P.O. Box 8067, New Orleans, LA 70182

[32]Fry-Miller, Kathleen, and Judith Myers-Walls. Young Peacemakers Project Book. Elgin, IL: Brethren Press, 1988, 43.

Dixon, Dorothy Arnett. Teaching Children to Care: 80 Circle Time Activities for Primary Grades. Mystic, CT: Twenty- Third Publications, 1981, 26.

[33]Illinois Chapter United Church of Christ Fellowship in the Arts. Songs of Hope and Peace. New York: Pilgrim Press, 1988, 3.

[34]Weiss, Evelyn, ed. Children's Songs for a Friendly Planet. Burnsville, NC: World Around Song, Inc., 1986, 110.

[35]The United Methodist Hymnal. Nashville: The United Methodist Publishing House, 1989, 431.

[36]Huber, Jane Parker. A Singing Faith. Philadelphia: The Westminster Press, 1987, 59.

[37]I Wonder Why. Robert Rosenthal, 1965. Available from: CRM/Mc Graw-Hill Films, 110-15th St., Del Mar, CA 92014.

[38]Hill, Elizabeth. Evan's Corner. New York: Holt, Rinehart and Winston, 1967.

[39]Aliki. Feelings. New York: Greenwillow Books, 1984.

[40]Shles, Larry. Hugs and Shrugs: The Continuing Saga of a Tiny Owl Named Squib. Rolling Hills Estates, CA: Jalmar Press, 1987.

[41]Ancona, George. I Feel. New York: E.P. Dutton, 1977.

[42] Simon, Norina. Why Am I Different? Niles, IL: Albert Whitman and Co., 1976.

[43]McDermott, Gerald. Anansi the Spider: A Tale from the Ashanti. New York: Holt, Rinehart and Winston, 1972.

CHAPTER THREE

PEACE IN THE
FAMILY

Introduction

To paraphrase author Jacqueline Haessly, single adults, married couples, parents with young children, families with older or grown children, the elderly, extended families, combined families, and families in need of healing need peacemaking skills at every stage of growth and development and in whatever life- stage they find themselves.[44]

Fred Rogers, creator of the children's television program, Mister Rogers' Neighborhood, offers reasons why.

> *"So why is peacemaking needed within families? Perhaps because the level of emotion and caring is so deep. Those whom we love so much are also the subjects of our dreams and the objects of our frustration, anger and disappointment. For all the times in which we reach out to nurture and support the ones we love, there are also times of crisis and stress when we do not know how to respond to, or how to include, the other members of our family.*

> *"Peacemaking is the effort to bring about that nurture and support — even in times of crisis. Peacemaking allows everyone to feel self-worth — to know that his or her own uniqueness is special and worth preserving and developing. Sometimes our actions communicate that message and sometimes they do not. When they do, we are being peacemakers, when they do not, we need to find ways to get back on track — to know what to do in order to be a peacemaker."* [45]

Rogers also suggests a model for family peacemaking based on the relationship between God and Jesus.

> *"The Christian faith shows us a model of giving and loving through the relationship between God and Jesus. God stayed with Jesus throughout his experiences on earth: through his joys, his friendships, his celebration, his grief, his anger, and his decision-making. Jesus shared the depth of his feeling with God in prayer. He found sustenance in the relationship. He was allowed to make choices of what to do with the power given to him by God. And, he struggled with the ultimate choice of whether or not to give his life in order that we might live. Throughout all of these experiences, God gave strength and support to Jesus. God was with him in his successes and in his struggles. That is what we can do as families - be with one another, lending our strength and support, but allowing the other persons to choose their own ways of life."* [46]

One of the most quoted resources in the peacemaking literature is Lorne Peachey's <u>Twenty Suggestions for Teaching Peace to Children in the Home</u>. In summary, they are:

1. Cultivate a home-life where children develop a sense of well-being and wholeness.

2. Join a parent support group.

3. Provide a good example.

4. Help children experience forgiveness.

5. Don't buy war toys.

6. Avoid entertainment glorifying violence.

7. Curb backyard fighting.

8. De-emphasize possessions.

9. Tone down war expectancy.

10. Talk about war and peace.

11. Stress cooperative play.

12. Tell stories.

13. Cultivate imagination.

14. Encourage autonomy.

15. Emphasize what it is that creates violence.

16. Have an abundance of peace materials in the home.

17. Cultivate friendships with other peacemakers.

18. Provide international experiences.

19. Support projects that express concern.

20. Send peace cards and letters.[47]

Activities, encompassing a broad range of creative methods and dealing with numerous concepts and concerns, are provided to promote the skills and strengths needed to foster peace in the family.

Architecture

PURPOSE:

To consider bridges of peace that are needed in a family.

PREPARATION:

Materials
- Pictures of bridges
- Blocks, Legos or Tinker Toys
- Newsprint
- Tape
- Markers

PROCEDURE:

A bridge may be a huge architectural structure which spans a major body of water or a board placed over a small stream to join two pieces of dry ground. Regardless of its size, its function is to connect two areas and to enable people to get from one place to another.

Show the students pictures of bridges or build one out of blocks, Legos or Tinker Toys. Talk about the ways in which bridges of peacemaking are needed in a family. Help the children think of some of them such as communication, honesty and imagination.

Post a large sheet of newsprint and draw the ends of a bridge on the right and left sides of the paper. Ask the children to communicate and cooperate together to connect the two sides by writing the family peacemaking words on the paper or by drawing pictures of these ideas on the sheet.

Art

PURPOSE:

To promote alternative giving as well as care and concern for family members.

PREPARATION:

Materials
- Paper
- Pencils
- Crayons or colored pencils
- Chalkboard or newsprint
- Chalk or marker

Advance Preparation
- Prepare a sample coupon on a chalkboard or newsprint.

PROCEDURE:

Ask the children to think about a family member to whom they would like to give a gift. Tell them to think of a gift they could give that would not cost any money. Name some things like washing the car, weeding the lawn, starting a photo album, or playing a game.

Pass out paper and pens or pencils. Show the children the sample coupon and ask them to copy the words on their paper. Suggest that they center the word "Coupon" and write "To," "For," and "From" on the left side. Help the children fill in their coupons. Invite the boys and girls to prepare additional coupons for other family members. Make crayons or colored pencils available so the gifts may be decorated.

Suggest that this is a good method to use to resolve conflicts in a family, as well as to express care and concern.

Art

PURPOSE:

To represent the major events of a family's life through a sculpture activity.

PREPARATION:

Materials
- Bases, wooden
- Dowel rods
- Drill
- Glue
- Clay
- Tempera paints
- Brushes
- Shellac
- Newspaper

Advance Preparation
- Drill holes into the centers of the wooden bases. Glue the dowel rods, in an upright position, into the bases.

PROCEDURE:

Totem poles are art pieces which tell the stories of Native American groups. Through the figures and carvings, major events and important forces were symbolized and remembered. The book Try This: Family Adventures Toward Shalom[48] suggests making family totem poles as a way to recall major events.

Pass out paper and pencils and ask the children to list some of the main events in their lives. These may be a family trip, the birth of a baby, or a special celebration. Have them design a symbol for each idea. Provide clay and ask

the students to make the various figures with it. Hand out the base pieces. Symbols of earlier events may be placed at the bottom and more current happenings at the top.

When the clay is dry the sculptures may be painted and sealed with a shellac coating. Invite volunteers to describe their symbols. Ask how they relate to peacemaking.

Suggest that the children repeat the exercise with their families participating in the project.

Art:
Draw Your Dream Of Peace

PURPOSE:

To illustrate peace in the family through a coloring and drawing activity.

PREPARATION:

Materials
- "PEACE IN THE FAMILY" coloring sheets
- Crayons or markers
- Paper

Advance Preparation
- Duplicate coloring sheets

PROCEDURE:

Pass out the coloring sheets and crayons or markers and invite the children to color the house. Tell the students to draw their own families in the pictures.

After the children have finished coloring, talk about the words on the door "Enter. Peace." Ask what attitudes and actions are needed to have peace in a family. Suggest that the boys and girls list some of these words, such as "care," "concern," and "commitment," on their sheets.

Art: Draw Your Dream Of Peace

ENTER   PEACE

Draw your own family in the picture.

List things that contribute to peace in your family.

Banners/Textiles

passed around, each student, in turn, may sniff the fragrance and take a pinch to place on his or her fabric square. Begin the process.

PURPOSE:

To consider the relationship of the statements of the Beatitudes to peacemaking in a family.

PREPARATION:

Materials
- Bible
- Fabric
- Yarn
- Scissors
- Containers, eight
- Herbs or dried fragrances:
  - Sage
  - Rosemary
  - Bay leaf
  - Lavendar
  - Marjoram or Roses
  - Mint
  - Thyme
  - Tansy

Advance Preparation
- Cut a three and one-half inch square of fabric for each person.
- Place a different herb or dried fragrance in each container.

PROCEDURE:

Read the Beatitudes, Matthew 5:3-10, to the children. Talk about how these attitudes, humility, love, honesty and others, are essential if there is to be peace in a family. Tell the children that they will have the opportunity to make a Beatitudes potpourri sachet[49] which may be kept in a special place in their family or given or sent to an extended family member, such as an aunt or grandmother.

Gather the children in a circle on the floor or around a table. Place a square of fabric in front of each person. Explain the procedure for the project. Show the eight containers of herbs or dried fragrances and explain that one relates to each Beatitude. The containers will be passed around the circle, one at a time. The significance of the herb and its relationship to peacemaking will be explained. As the container is

BEATITUDE:

Blessed are the poor in spirit...
theirs is the kingdom of heaven.

Herb: Sage
Symbolism: Humility
Relationship to Peacemaking: Emphasize humility in the sense of trusting God rather than self. Stress that praying and seeking God keeps a person in the right spirit.

BEATITUDE:

Blessed are those who mourn...
they shall be comforted.

Herb: Rosemary
Symbolism: Remembrance
Relationship to Peacemaking: Think of those who are sad or oppressed and ways to show care for them.

BEATITUDE:

Blessed are the meek...
they shall inherit the earth.

Herb: Bay leaf
Symbolism: Victory
Relationship to Peacemaking: Jesus taught people not to brag or to be boastful and to know that they need his forgiveness and love, as well as that of others. This makes them victorious.

BEATITUDE :

Blessed are those who hunger after
righteousness... they shall be satisfied.

Herb: Lavender
Symbolism: Virtue and purity
Relationship to Peacemaking: People in a family should desire and work for what will be good for all of God's people, because it will also be good for them.

BEATITUDE:

Blessed are the merciful...
they shall obtain mercy.

Herb: Marjoram or Roses
Symbolism: Happiness or Love
Relationship to Peacemaking: People in a family show love to each other and also show love and care for other people no matter who they are.

BEATITUDE:

Blessed are the pure in heart...
they shall see God.

Herb: Mint
Symbolism: Purity
Relationship to Peacemaking: People in a family need honesty and should strive to seek God's way and reward rather than being self-seeking.

BEATITUDE:

Blessed are the peacemakers...
they shall be called children of God.

Herb: Thyme
Symbolism: Courage
Relationship to Peacemaking: It takes courage to live as a peacemaker. People who do live as a peacemaker work to make the world a better place for all of God's people and to settle conflicts in a caring way.

BEATITUDE:

Blessed are those who are persecuted for
righteousness' sake... theirs is the kingdom of
heaven.

Herb: Tansy
Symbolism: Immortality
Relationship to Peacemaking: Those who do God's will, regardless of being teased or rejected, will be with God forever.

When the eight herbs have been passed around, tell the children to bring up the corners of the fabric and to use a piece of yarn to tie a little bundle.

Remind them to share the significance of the potpourri with the person who receives it.

51

Cartoons

PURPOSE:

To use cartoons to suggest solutions to "unfair" situations in a family.

PREPARATION:

Materials
- Paper
- Pens
- Markers
- Tape

PROCEDURE:

Ask each student to think of a situation in his or her family that sometimes seems unfair. Invite volunteers to share ideas. These situations might involve daily and weekly tasks such as taking out the garbage, cleaning a room or doing the dishes. The things mentioned could center on allowance, food, trips, bed times, and so forth.

Tell the children they will be making cartoons which have two parts. The first part will be a drawing of the "unfair" situation and the second part will depict a solution to the problem. For example, if a child complains that his or her family never gets to go anywhere, the solution portion of the picture might show the group obtaining free videos or books from the library and taking a "trip" around the world.

Pass out paper, pencils and markers. Tell the pupils to use the top half of the sheet to draw the unfair situation and the bottom half for the solution.

Hang the cartoons around the room and allow the students to walk around to look at them.

Clown/Mime

PURPOSE:

To transform the children into "Kindness Klowns" who promote peace in the family.

PREPARATION:

Materials
- Watercolor paints
- Water
- Containers
- Brushes
- Dictionary
- Construction paper
- Scissors
- Markers

PROCEDURE:

Transform the children into kindness clowns. Think with the young people, or look up, words that have the same meaning as "kindness." Some are "friendliness," "graciousness" and "mercifulness." Ask the boys and girls to name ways to show kindness in a family. Using manners, doing someone else's job because he or she has extra homework, and giving someone a pleasant surprise are all important ways. Ask how all of these things contribute to peace in a family. Invite the children to become Kindness Klowns and to do special things for their families. Have each person think of one simple design to paint on his or her cheek to symbolize the Kindness Klown. Mention a heart, flower, balloon or cross as possibilities.

Provide watercolor paint, water and brushes and have or help the children paint on the design.

Enable the children to plan special, kind surprises to do for their family members. One might be to give away hug coupons. Pass out construction paper, scissors and markers and let each person cut out several heart shapes. On each, have them write "Good for one free hug." These may be given to family members as kind acts, too.

Creative Writing

PURPOSE:

To use creative writing as a way to affirm family members.

PREPARATION:

Materials
- Paper
- Pens
- Ribbons, trims
- Scissors
- Glue
- Envelopes
- Stamps

PROCEDURE:

Invite each child to write a note to a member of his or her immediate or extended family.[50] Tell the group that the letters should be positive and affirming. Inform the children that many Japanese people write notes to relatives which include specific details and examples of ways in which the person is important to the writer. Ask the children, who are willing, to share some unique things they could include in their notes. These might be:

Grandma,
I think of you every time I wear the warm blue scarf you made for me.

Dad,
Riding to school with you every morning is neat! It's our special time together.

Offer attractive stationary, or have the participants design their own by gluing ribbon or trim to pieces of paper. As the letters are being written, help any child who needs ideas or encouragement.

Ask the youth to deliver or mail their letters. Suggest that they repeat the process for other people in the family.

Creative Writing: Poetry

PURPOSE:

To identify concepts which promote peace in a family and to illustrate one of them by writing a limerick.

PREPARATION:

Materials
- Paper
- Markers

PROCEDURE:

Brainstorm concepts the students associate with the theme "Peace in the Family." These could be words such as "love," "trust," "cooperation," "sharing" and "understanding." Encourage the pupils to give specific examples from their own experience.

Ask the children to illustrate some of these ideas by writing limericks. Explain that a limerick is a five line poem which has a specific pattern of rhyme and rhythm. Lines one, two and five have eight beats and the last words of each phrase rhyme. The third and fourth lines contain five beats and also rhyme. Clap out the rhythm for the students. Try clapping it together so the children begin to feel the pattern.

Write a limerick together as a group. Recall three words or themes from the original list to use as the subject matter. Provide an opportunity for each learner to contribute his or her idea to the project.

An example of a limerick using the three words "family," "chore" and "help" is:

There once was a family of four.
Each one in the house had a chore.
When Bob's job was through,
He knew what to do,
He'd help out someone who had more.

Another example, using the theme of caring, is:

Each night as their dinner was shared,
The family let each other know they cared.
They talked of their day,
Found kind words to say.
Their joys and their problems were aired.

Distribute paper and markers and guide the participants as they write their own family peace poems. Suggest that the students use the markers to draw illustrations for the words they have written.

Encourage the boys and girls to share their limericks with their families.

Culinary Arts

PURPOSE:

To let the children taste various types of bread and to teach that bread is the mainstay of the diet of many people in the world.

PREPARATION:

Materials

- Bread, all types
- Knife
- Napkins
- Paper
- Scissors
- Pens or pencils

Advance Preparation
- Cut paper into the shape of a slice of bread.

PROCEDURE:

Ask the children to name a type of food which is part of almost every meal. Bread, in various forms and flavors, is generally served three times a day. It may be toast for breakfast, sandwiches for lunch and rolls for dinner. Tell the young people that for many people of the world bread is the mainstay of their diet. For some, it may be all they eat in a day. Acquaint the pupils with various types of bread which are commonly used on the seven continents of the world. These may include cornbread from North America, tortillas, commonly used in South and Central America, rye, representing Europe, rice cakes for Asia, chapatis from Africa, wheat bread, common in Australia, and marbled bread, depicting people from many continents who live and work in Antarctica. Invite the group to sample several selections. Encourage the pupils to ask their families to use a different type of bread each day for a week as a way to become more aware of people around the world.

Continue the activity by talking with the girls and boys about ways in which bread is used in their own families. Brainstorm how this taken-for-granted staple may be used more sparingly. These ideas may range from buying it at a surplus store, finding out what grocery stores and bakeries do with day old bread, to using stale bread for crumbs or croutons rather than throwing it away.

Pass out paper which has been cut into the shape of a slice. Provide pens or markers and ask each child to write or draw a way in which he or she will commit to using this resource more carefully and creatively.

Dance

PURPOSE:

To use a Shaker dance to emphasize the importance of simplicity in a family.

PREPARATION:

Materials
- "Simple Gifts" music[51]
- Accompaniment, optional
- Resources on the Shaker tradition

Advance Preparation
- Obtain information on the Shakers. Use resources from a library or contact:

  Shaker Town
  3500 Lexington Road
  Pleasant Hill, KY 40330
  (502) 734-5411

PROCEDURE:

Share information on the Shakers and the simple lifestyle which they lived. Talk with the children about the importance of a simple lifestyle in a family. Tell the students that the Shakers were a people who sought peace, justice and equality not only for themselves, but also for others.

One of the most famous Shaker songs is "Simple Gifts." Movements were added to it and it was used as a dance. The shaking hands signified shedding tensions and evils and the gathering in, or scooping, symbolized receiving God's blessings. Invite the children to try this dance together based on movements from the National Peace Day Celebrations book.[52]

Form a circle and use the following movements. Tell the children to take a partner.

'Tis the gift to be simple, 'tis the gift to be free, 'Tis the gift to come down where we ought to be,

Move to the center of the circle holding arms in front, elbows bent, and with relaxed wrists, shake the hands.

And when we find ourselves in the place just right, 'Twill be in the valley of love and delight.

Move back and re-form circle, with arms still extended in front, but with palms up and a scooping gesture.

When true simplicity is gained, To bow and to bend we shan't be ashamed.

Face partner and bow.

To turn, turn will be our delight.

Turn and bow to person on the other side.

'Til by turning, turning we come round right.

Turn in place. End facing the center so the dance may be repeated.

Drama

PURPOSE:

To teach children problem solving methods and to use drama to act out possible solutions.

PREPARATION:

Materials
- Newsprint or chalkboard
- Marker or chalk
- Paper
- Pencils

PROCEDURE:

Teach the children a step-by-step method for solving interpersonal problems. Focus on the theme of peace in the family for this activity. Use drama to act out the alternatives and options for resolving conflict situations.

Present the key words of the problem-solving plan to the students. List them on newsprint or on a chalkboard. Discuss each of them as it is listed. The steps are:

1. **Stop**. Think. Remain calm.

2. **Identify**. Identify the problem. What is causing the problem? What does the other person need and want?

3. **Brainstorm**. Generate a list of all the possible ways to solve the problem.

4. **Select**. Have each person select three acceptable solutions and one unacceptable solution. Star the solutions that are acceptable to everyone.

5. **Evaluate**. What will happen with each of the ideas? What are the consequences? How practical will they be to implement? Why will they be effective?

6. **Decide**. Make a group decision on which solution will meet the needs of the most people in the most acceptable way.

7. **Plan**. Decide the best way to carry out the idea.

8. **Re-evaluate**. Plan to re-evaluate the decision within a certain time.

Have the children suggest problems common in a family. Brainstorm all of the possible solutions and give individuals and small groups an opportunity to act them out. This will aid the learners in understanding why some possibilities will work better than others.

Pass out paper and pencils and encourage the children to write down and to remember this peacemaking formula and to suggest it to their families when conflict situations arise.

Drama: Plays

PURPOSE:

To play out experiences in the life of a cross-cultural family.

PREPARATION:

Materials
- Kimchi Kid[53]

PROCEDURE:

Not only is the topic of parent-child relations addressed in Kimchi Kid, but also the subject of merging cultures is covered. An Amerasian child is adopted into an American family and, although all parties work hard at the new relationships, there are cultural expectations from both sides. The play addresses issues that are painful as well as amusing.

Kimchi Kid is one hour and calls for a cast of nine male and seven female characters. It would be most suitable for older youth.

Games

PURPOSE:

To encourage children to play with constructive, creative toys.

PREPARATION:

Materials
- Toys
- Newsprint
- Markers
- Tape

PROCEDURE:

Brainstorm with the children toys they have at home that are peaceful and unpeaceful. Ask the boys and girls to bring examples and make a display in the room.

Tape up a sheet of newsprint with each of the following headings: "exercise/activities," "science/nature," "imaginative play," "constructive arts," "games," "music," "farming and gardening," and "reading and learning." On each sheet list constructive, creative toys that fall into these categories.

Ask each child to describe in words a peaceful toy he or she would invent. Ask questions like the following: "Out of what would it be made?" "How would it work?" and "For what would it be used?" Encourage the children to talk about these ideas with their parents.

Music

PURPOSE:

To tape record a musical peacemaking message for families.

PREPARATION:

Materials
- Records
- Record player
- Tapes
- Tape players (two)
- Blank tape

PROCEDURE:

Prepare a powerful musical message that families should hear. Choose a theme like cooperation, lifestyle, diet or stewardship around which to center this creative communication.

Gather records or tapes of popular songs or traditional music. Play some and listen carefully to the content. Choose words, phrases and lines that are meaningful and put them together to form a peace message.

Play the selected segment and record it onto a blank tape. Continue adding sections until the message is completed. The book, Try This: Family Adventures Toward Shalom, suggests a helpful way to do this. "Find the phrase to be recorded on the record. Start playing the record just before that point. When the record reaches the chosen phrase, quickly press the 'record' button on the tape recorder. When the chosen phrase is over, press the tape recorder's stop button. Go on to another record and repeat the procedure."[54]

The entire class may work on the project together or it may be done individually or in small groups.

Allow the children to take turns sharing the message with their own families, or set up a special display or demonstration so families of the church may hear it.

Music: Song Adaptation

PURPOSE:

To write verses of a song on the theme "peace in the family."

PREPARATION:
Materials
- Music, "Skip to my Lou"
- Accompaniment, optional
- Posterboard
- Marker

Advance Preparation
- Write the sample stanza on posterboard.

PROCEDURE:

Hum the tune "Skip to my Lou" with the students. Invite them to think of new words to convey a message of peace in the family. Show them a sample stanza, such as:

Help our family be a place
That's full of love and full of grace.
Help our family be aware
Of each one's needs, and show we care.

Pass out paper and pencils. Continue writing verses as long as the students are interested in the activity. Sing the new songs together.

Music: Song Suggestions

PURPOSE:

To promote the concept of peace in the family through music.

PREPARATION:
Materials
- Music
- Accompaniment, optional

PROCEDURE:

Help the children use songs to explore the theme of peace in the family. A few are:

"Give Me Peace, O Lord, I Pray" [55]

"God, Teach Us Peacemaking" [56]

"Tis the Gift to be Simple" [57]

"We Have Come to This Moment" [58]

Photography

PURPOSE:

To provide a project that will help children identify attitudes and actions that contribute to peace in a family.

PREPARATION:

Materials
- Magazines or catalogs
- Scissors
- Plastic bag
- Twist tie
- Waste basket

PROCEDURE:

Talk with the children about attitudes and actions that contribute to peace in a family and those which detract from it. The manual, Let Peace Begin with Me, suggests an excellent way to do this.[59]

Provide magazines and catalogs and help each child find at least one picture of something that could be eliminated so that his or her family might be a more peaceful place. These illustrations may range from arguing with another person to accumulating material possessions. Once the pictures are selected, invite the children to share some of the reasons they were chosen.

Open a large paper or plastic garbage bag. Take turns allowing each child to place his or her picture in it. After everyone has participated, tie up the bag and throw it into the wastebasket. Offer a prayer that reflects the participants' commitment to strive for peace in their families. Suggest that the boys and girls repeat this activity at home with their own families.

Photography: Media

PURPOSE:

To use a film to center children's attention on the theme "peace in the family."

PREPARATION:

Materials
- Film, People Are Different And Alike [60]
- Projector
- Screen
- Extension cord

PROCEDURE:

Show the film People Are Different And Alike. It can aid children in understanding that people are a family. This eleven minute film shows that people may be different races and colors and still be alike in many important ways.

Puppetry

PURPOSE:

To make and use spoon puppets to stress cooperation in a family.

PREPARATION:

Materials
- Spoons, plastic or wooden
- Markers, permanent
- Scissors
- Glue
- Yarn, cotton or felt
- Fabric scraps
- Trims
- Pipe cleaners, optional

PROCEDURE:

Cooperation in a family helps to make the home a peaceful place. Stress this important concept by making and using spoon puppets. Talk about this theme with the children and tell them they will be making puppets representing themselves to use in simulations of situations which take place where they live.

Set the supplies within reach of the students. Tell them to each take a spoon and to use a permanent marker, or several colors of markers, to draw a face on the curved, bottom side of it. Demonstrate how to make hair from yarn, cotton or felt and to glue it to the top of the spoon. Simple clothes are made from fabric scraps. Have each person chose a piece of material and cut it into a rectangle or triangle the length of the distance from the neck to the bottom of the spoon. Instruct the learners to glue it to the front of the spoon at the neck. Trims may be added. Arms, made from pipe cleaners, can be twisted around the spoon.

Form pairs or small groups of children and have them think up and act out family situations which require cooperation skills. Suggestions are doing extra tasks because a parent is sick, cleaning up the yard after a storm, and preparing food for visitors.

Additional "family members" may be made from more spoons, or by gluing or drawing faces on kitchen gadgets and utensils like spatulas, brushes and turners.

Storytelling

PURPOSE:

To encourage an awareness of and an appreciation for nature.

PREPARATION:

Materials
- Nature items
- Paper
- Glue
- Wax paper
- Iron
- Stapler
- Staples

PROCEDURE:

Take the children on a nature walk. Encourage them to use all of their senses to explore the beauty of God's creation. Suggest that they pick up interesting leaves, grasses and other fairly flat items to use to compile a book to record the event.

After the walk, help the boys and girls make the pages. Provide paper and glue and show them how to attach items to the pages. Another method would be to give everyone two sheets of wax paper, to demonstrate how to arrange the nature items between

the sheets, and to help the students iron the paper until the sides stick together. Make a stapler available and help the children put their pages together to form a book.

Invite each student to read the "book" to tell about his or her walk. Urge the children to repeat the activity with their caregivers at home.

Storytelling: Children's Books

PURPOSE:

To share books with pupils which highlight the theme "peace in the family."

PREPARATION:

Materials
- Books

PROCEDURE:

Peace in the family is the focus of many children's books, and a variety of subjects, such as death, divorce, sibling rivalry, moving and illness, are covered in them. Discuss some of these topics after reading books like:

All Kinds of Families.[61] Themes of love, trust and belonging are shown through a series of pictures on the theme of family.

Is That Your Sister?[62] Sensitive treatment of inter-racial adoption told by one of the adopted children. Emphasizes that parents and children do not have to be biologically related to be a genuine, caring family.

My Mother is the Most Beautiful Woman in the World.[63] Adaptation of a Russian folktale which points out that inner beauty is more important than outer beauty.

The Quarreling Book.[64] The dog reverses a chain reaction of unhappiness that has been passed to each member of the family to one of happiness that is passed back to everyone.

The War With Grandpa.[65] Peter has to give up his room when his grandfather moves into his house, and he isn't happy about it. He declares "war" on grandpa and plays tricks on him, until grandpa begins to play tricks on Peter. Peter realizes, not only that war isn't fun, but that grandfather is important to him.

Storytelling: Folktales

PURPOSE:

To remind young people, through the use of Beauty and the Beast, to look at the inner rather than the outer qualities of a person.

PREPARATION:

Materials
- Folktale, Beauty and the Beast
- Bible
- Construction paper, red
- Scissors
- Markers

PROCEDURE:

From France, the story of Beauty and the Beast can remind young people to look at the inner qualities and worth of a person rather than at their outward, physical appearance. Despite the Beast's obvious ugliness, Beauty loved him because of his kindness and virtue, and he was transformed into a handsome prince.[66]

Help the children think of and talk about ways in which they can look at the inner beauty of all people, especially the members of their own families. Suggest and discuss inner qualities such as empathy, listening skills, warmth, kindness and patience.

Follow up this discussion by sharing the story of David's Anointing from I Samuel 16. God chose David to be the next king of Israel because of what was in his heart rather than for his outward appearance.

Conclude this activity by passing out a piece of red construction paper, a scissors and a marker to each person. Ask the boys and girls to cut a large red heart out of the paper and to use the marker to write a word on it which describes an inner quality that helps him or her be a peacemaker at home.

[44]Haessly, Jacqueline. _Peacemaking: Family Activities for Justice and Peace_. New York: Paulist Press, 1980, 1.

[45] Rogers, Fred, and Barbara Marsh. _Peacemaking in the Family by Mister Rogers: Four Intergenerational Events for Your Church_. New York: Presbyterian Peacemaking Program, n.d., 2.

[46] _Ibid._, 2.

[47] Peachey, J. Lorne. _How to Teach Peace to Children_. Scottdale, PA: Herald Press, 1981, 11-19.

[48] Ecumenical Task Force on Christian Education for World Peace. _Try This: Family Adventures Toward Shalom_. Nashville: Discipleship Resources, 1979, 58.

[49] Mueller, Jeanne, and Judy Wood. _Called to be Peacemakers_. Hinton, WV: First Presbyterian Church, 1985, 13-14. Adapted with permission.

[50] Fry-Miller, Kathleen, and Judith Myers-Walls. _Young Peacemakers Project Book_. Elgin, IL: Brethren Press, 1988, 38.

[51] Strain, Marie M., ed. _Ideas for Celebration of Peace_. Concord, MA: National Peace Day Celebrations, 1985, 24.

[52] Strain, Marie M., ed. _Ibid._, 24. Adapted with permission.

[53] Kraus, Joanna Halpert. _Kimchi Kid_. Bethel, CT: New Plays, Inc., 1985. Available from: New Plays, Inc., Box 371, Bethel, CT 06801.

[54] Ecumenical Task Force on Christian Education for World Peace. _Try This: Family Adventures Toward Shalom_. Nashville: Discipleship Resources, 1979, 18.

[55] _Their Words, My Thoughts_. Oxford: Oxford University Press, 1981, 69.

[56] Huber, Jane Parker. _A Singing Faith_. Philadelphia: The Westminster Press, 1987, 64.

[57] Hawkes, Mary, and Paul Hamill, eds. _Sing to God: Songs and Hymns for Christian Education_. New York: United Church Press, 1984, 135.

[58] Illinois Chapter United Church of Christ Fellowship in the Arts. _Songs of Hope and Peace_. New York: Pilgrim Press, 1988, 39.

[59] Kownacki, Mary Lou, and Carol Clark. _Let Peace Begin With Me: Teacher Manual_. Chicago: International Catholic Movement for Peace, n.d., 12.

[60] _People Are Different And Alike_. Coronet Films, n.d. Available from: Mennonite Board of Congregational Ministries Audio Visual Library, Box 1245, Elkhart, IN 46515.

[61] Simon, Norma. _All Kinds of Families_. Chicago: Albert Whitman and Co., 1976.

[62] Bunin, Catherine, and Sherry Bunin. _Is That Your Sister?_ New York: Pantheon Books, 1976.

[63] Reyher, Becky. _My Mother is the Most Beautiful Woman in the World_. New York: Lothrop, Lee and Shepard Co., Inc., 1962.

[64] Zolotow, Charlotte. _The Quarreling Book_. New York: Harper and Row, 1963.

[65] Smith, Robert Kimmel. _The War with Grandpa_. New York: Delacorte Press, 1984.

[66] Spy, Deborah, ed. _Beauty and the Beast_. Illus. Michael Hague. New York: Holt, Rinehart and Winston, 1980.

CHAPTER FOUR

PEACE IN THE CONGREGATION

Introduction

Stephanie Judson, writing in <u>A Manual on Non-violence and Children</u>,[67] believes that there are five elements which must be cultivated in a home where children learn to be peacemakers. These components are also essential in a child's church home, or congregation. They are:

1. Affirmation of all people.

2. Sharing of feelings, information and experiences to promote understanding between individuals and groups.

3. A supportive community that allows people to work together on problems.

4. Practical experience for children on different ways to solve problems.

5. Sense of enjoying life together.

Children in a congregation need to develop this sense of well-being and wholeness to help contradict feelings of helplessness and powerlessness.

The activities included in the theme, "Peace In The Congregation," center on enabling young people to understand and to put into practice God's teachings on peace and justice and the biblical vision of <u>shalom</u>. The exercises suggest actions and activities through which people in a congregation may become involved in peacemaking.

Architecture

PURPOSE:

To show children how the beliefs of a congregation influence the architecture of its building.

PREPARATION:

Materials
- Pictures of religious structures
- Newsprint
- Tape
- Markers

Advance Preparation
- Arrange to tour historic congregations in the area.

PROCEDURE:

Take a field trip by foot, car, bus or picture. Visit historic congregations in the area that have an ethnic heritage. If possible, pre-arrange to have someone from each congregation talk with the children about the building's and the believers' backgrounds. Note how the structure was designed and built to reflect the religious heritage of its original worshippers. Point out ways that this is depicted in the architecture.

Continue a study of the world of faith by using a suggestion from the book Worldways: Bringing the World Into the Classroom.[68] Show the resource book, Caves To Cathedrals: Architecture of The World's Great Religions.[69] It portrays, in one hundred-fifty photographs, the architecture of six of the world's major religions.

Tape newsprint to the wall and have the students make a mural depicting a sample of symbols and architecture of the religions of the world.[70]

Christianity

Judaism

Buddhism

Islam

66

Art

PURPOSE:

To link participants together in an activity symbolizing their peacemaking potential.

PREPARATION:

Materials
- Construction paper
- Paper cutter or scissors
- Markers
- Stapler
- Staples

Advance Preparation
- Cut sheets of construction paper into one inch strips.

PROCEDURE:

Join the people in a congregation together by using an activity to symbolize the importance of their individual and collective contributions to peacemaking. Pass around construction paper strips and have each participant choose a piece. Distribute markers. Instruct each person to write his or her name on the strip. Also ask each individual to write one way he or she is a peacemaker. Alternative topics to suggest include:

One way they work for justice.

One way they are involved in global concerns.

One way they work to alleviate hunger.

One way they work for global or local missions.

Go around the group and have each person share the information that has been written on the strip. When the first person finishes, have him or her staple the strip to form a link. As others finish, have them add their links to the chain. Continue the process of introducing and linking until everyone has had a turn. Discuss the importance of working as individuals and as a congregation to promote peace concerns.

Art

PURPOSE:

To make peace lanterns and to discuss ways each person can let his or her light shine for peace.

PREPARATION:

Materials
- Tin cans
- Markers
- Nails
- Hammers
- Towels
- Wire
- Scissors
- Newspaper
- Bucket(s)
- Water
- Tape
- Candles, short
- Matches

Advance Preparation
- Remove labels and clean tin cans.
- Shred and soak newspaper.

PROCEDURE :

Talk with the children about ways in which each person can let his or her light shine for peace. This could be by praying for children in another part of the world, contributing allowance to a special peacemaking offering, or helping an elderly member of the congregation with yard work.

Tell the children they will be making peace lanterns to help them remember to let their lights shine. Demonstrate the method for making the lanterns before the children begin the project.[77]

Fill an empty tin can with wet, shredded newspaper. Pack the paper solidly and tape the top shut to secure it in place. Use a marker and draw a dot design on the can in the shape of a peace symbol or word.

Place the can on a folded towel. Use a nail and a hammer to make a hole in each dot. Hold the nail to the dot and hammer it until the hole is

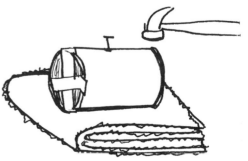

67

formed. Various sized nails may be used. Also hammer in two holes at the top and add a piece of wire to make a hanger. Remove the newspaper and dry the can.

Light a candle and drip some wax from it into the bottom of the can. Blow it out. Position the candle into the soft wax, relight it, and watch the lantern glow.

Provide supplies and guide the boys and girls as they make their own lanterns.

When the project is completed, suggest that the lanterns be used in worship, either in the classroom or in the sanctuary. Talk about the light intensifying as many candles are placed together. Compare this to the light of peace burning brightly as many people put their efforts together.

Art:
Draw Your
Dream Of Peace

PURPOSE:

To compose prayers for peace in conjunction with an art activity.

PREPARATION:

Materials
- "PEACE IN THE CONGREGATION" coloring sheets
- Crayons or markers
- Paper

Advance Preparation
- Duplicate coloring sheets

PROCEDURE:

An important component of peacemaking is prayer. Inform the students that a child originally drew this picture of children in prayer. Ask the boys and girls what they think the children might be saying. Talk about what they would say in their own peace prayers.

Pass out the activity sheets and crayons or markers. Invite the learners to color their pictures.

Gather the children in a circle and offer a prayer for peace.

Art: Draw Your Dream Of Peace

What might the children be saying in their prayers?

What would your prayer for peace include?

Banners/Textiles

PURPOSE:

To combine the children's thoughts and talents in a patchwork banner or quilt activity.

PREPARATION:

Materials

- Fabric
- Scissors
- Markers, permanent, or liquid embroidery pens
- Fabric and felt scraps
- Glue
- Sewing equipment
- Pole or rod, optional
- Backing material, optional

Advance Preparation

- Cut a 4" x 4" fabric square per person. If only a few people participate, larger squares should be used.

PROCEDURE:

"'The patchwork quilt is really a symbol of the world which must come,' Pete Seeger has said. 'One new design made out of many old designs. We will stitch this world together yet.'"[72]

Combine the thoughts and talents of the children, or of an entire congregation, as they work together to make a patchwork banner or quilt. This project involves the cooperation and invites the contributions of many individuals. The finished product, however, serves as a reminder of what can be accomplished when people work together.

Discuss a topic or theme for the banner or quilt. Here are a patchwork of ideas from many sources to consider. The handbook, Make a World of Difference, suggests "ways to alleviate hunger, ideas for justice, names of peace workers, children's dreams of peace, visions of a new tomorrow, names of countries, traditional peace and justice symbols and new, fresh peace and justice symbols."[73] Peacemaking for Little Friends proposes having each child write his or her hope for the world on a square.[74] The cover of the Young Peacemakers Project Book II contains a beautiful graphic of a patchwork piece. Each square contains a letter of the alphabet, a peacemaking word that begins with that letter, such as "assist," "bless," " cooperate," and "dream," and an illustration of children acting out the word.[75] In the first book by Fry-Miller and Myers-Walls, possibilities for square designs are "peace in many languages," or "pictures of peace and beauty."[76]

Regardless of the theme selected, the process for completing the project is the same. Distribute the patches and the supplies needed to decorate them. Encourage the use of drawings, symbols and words. Talk with the children as they work on the project.

Sew the squares together. This should be done on a sewing machine by an adult. Back the piece, if desired. If the patchwork project is a banner, insert a rod at the top through a casing or loops.

Display the piece in a prominent place to remind the children, and the congregation, of their commitment to peacemaking. The finished product may also be sold and the money donated to a peace cause.

Cartoons

PURPOSE:

To study biblical teachings about hunger and to use comic books on the subject to explore causes and solutions.

PREPARATION:

Materials
- Comic books on hunger, such as:
  - About World Hunger[77]
  - About World Hunger: A Coloring and Activity Book[78]
  - Food First Comic[79]
  - Let's Learn About World Hunger: An Information and Activity Book[80]

Advance Preparation
- Obtain comic books from the publisher.

PROCEDURE:

Comic books are an engaging and lively way to acquaint children with issues of peace and justice. This is an important medium to use since young people are so attracted to this type of reading material. Unfortunately, many of them emphasize themes of war and violence.

There are several inexpensive comic style books appropriate for various age groups which address the issue of hunger. These would be good to use in a congregation's youth programs to study this critical topic.

Distribute a hunger comic book to each student. Have them read the material and do the activities individually or as a group.

Discuss what has been read and learned and determine specific ways in which children and congregations can work to make a difference.

Clown/Mime

PURPOSE:

To portray scripture passages on peace and justice through clowning.

PREPARATION:

Materials
- Bibles
- Index cards
- Markers
- Hats
- Stickers, red circles

Advance Preparation
- Write a scripture passage related to peace on an index card. Prepare one per person. Use verses like:
  - Matthew 25:34-40
  - Hebrews 13:1-3
  - Isaiah 2:4
  - Matthew 5:3-14
  - Leviticus 19:9-15

PROCEDURE:

Give each child a Bible and an index card on which a peace related scripture passage has been written. Ask the individual to look up the verses and to read them silently. Form pairs or small groups and have the pupils share summaries of the verses. Tell each group to choose one passage to act out as a clown skit.

Create "Quick Clowns" by asking the children to change three things about their clothing. Suggest ideas like rolling up one pant leg, putting a shirt on backwards and wearing shoes on the wrong feet. Let each person choose a hat to wear. Place a red circle sticker on everyone's nose to signify the mark of the clown.

Provide an opportunity for each group to present its skit. After the clown acts, summarize some of the biblical teachings on peace and justice.

Creative Writing

PURPOSE:

To enable participants to write petitions for a peace prayer calendar.

PREPARATION:

Materials
- Paper
- Pens
- Copy machine
- Newsprint
- Tape
- Markers
- Globe, optional

PROCEDURE:

Prepare a prayer calendar with specific petitions that can be used every day for a month. Give each child the opportunity to write one or more of the sentences. Think with the children of causes for praise, specific people who work for peace, situations in which conflicts have been resolved, countries where needs are great, places where missionaries work, organizations that provide education and assistance, and local opportunities for involvement.

Distribute paper and pencils and have the pupils record their thoughts. Compile the requests into a calendar that can be duplicated and distributed, not only to each participant, but also to the entire congregation.

This project may also be done in another way. Divide the participants into seven groups. Distribute paper and pens. Show the globe, if one is available, and ask the children to name the seven continents. Assign each group one continent, e.g., Africa, and one day of the week, e.g., Sunday. Ask them to discuss the needs and concerns of the people in that particular region of the world. Have them decide on one prayer request to convey these needs.

Reconvene the total group. Begin with the group that was assigned "Sunday." Invite them to share their continent and prayer request. Ask someone else from the group to record this on a piece of newsprint which

has been taped to the wall. Continue through the remaining days of the week. Have each group offer its petition beginning with the Sunday group and continuing through all the groups. Challenge the participants to raise these requests in prayer on the specific days of the week for one month.

Creative Writing: Poetry

PURPOSE:

To read a scripture passage and a poem concerning Jesus' teaching on peace and justice and to write a response to them.

PREPARATION:

Materials
- Bibles
- "Listen Christian" poem
- Paper
- Pens

PROCEDURE:

Distribute Bibles and ask the class to look up Matthew 25:37-40. Read the verses in unison. Share the poem, "Listen Christian," with the students. It is based on this passage.

*"I was hungry
and you formed a
humanities club
and discussed my hunger.*

*"I was imprisoned
and you crept off quietly
to your chapel in the cellar
and prayed for my release.*

*"I was naked
and in your mind
you debated the morality
of my appearance.*

*"I was sick
and you knelt and
thanked God for your health.*

*"I was homeless
and you preached to me
of the spiritual shelter
of the love of God.*

*"I was lonely
and you left me alone
to pray for me.*

*"You seem so holy;
so close to God,*

*"but I'm still very hungry
and lonely and cold.*

"So where have your prayers gone?

"What have they done?

*"What does it profit a
man to page through
his book of prayers
when the rest of the
world is crying for
his help?"* [81]

After reading the poem, form six groups. Assign each group the first line of one of the first six verses. Tell Group One to take, "I was hungry," give Group Two, "I was imprisoned," and so forth. Have each group compose lines which describe what could be done to aid the people depicted in the phrase. For example:

*I was hungry
and you donated canned
goods to a food pantry
so I could eat.*

*I was imprisoned
and you visited my
family and offered
them your aid.*

Put the new verses together to form a positive response to these needs and one to which Jesus would reply, "Well done." Beginning with Group One, ask the students to take turns reading the lines they have written.

Remind the children that the congregation is a place to learn more about promoting peace and justice and to find ways to put these ideas into action.

Culinary Arts

PURPOSE:

To use holiday foods to introduce children to major world religions.

PREPARATION:

Materials
- Food items

PROCEDURE:

The culinary arts may be used to introduce children to several major world religions. This activity can promote an understanding of their beliefs and of the people who practice them. The book Religion: A Reference First Book by Gilda Berger[82] is a good resource to use with this learning experience.

Food is often a focal and festive part of the commemoration of religious holidays. This would be an interesting way to introduce the topic of various faith traditions. Bring information and food items related to the specific occasion. Some ideas follow:

Christianity: On Easter Christians often have large dinners which include lamb, representing Jesus the Lamb of God, and boiled eggs, symbolizing new life.

Judaism: Passover meals involve unleavened bread and other foods which are used to re-tell the story of the Israelites deliverance from Egypt.

Hindu: In celebration of the Hindu New Year, which falls in April or May, people go to the temples for prayer and then return home for elaborate feasts and gift exchanges.

Buddhism: During a three day festival which reminds people of the life of Buddha, everyone goes to the temple to listen to the holy scriptures and in the evening they light candles, eat and celebrate together.

Baha'i: On the first day of Spring, which is also the first day of their new year, Baha'i's break a fast with special prayers and potluck dinners.

Islam: Muhammad's birthday is commemorated with nine days of fairs and parades. Favorite foods are tabbouli (wheat, mint, onions and tomatoes) and roast chicken filled with rice, spices and ground lamb.

Dance

PURPOSE:

To involve children in an interpretive version of passing the peace.

PREPARATION:

Materials
- "Shalom Chaverim" music[83]
- Accompaniment, optional

PROCEDURE:

A spiritual dimension in a child's life adds a special type of peace, or shalom. This spirituality contributes to a sense of meaning and purpose. The sacred writings, or scriptures, provide guidance and direction and in stress-filled times, can also be a source of strength and comfort.

A child develops a sense of belonging and a means of fellowship by being part of a congregation. This activity incorporates the congregational ritual of passing the peace. Through music and movement, shalom is exchanged.

Interpret the words of the Hebrew round "Shalom Chaverim" through simple movements. Gestures are suggested for each phrase.[84] Have participants form pairs and stand facing each other.

Shalom, my friend: Partners bring palms of one hand together as in a mirror image. (i.e., partner one uses right hand, partner two uses left hand.)

Shalom, my friend: Repeat, using opposite hands.

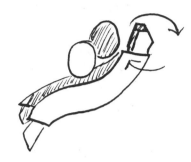

Shalom: Keeping palms together, move hands up and outward in a circular motion until circle is completed.

Shalom: Each partner brings his or her palms together in front of the chest as in a Hindu greeting.

May peace be with you: Partners bow heads, hands and upper bodies towards each other.

May peace be with you: Repeat action.

Shalom: Each person raises hands, repeating the circle movement.

Shalom: Cross hands over chest, touching fingertips to opposite shoulders.

Drama

PURPOSE:

To use biblical peacemakers as role models and to dramatize their stories.

PREPARATION:

Materials
- Bible(s)
- Tapes of Bible stories
- Bible story books
- Tape recorder
- Tapes, blank

PROCEDURE:

Introduce the students to some of the people of peace of the Bible by involving the boys and girls in a project to dramatize a few of these scripture passages.

Find tapes of the stories of Abraham and Lot dividing the land, Solomon resolving the conflict between the two mothers with the baby, or Ruth's decision to stay with Naomi. If tapes are not available for the selected scripture, read, or have the children read, the story from the Bible or Bible story book, into a tape player, and record it.

Assign parts or ask for volunteers and have the children act out the story to this narration.

Discuss the peacemaking actions taken by the Bible characters. Stress that skills like conflict resolution, cooperation and compassion are important for any age and time in history.

Drama: Plays

PURPOSE:

To address issues members of congregations face as they deal with peace and justice concerns.

PREPARATION:

Materials
- La Llmada[85]

PROCEDURE:

La Llmada is a drama to be performed by adults for mixed audiences which may include children. It focuses on the issue of churches providing sanctuary for refugees. As the life experiences of one refugee from Guatemala are shared, church members struggle with the issues of involvement in the situation.

Six demanding adult roles are required.

Games

PURPOSE:

To provide young people with a children's bulletin containing games with peace themes.

PREPARATION:

Materials
- Paper
- Pencils
- Typewriter or computer
- Duplicating equipment

Advance Preparation
- Design a children's bulletin which includes games involving peace themes, and duplicate a copy for each person. Suggested activities are:

Alphabet Challenge: Print the alphabet down the left side of the paper. Challenge players to write a word associated with peace for each letter.

Code: Prepare a code for every letter of the alphabet. Write a peace related scripture verse in the code and have players decipher it.

Connect The Dots: Form the outline of a peace symbol with dots. Place a number by each one and have players connect the dots to discover the picture.

Crossword Puzzles: Create a crossword puzzle using words related to peace and justice.

Matching: In random order, make two columns of ten items each. The first should be the names of countries and the second the word peace written in another language. Have players draw lines to match correct answers.

Scrambled Words: Scramble familiar words associated with peace, like "vedo" for "dove." Ask players to unscramble them.

Who Am I?: Write short sentences describing people in the Bible who made peace and ask players to name them.

Word Find: Write a phrase such as "Blessed are the peacemakers" and challenge players to see how many words, especially related to peace, they can make from the letters.

Word Search: Make a word search and ask children to circle the hidden words.

PROCEDURE:

Distribute the children's bulletins and pencils and have young people complete the games.

Music

PURPOSE:

To identify peace songs in hymn books and to make visuals to illustrate their messages.

PREPARATION:

Materials
- Hymn books
- Scissors
- Markers
- Punch
- Yarn or string
- Wire hangers
- Construction paper

PROCEDURE:

Take special note of songs with peace themes. Provide several copies of the hymn books that are used in worship, together with a variety of other song books. Guide the students in looking through the subject headings and indexes to find songs which pertain to peace. Some are "Peace Like a River" and "Let There Be Peace on Earth." Songs for younger children could be "I Am A Promise, I Am A Possibility" and "If I Were A Butterfly." A folk song might be "If I Had A Hammer."

Tell the students that they will be making mobiles to illustrate the messages of the songs. Pick one song for the entire class to depict or have each person pick a song to use. Distribute construction paper, scissors and markers. Have each person cut out three shapes. Instruct them to write the name of the song on one, to record information about the piece, such as composer, history or key lines, on the second, and to draw a picture portraying its message on the third. Punch a hole in the top of each piece. Pass out three lengths of yarn or string and a hanger to each individual. Help the children run yarn or string through the holes and attach the pieces to their hangers. Display the mobiles. If time allows, sing several of the songs.

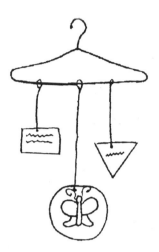

Music: Song Adaptation

PURPOSE:

To set a scripture passage on peace to music.

PREPARATION:

Materials
- Scripture passage list
- Bibles
- Paper
- Pens

Advance Preparation
- Prepare and duplicate a list of scripture passages on peace.

PROCEDURE:

Pass out a list of scripture verses on peace such as Leviticus 19:9-15, Isaiah 2:4, Isaiah 11:6, Matthew 5:38-42, and Matthew 5:43-48. Form pairs of students and ask the partners to look up and read a passage out loud.

Tell each pair to pick a familiar tune and to set their passage to that music. A sample is:

Tune: Joy To The World
Scripture: Matthew 25:34-40

*Peace in the World, we'll do our part,
To do what Jesus taught.
We'll collect food for the hungry,
Find shelter for the homeless,
Spread peace to everyone,
Spread peace to everyone,
Spread peace, spread peace to everyone.*

If the partners are willing, ask them to sing their musical messages for each other.

Music: Song Suggestions

PURPOSE:

To help children express the theme, peace in the congregation, through music.

PREPARATION:

Materials
- Music
- Accompaniment, optional

PROCEDURE:

Explore the concept of peace in the congregation with the participants by singing:

"Christ Has Come to Bring Us News"[86]
"Come, Peace of God"[87]
"Go, Tell It On The Mountain"[88]
"A Ship That Calls Itself The Church"[89]

Photography

PURPOSE:

To make caring cards and distribute them to the senior members of the congregation.

PREPARATION:

Materials
- Photograph of each child
- Index cards, 5" x 7"
- Glue
- Markers

Advance Preparation
- Request or take a photo of each child.
- Obtain names and addresses of senior members of the congregation.

PROCEDURE:

In advance, ask each child to bring his or her photo to use for a special project. School photographs would be ideal for this purpose. Alternatively, take the children's pictures in advance and have them available for their use.

Give each person an index card. Pass out glue and tell the children to glue their pictures to their cards. Allow the learners to choose markers to use. Have each person write his or her name on the paper. Additional information such as birthday, age and hobbies may also be written.

Turn the picture pages into caring cards by distributing them to senior members of the congregation. Invite these faithful friends to pray for the children daily. At some point during the year, encourage the adults to come to a church school class so the children may meet the people who are remembering them in this special way.

Photography: Media

PURPOSE:

To focus people's attention on a film suggesting ways for a congregation to become involved in peacemaking.

PREPARATION:

Materials
- Walter Fish[90]
- Projector
- Screen
- Extension cord

PROCEDURE:

Show the five minute filmstrip, Walter Fish. The theme of the parable of the Good Samaritan is depicted in this story about a fish, stranded on the shore, who attempts to find someone to throw him back into the sea and save his life. The message suggests people's responsibility to help others help themselves. Use the film as a discussion starter.

Puppetry

PURPOSE:

To help children learn experientially that all people, though unique, are children of one Creator.

PREPARATION:

Materials
- Brown paper grocery bags
- Fabric
- Rubber bands, medium; two per person
- Stapler
- Markers
- Construction paper, optional
- Glue, optional

Advance Preparation
- Cut two 18" x 3" fabric strips per person, for puppet arms.
- Cut one 30" x 3" strip per person for neck piece.
- Attempt to locate the 16mm film, <u>The Toymaker</u>. If found, obtain 16mm projector and screen.

PROCEDURE:

Master puppeteer Martin Stevens, one of the founders of the Puppeteers of America, created a classic performance called "The Toymaker." He later produced it as a film, which is out of print, but may be obtained from the Puppeteers of America Audio-visual library. Contact Norman L. Gibson, Curator, 30207 - 27th Avenue, South, Federal Way, WA 98003-4212, for information. In the story two friends, Spot and Stripe, begin to fear each other because they are different, and they build a wall to separate themselves. They discover, however, that they were both made by and are being held by the same Creator, and soon become part of a loving family again.

If the fifteen minute film can be found, show it to the children. If not, tell them about the story. Follow this by having the participants make Spot and Stripe body puppets to act out the story. Form pairs and have one person make Spot and the other make Stripe.

Distribute a bag to each person. Make markers, construction paper, scissors and glue available. Tell the children to decorate the bottom flap of the bag as the head and the remainder of the bag as the body.

Help the young people attach the arms and neck piece in the following way. Staple the center of the long piece of fabric to the top center of the bag. For the arms, tie a rubber band to the end of each piece of fabric. Staple the other end of each arm strip to the paper bag, just below the flap.

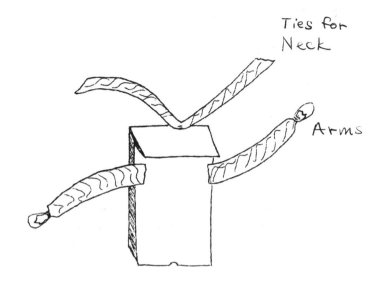

When all the children have finished, assist them, or ask them to assist each other, in putting on the puppets. Tie the neck ribbon around the child's neck and slip the rubber bands over the wrists.

Ask the children to "become the puppets," and to act out the story.

Re-gather the group and ask questions like:

What are some of the ways we are the same? Different? Would it be good if everyone looked exactly alike?

Would a flower garden be pretty if there were only one kind of flower?

Which kind of flower would you choose to be the only kind of flower?

Would you miss seeing the others?

Storytelling

PURPOSE:

To engage children in chanting a rhythm story about the dove and the olive branch.

PREPARATION:

Materials
- Rhythm story

Advance Preparation
- Practice the story to establish the rhythm.

PROCEDURE:

A rhythm or echo story is a participatory method in which the leader chants a line and the group repeats or echoes it back. Present the story of Noah in which the dove and the olive branch become symbols of peace. Begin by establishing a clapping rhythm to accompany the lines. A slap on the knees and a clap of the hands works well. Involve the students in the story.

There was a man named Noah,
He loved and served the Lord.
When God told him to build an ark,
Poor Noah, he was floored.

He hammered and he pounded.
His neighbor laughed and jeered.
"There is no rain in sight," they said.
Noah's flipped his lid, they feared.

Noah followed God's instructions.
His family would be spared.
A flood would destroy the rest of the earth
Because people had sinned and erred.

Noah gathered all his family,
And many animals, two by two.
They boarded the ark as God had planned.
It was a traveling zoo.

The rain came down for forty days.
Water covered all the land.
They stayed aboard for many months,
And were guided by God's hand.

When the water began receding
Noah wondered how he would know
When it was safe to leave the ark,
To pack up his things and go.

Noah sent out a bird, the raven,
To see if dry land could be found.
But since the raven never returned,
It meant there was no dry ground.

Then Noah sent out a special bird,
A dove, so white and pure.
It returned to the ark with an olive branch.
Noah knew it was safe for sure.

The dove has become the symbol
Of peace throughout the land.
The olive branch reminds us
That peace is part of God's plan.

Storytelling: Children's Books

PURPOSE:

To explore concepts involved in peace in the congregation by reading children's books.

PREPARATION:

Materials
- Book(s)

PROCEDURE:

Books about God's world, religious leaders, scripture stories and modern day parallels of biblical accounts are just some of the subjects to consider under the theme "peace in the congregation." A few titles to use are:

Francis, the Poor Man of Assisi.[91] Written to celebrate the eight hundredth anniversary of Saint Francis of Assisi, the book tells the story of a man who exchanged a life of wealth and luxury to serve the poor and needy for the cause of peace.

God's Creation — My World.[92] Book which affirms God as the creator of the world and the one who enables people to love and serve others.

Marty Finds A Treasure.[93] Modern day story of the prejudice of a boy for the Mexican people forms an analogy to the New Testament story of the Good Samaritan.

Naja, the Snake and Mangus, the Mongoose.[94] Jamaican folktale which parallels the biblical story of the lion lying down with the lamb. Although the snake and the mongoose thought they would like to fight each other, they discover instead that they like each other and that a special bond exists between them.

Why Noah Chose the Dove.[96] Illustrations by Eric Carle highlight this re-telling of the story of Noah and why the dove was chosen to be the bird of peace.

Storytelling: Folktales

PURPOSE:

To read the Rabbit in the Moon and to point out that personal sacrifice may enable peace for others.

PREPARATION:

Materials
- Folktale, The Rabbit in the Moon[97]
- Sticks

PROCEDURE:

Read the Japanese folktale The Rabbit in the Moon to the group. It tells the story of an old man who turns himself into a beggar in an attempt to discover the kindest animal in the world. When the man declares he is hungry, the forest and the meadow animals search for food, and each one supplies him with something to eat. The rabbit, who cannot find food, brings the beggar sticks for a fire and tells him that rabbit meat is very delicious. The man realizes that this animal is willing to give up his own life to feed him.

Compare the ways in which the sacrifice the rabbit is willing to make for the man points to Christ's sacrifice for His people. Also point out to the participants that both stories illustrate that individuals must make sacrifices to help each other. Brainstorm ways a congregation, and especially the children, can get involved in meeting the needs of people near and far.

Before the boys and girls leave, give each of them a stick to keep to remind them of both stories.

[67] Quoted in Peachey, J. Lorne. How to Teach Peace to Children. Scottdale, PA: Herald Press, 1981, 11-12.

[68] Elder, Pamela, and Mary Ann Carr. Worldways: Bringing the World Into the Classroom. Menlo Park, CA: Addison-Wesley Publishing Co., 1987.

[69] Hiller, Carl E. Caves to Cathedrals: Architecture of The World's Great Religions. Boston: Little, Brown and Company, 1974.

[70] Elder, Pamela, and Mary Ann Carr. Worldways: Bringing the World Into the Classroom. Menlo Park, CA: Addison-Wesley Publishing Co., 1987, 96.

[71] Obold, Ruth. Prepare for Peace: A Peace Study for Children. Part III: Grades 7-8. Newton, KS: Faith and Life Press, 1986, 26.

[72] Wollman, Neil, ed. Working for Peace: A Handbook of Practical Psychology and Other Tools. San Luis Obispo, CA: Impact Publishers, 1985, 242.

[73] Office on Global Education for Church World Service [McFadden, Sandra L., Phyllis Vos Wezeman, Tom Hampson, and Loretta Whalen]. Make a World of Difference: Creative Activities for Global Learning. Baltimore: Office on Global Education, National Council of Churches, 1989, 139.

[74] Park, Mary Joan. Peacemaking for Little Friends: Tips, Lessons and Resources for Parents and Teachers. Saint Paul, MN: Little Friends for Peace, 1985, 8.

[75] Fry-Miller, Kathleen, Judith Myers-Walls, and Janet Domer-Shank. Peace Works: Young Peacemakers Project Book II. Elgin, IL: Brethren Press, 1989, cover.

[76] Fry-Miller, Kathleen, and Judith Myers-Walls. Young Peacemakers Project Book. Elgin, IL: Brethren Press, 1988, 94.

[77] Church World Service. About World Hunger. South Deerfield, MA: Channing L. Bete Company, 1987.

[78] Channing L. Bete Company, Inc. About World Hunger: A Coloring and Activities Book. South Deerfield, MA: Channing L. Bete Company, 1986.

[79] Rifos, Leonard. Food First Comic. San Francisco: Food First, 1982.

[80] Channing L. Bete Company, Inc. Let's Learn About World Hunger: An Information & Activities Book. South Deerfield, MA: Channing L. Bete Company, 1986.

[81] Poem, anonymous.

[82] Berger, Gilda. Religion: A Reference First Book. New York: Franklin Watts, 1983.

[83] Obold, Ruth. Prepare for Peace: A Peace Study for Children. Part III: Grades 7-8. Newton, KS: Faith and Life Press, 1986, 52.

[84] Office on Global Education for Church World Service [McFadden, Sandra L., Phyllis Vos Wezeman, Tom Hampson, and Loretta Whalen]. Make a World of Difference: Creative Activities for Global Learning. Baltimore: Office on Global Education, National Council of Churches, 1989, 158.

[85] Hansen, Brian, and students at University of New Mexico. La Llmada. Albuquerque: University of New Mexico Theatre Department, 1986. Available from: Brian Hansen, Theatre Department, University of New Mexico, 501 Carlisle Blvd., N.E., Albuquerque, NM 87106.

[86] Illinois Chapter United Church of Christ Fellowship in the Arts. Songs of Hope and Peace. New York: Pilgrim Press, 1988, 5.

[87] Ibid., 9.

[88] Ibid., 11.

[89] Ibid., 1.

[90] Walter Fish. Alba House Communications, 1976. Available from Church World Service, P.O. Box 968, Elkhart, IN 46515. (219) 264-3102

[91] De Paola, Tomie. Francis, the Poor Man of Assisi. New York: Holiday House, 1982.

[92] Schindler, Regine. God's Creation - My World. Nashville: Abingdon, 1982.

[93] Blaufuss, Deloris, comp. Building a Foundation for Peace: Bibliography of Peace Books for Children and Young Adults. 2nd ed. Burlington, IA: Saint Luke United Church of Christ Peace Fellowship, 1986.

[94] Richards, Dorothy Fay. Marty Finds a Treasure. Chicago: The Dandelion House, 1982.

[95] Kirkpatrick, Oliver. Naja, the Snake and Mangus, the Mongoose. Garden City, NY: Doubleday and Co., Inc., 1970.

[96] Singer, Isaac Bashevis. Why Noah Chose the Dove. New York: Farrar, Straus and Giroux, 1974.

[97] Pratt, Davis, and Elsa Kula. "The Rabbit in the Moon." Magic Animals of Japan. Berkeley, CA: Parnassus Press, 1967, 21.

CHAPTER FIVE

PEACE IN THE SCHOOL

Introduction

According to the Infusion Curriculum Training Workshop[98] manual, peace and justice education in a school should involve six characteristics, described by Rev. Robert J. Starratt, S.J. in his booklet, "Sowing Seeds of Faith and Justice" (Washington, DC: Jesuit Secondary Education Association, n.d.). They are:

1. Authentic Involvement. Every aspect of the school program must reflect a peace and justice perspective.

2. Appropriate to Schools. The school is not a social service agency or political organization, but rather a place where learning is the primary goal. Schools must prepare students for what will take place all through their lives.

3. Appropriate for the age group. Goals must be attainable and developmentally appropriate for the particular age group.

4. Appropriate to our culture. A school program should be appropriate to the cultural context of the United States, however, it should also stress global citizenship.

5. Involvement of the whole faculty. The whole faculty should be involved in building a concern for peace and justice.

6. Collaboration with the family. Parents must be included in the program to be sure the home and school are promoting the same goals.

The arts related activities in the "peace in the school" section suggest ways in which students can make their educational environment a more cooperative and caring place.

Architecture

PURPOSE:

To use landscape architecture as a way to help children reflect on things shared by people throughout the world.

PREPARATION:

Materials
- Labeling materials

Advance Preparation
- Arrange for a landscaper to speak to the group.

PROCEDURE:

The landscaping around many places of worship and schools frequently contains plants, shrubs, trees and flowers which originate in various countries. Invite someone from a landscaping service to speak to the participants and to help them identify where some of the vegetation on their grounds is found throughout the world.

Create a miniature international garden by labeling these plants in some attractive way. Also prepare a diagram of the premises to help people locate different plants and to identify their country of origin.

Art

PURPOSE:

To encourage participants to share information about themselves as individuals and as peacemakers with the total group.

PREPARATION:

Materials
- Paper, white
- Markers
- Masking tape

PROCEDURE:

Improving and maintaining the self-esteem of all students is essential to promoting peace in the school. This activity will provide a way for each child to share some of his or her strengths and successes with the total group.

Distribute a sheet of paper and a marker to each participant. Instruct the group to fold the paper in quarters and then to re-open it. Ask each person to write the following information in the quarters of the paper as indicated:

Upper left: Name
Upper right: Favorite book or movie
Lower left: Favorite hobby
Lower right: One special talent or skill

Substitute specific peacemaking themes in some of the blocks by using topics like favorite peacemaker, favorite country, favorite ethnic food, one action for peace, or one peace-related scripture passage.

When the sheets are completed, have each person get a piece of masking tape and tape the paper to the wall. When all participants have posted a sheet, invite the group to walk through the "art gallery" to learn about the others in the class. Encourage everyone to browse, read and note interesting things about the people. After a short time, invite each person to stand by his or her sheet on the wall. Take turns having people introduce themselves by name, and tell one thing they would like others to remember about them. Affirm each other by clapping for the multiple gifts and talents that have been shared in the class.[99]

Art

PURPOSE:

To review peace and justice concepts and to represent them in a three dimensional sculpture.

PREPARATION:

Materials
- Wire
- Wire cutter or scissors

Advance Preparation
- Cut a long piece of wire for each person.

PROCEDURE:

The Infusion Curriculum Training Workshop material lists several peace and justice concepts. The most basic one is human dignity. Others include communication, conflict analysis, cooperation, non-violence, global community, interdependence, multicultural understanding, and stewardship.[100] Discuss these with the students and check for understanding by having them describe the ideas in their own words.

Ask the children to try to represent the concepts in a three dimensional way. Provide each person with a long piece of soft, bendable wire and ask him or her to pick one concept and to form a sculpture to symbolize it.

Display the sculptures. Notice how people may have picked the same concept, yet interpreted it very differently. Ask the children what this tells them about working for peace in a school setting.

Art:
Draw Your
Dream Of Peace

PURPOSE:

To involve children in an art project to picture cooperation between people.

PREPARATION:

Materials
- "PEACE IN THE SCHOOL" coloring sheets
- Paper
- Pencils
- Crayons or markers

Advance Preparation
- Duplicate coloring sheets.

PROCEDURE:

Pass out paper and pencils and ask the children to list ways in which they use their hands to cooperate with other people. After a few minutes, invite each student to share one or more ideas from his or her list. These may include playing catch, sweeping the floor, holding open a door, turning down the television or radio and carrying groceries.

Pass out the "Peace In The School" coloring sheets. Let the students know that the person who made the original drawing colored the hands three different colors, brown, yellow and red, to represent people cooperating together. Request responses of ways in which people in a school or class cooperate together.

Following the coloring, form groups of three. Pass out paper and ask the trios to cooperate together to make one drawing of their hands. Recommend that the pupils take turns tracing each other's hands onto the paper. These pictures may also be colored. Propose that each group lists one thing they will cooperate to do together today.

Display the pictures.

Art: Draw Your Dream Of Peace

Find two other children and trace each other's hands to form one picture.

List ways you could use your hands to cooperate with other people.

Banners/Textiles

PURPOSE:

To establish connections between people working for peace.

PREPARATION:

Materials
- Paper clips
- Fabric or paper
- Scissors
- Thread or glue
- Stationery
- Pens or pencils
- Envelopes
- Stamps
- Marker, permanent

Advance Preparation
- Prepare the banner background from fabric or paper. Any size is appropriate.
- Cut out the shapes, corresponding in size to the banner background, of a boy and a girl standing together. Their inner hands should be joined and their outer hands are to be extended. Attach a paper clip to each one's outer hand. Sew or glue the figures to the background piece.
- Add the words "We're Hooked on Peace" to the top of the banner. These may be written on with permanent marker or cut out of fabric or paper and sewn or glued in place.

PROCEDURE:

Form a short chain of paper clips. Explain to the children that people need to be as firmly hooked on peace as the paper clips are hooked to one another.

Show the group the banner. Pass out a paper clip to each person and invite the boys and girls to symbolize a commitment to peace by attaching a clip to the chain. If possible, invite a whole church school or public, private or parochial school to participate in the project.

The banner may be exhibited. It may also be sent to a local, national or international public official requesting actions for peace. It could be delivered or mailed to a parent-teacher organization with a request to hold a peace festival, or sent to the school board suggesting peace education opportunities in the classroom. Be sure to identify and articulate in the letter why a world hooked on peace is so important.

Cartoons

PURPOSE:

To create a bulletin board of cartoon strips and comics which address peace concepts.

PREPARATION:

Materials
- Magazines
- Newspapers
- Bulletin Board
- Tacks or pins
- Book(s) on peace cartoons, optional

PROCEDURE:

Ask the children to name their favorite comic strips. Inquire if any of these ever address issues of peace. Suggest that "Family Circus" spotlights the theme of peace in the family, "Peanuts" often centers on self-esteem or cooperation and "Doonesbury" is intended to be a political satire. If possible, show the book Comic Relief.[101] which includes drawings from the cartoonists' Thanksgiving Day Hunger Project. Mention that cartoons which appear on the editorial pages of a newspaper help to focus people's attention on current events of local, national and international scope.

Tell the students that they will be starting a cartoon bulletin board in the classroom. Decide if it will be organized by themes, such as self, family and world, or by concept like cultural understanding, global awareness and human dignity.

Make the materials available and start the students on a search for cartoons and comics which address the chosen topics.

Display the clippings on a bulletin board. Ask the children to continue to bring materials to add to the collection.

Clown/Mime

PURPOSE:

To mime verbs associated with positive, powerful actions for peace.

PREPARATION:

Materials
- Chalkboard or newsprint
- Chalk or marker
- Dictionary

PROCEDURE:

People of all ages, and especially children, need to discover that peace is active and exciting rather than passive and dull. Use this exercise to have the pupils name and mime verbs that describe positive and powerful actions needed in peacemaking. As much as possible, focus on actions needed to promote peace in a school.

Write the alphabet on a chalkboard or a piece of newsprint. Challenge the children to name a verb for each letter. Start the process by suggesting words like forgive, join, praise, strengthen, trust and risk.

Take turns having the boys and girls pick a verb and mime it. The other children may guess the word, or the presenter may share the answer. Select one or two letters and work together to see how many positive, powerful peacemaking verbs can be found for them.

Creative Writing

PURPOSE:

To research information on life in another country and to report on it.

PREPARATION:

Materials
- Paper
- Pens or pencils
- Resource materials
- Costumes, optional
- Props, optional

PROCEDURE:

Researching the way people in another country live, and particularly what the average school day is like, and reporting on it, helps students gain a better understanding of all of God's people throughout the world.

Provide resource material such as magazines, newspapers and encyclopedias. Show photographs and films. An excellent series of books to share with the class are the A Day in the Life set. Some of the featured countries include the Soviet Union, Japan, Spain, Australia and Canada. Beautiful colored photographs of school children are featured on many of the pages of A Day in the Life of the Soviet Union.[102] Guide the learners as they explore these sources and gather material.

Furnish paper and pens or pencils and have the children write their information from a personal perspective such as "My Day in Australia." Suggest that they include information about the similarities to and differences from life in their own school and country.

Add fun and excitement to the project by having the students use hats, costumes or props while they read their story to the entire group.

Creative Writing: Poetry

PURPOSE:

To use the ABC's to have the children write statements which describe ways in which peace, especially at school, may be accomplished.

PREPARATION:

Materials
- Paper
- Pencils
- Posterboard, optional
- Marker, optional

PROCEDURE:

Assign a letter, or several letters, of the alphabet to each student. Instruct them to compose a "Quick Couplet"[103] for each of them. Tell the pupils that their poem should contain two lines, with three syllables in each line. Here are two examples:

P: Peace must start, in the heart.
Q: Quarrels end. Make a friend.

Encourage the sharing of ideas between students, especially if someone is having difficulty developing a rhyme for his or her letter. When everyone has finished, give each child, in turn, an opportunity to read and to contribute to the "Peace at School" alphabet.

If desired, print the ABC's of peace on posterboard and display it in the classroom.

Culinary Arts

PURPOSE:

To have students work cooperatively to plan and produce a meal.

PREPARATION:

Materials
- Ingredients for recipe(s)

PROCEDURE:

Cooperation is essential in a classroom and school. It is also a key ingredient in peacemaking. Invite the children to share a special lunch or snack to which everyone contributes an item and cooperates in the planning and preparation process.

Discuss some meals that could be made in this manner. These might be tacos where the shells, tortillas, are provided and cheese, lettuce and tomato are purchased; rice with a variety of items like chicken, celery, pineapple and coconut to put on top; fruit salad for which each person brings one ingredient; broth or stock combined with various vegetables to make soup; waffles or pancakes with unusual toppings; or bread with several selections of spreads and condiments. The More with Less Cookbook has detailed suggestions on how to build cooperative meals.[104] In advance, assign each participant a specific item to bring for the meal. Prepare or purchase the base, such as bread or rice.

Include preparation time as part of the process. Guide the children as they chop or combine the ingredients to be used.

As the meal is shared together, talk about ways in which the contributions and cooperation of many people could help eliminate world hunger.

Dance

PURPOSE:

To add movement to Saint Francis' prayer and to use it as a catalyst for exploring peace in the school.

PREPARATION:

Materials
- Paper
- Pencils

PROCEDURE:

"Lord, make me an instrument of your peace..." are the familiar words of Saint Francis of Assisi. They are often called a peace prayer. Read the familiar lines to the children:

"Lord, make me an instrument of your peace.
Where there is hatred, let me so love,
Where there is injury, pardon,
Where there is darkness, light,
Where there is sadness, joy,
Where there is doubt, faith,
And where there is despair, hope.

"O Divine Master,
Grant that I may not so much seek
To be consoled as to console,
To be understood as to understand,
To be loved as to love.
For it is in giving that we receive,
It is in pardoning that we are pardoned,
And it is in dying that we are born to eternal life."

Invite the class to add movements and gestures to the words to express their meaning. Take turns having different children interpret a phrase.

The activity book, Peace, suggests having children re-write Saint Francis' thoughts using their own words to form prayers.[105] Instruct the pupils to focus, in the poems, on ways in which they can be peacemakers at school.

Share an example:

Lord, make me an instrument of your peace.
Where there is name calling,
Let me bring kind words.
Where there is arguing,
Let me bring problem solving.

Encourage the children to interpret the new peace prayers through movement, too.

Drama

PURPOSE:

To role-play conflict situations which arise in a classroom or school.

PROCEDURE:

Role play, a dramatic method, is intended to enable a person to experience the feelings of other individuals. It can be used as a means of conflict resolution between pupils in a classroom or a school.

Begin by talking about classroom situations which require peacemaking skills. Ask the children for suggestions. Some might be dealing with hard feelings over not being chosen for a special task, name-calling, or stealing. Let the group decide on a situation to role play. Pose questions for the children to ponder like what might have happened before this situation? After?

Decide on the characters in the scene and ask for volunteers. Briefly review the situation. Do not offer suggestions for playing the roles, rather, help each person clarify his or her part by asking questions.

When the people playing the roles are ready, spontaneously enact the situation. Have the rest of the group watch. After several minutes, or when a climax is reached or the players run out of dialogue, stop the action. Discuss the situation. Help group members attempt to understand how the people in the scene felt and why. Play the scene again, with new people playing the roles, or choose a new situation to illustrate through this drama technique.

Drama: Plays

PURPOSE:

To involve children in a dramatic performance exploring ways in which young people can bring peace to the world.

PREPARATION:

Materials
- Peace Child[106]

PROCEDURE:

Do a production of the play Peace Child, a musical fantasy, set in the future, which tells the story of the way in which peace came to the world. The play can be performed by casts ranging from a few to several hundred children. It is especially suitable for schools. There are speaking roles which can be combined or expanded to accommodate the number of people involved, as well as parts for a chorus and dancers. The production is performed on an open stage.

The show is the story of an American boy and a Soviet girl who become friends and who make a plea for peace to the leaders of the world. They mount a campaign to establish an exchange of children between countries, as is done in the Peace Child legend of Papua, New Guinea, to build and maintain peace.

New versions of the play dealing with conflicts in Central America, Ireland and Israel, as well as environmental issues, have been written or are in process.

The Peace Child Foundation sponsors international youth exchange programs between the Soviet Union and the United States as well as to several other countries. Children who have participated in local productions and international tours are also eligible to be part of the United Nations Peace Day concert, a world-wide television event.

Games

PURPOSE:

To learn and play cooperative games.

PREPARATION:

Materials
- Cooperative games books
- Game supplies

PROCEDURE:

Introduce the children to a variety of cooperative games by presenting a new one each week. Play it during class or recreation time.

Make several game books available like:

The New Games Book: Play Hard, Play Fair, Nobody Hurt.[107]

More New Games and Playful Ideas from the New Games Foundation.[108]

The Cooperative Sports and Games Book.[109]

Play Fair: Everybody's Guide to Noncompetitive Play.[110]

Allow a different student to choose the game that will be highlighted for the week. Have that person teach the rest of the class the directions.

Help the children learn to play and to work together to achieve common goals. Emphasize how this cooperative spirit, which nurtures caring and sharing attitudes, is needed in school activities.

Music

PURPOSE:

To play musical chairs as a cooperative game.

PREPARATION:

Materials
- Chairs, one per person
- Records
- Record player

PROCEDURE:

Try playing "Musical Chairs" in ways that will stress cooperation rather than competition among students. For background music use folk songs with peace messages. Some folk and rock musicians who have written peace songs or been involved in peace efforts are Pete Seeger, John Denver, Peter, Paul and Mary, Paul McCartney and Harry Chapin.

Explain to the children how the game will be played. Remove a chair each time the music stops, but do not eliminate any young people from the game. Watch the fun begin when only one chair remains and all the students attempt to get on it.

A variation of the game is to have each student hug a person when the music stops.[111]

Continue playing as long as the children are having fun. At the conclusion of the game, ask the students to find a comfortable seat and to listen to the words of the music.

Music: Song Adaptation

PURPOSE:

To listen to recordings of and to learn children's peace songs.

PREPARATION:

Materials
- Tape, I Can Make Peace[112]
- Tape, Teaching Peace[113]

PROCEDURE:

Gather the learners and invite them to listen to children's peace songs. Play selections from the tapes I Can Make Peace and Teaching Peace. The two title songs would be good ones to learn.

Provide kazoos and teach the students how to play them. Form a kazoo peace orchestra and perform some of the music.

Music: Song Suggestions

PURPOSE:

To teach children songs containing the theme peace in the school.

PREPARATION:

Materials
- Music
- Accompaniment, optional

PROCEDURE:

Songs emphasizing children and children's actions and activities may be included during a study of the theme, peace in the school. Try the following:

"Friendship Song"[114]

"May There Always Be Sunshine"[115]

"Faraway Friends"[116]

"We Thank You For Our Friends"[117]

Photography

PURPOSE:

To use calendars in the school environment to explore peace themes.

PREPARATION:

Materials
- Calendars, current and used

PROCEDURE:

Calendars, available from places like UNICEF, Church World Service or denominational mission committees, are an excellent and plentiful resource for exploring themes such as cultural diversity and global perspectives. Use the calendars and individual pictures from them for curriculum enrichment and classroom activities. Create bulletin boards to illustrate various themes or include them in reports on different cultures and regions. Some special projects, suggested in an issue of "Teachable Moments," follow.[118]

Use the whole calendar and try these ideas:

Select a calendar with pictures that promote global awareness. Display it in a classroom, hallway or fellowship hall. Each time a person glances at it, checks a date, or writes something on it, global perspective will be heightened.

To help the children experience and understand the value of multiple perspectives, divide the participants into trios or quartets. Give each group several calendars. Tell each person to privately select a favorite and least favorite picture. Each person could then share his or her choices and the reasons

for them with the small group. Re-convene the total group. Ask if everyone chose the same picture and if there were right and wrong choices. Then discuss with the participants what the exercise taught them about people's opinions and the way they act with one another.

Take the calendars apart and use these activities:

Have participants select a picture and then group with four or five other students who have pictures that they think illustrate a common theme or category, e.g., water, nature, children, conflict. Instruct them to re-group to create new themes or categories.

Invite individuals or groups to choose a theme and to use calendar pictures to create a collage.

Select a picture, or series of pictures, as a focus for a story or poem.

Involve students in a cooperative project and have them use pictures from calendars to make a bulletin board on a certain theme.

Some calendar sources include:

Children of the World Calendar. Also: "One World," One Family," and "Around the World." Pomegranate Calendars and Books, Box 980, Corte Madera, CA 94925.

Church World Service Global Calendar. Beautiful pictures with diagrams, illustrations, charts and short stories. Church World Service, P.O. Box 968, Elkhart, IN 46515-0968.

UNICEF Engagement Calendar. Many photographs centered around one theme. United States Committee for UNICEF, One Children's Boulevard, Ridgely, MD 21685.

UNICEF Wall Calendar. Illustrated with art from children around the world. United States Committee for UNICEF, 331 E. 38th Street, New York, NY 10016.

The World Calendar. Information on worldwide religious holidays, civil holidays of many countries, birthdays of world leaders. Teachers guide of 22 calendar related projects. Educational Extension Systems, P.O. Box 11048, Cleveland Park Station, Washington, DC 20008.

Photography: Media

PURPOSE:

To picture, through the use of media, issues which effect peace in the school.

PREPARATION:

Materials
- Video, <u>Buster And Me: Getting Active</u>[119]
- VCR
- Monitor or TV

PROCEDURE:

Show the twenty-five minute video <u>Buster and Me: Getting Active</u>. It is a puppet program which addresses children's fear and confusion about the threat of nuclear war. The point is made that the cost of the arms race means less money is available for education and school programs. It promotes action and discussion.

Puppetry

PURPOSE:

To introduce, through a shadow puppet project, a study of trees of the world and to discuss ways to preserve natural resources.

PREPARATION:

Materials
- Posterboard, black
- Scissors
- Paper punches
- Cellophane, various colors
- Straws
- Masking tape
- Shadow puppet screen
- Light source
- Resource materials, trees of the world
- Egg cartons, optional
- Markers, optional
- Construction paper, optional

Advance Preparation
- Make or set up a shadow puppet screen and light source.
- To make a simple shadow puppet screen, cut the flaps off of the top of a medium-sized cardboard box. Turn the box bottom up. Leaving a three inch border around the edges, cut out the center of the bottom. The border helps to support the box.

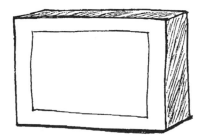

- Working from the inside of the box, cover the opening just created with white paper. Tape it in place.
- Light the shadow puppet screen from behind with a light bulb, slide or over-head projector, or with natural light from a window.

PROCEDURE:

With a renewed emphasis on environmental and stewardship issues, a class project involving shadow puppetry is a perfect opportunity to focus on trees of the world. In light of the rapid decline of the number of trees and the emphasis on preserving and planting them, this is an especially important topic.

Form small groups of children and tell them they have the opportunity to study the diverse regions of the world and the types of trees that are found in them. They will then make shadow puppets to illustrate the trees that are typical of that specific area. Each group or child may make a tree. Some areas to assign are mountains, meadows, deserts, jungles, rain forests and islands. Make resource material available for the students to use in exploring these regions.

Pass out the shadow puppet supplies. These include posterboard, scissors, paper punches, colored cellophane, straws and tape. Irregularly shaped, rather than square or rectangular, pieces of posterboard often spark children's creativity and imagination when working on a shadow puppet project. Tell each person or group to cut the tree shape out of posterboard. Remind them that it is to be illustrative of the type of trees found in the region they researched. Suggest that they add detail and decoration to the trees by cutting intricate and interesting designs to highlight branches, leaves, needles and so forth. Paper punches are helpful for this purpose. Show the boys and girls how to tape pieces of colored cellophane behind some of the cut-out areas. To form the rod by which the shadow figure is operated, tell the people to tape the top inch, or bendable portion, of a straw to the center of the puppet. This should be placed on the back side.

Invite the children to take turns sharing their puppets behind the shadow screen. Ask them to give information on the tree and the region in which it is found.

To introduce animals that live in or feed off of these trees, as well as another puppetry style, make simple finger puppets by cutting off the tall crowns that separate cardboard egg cartons. This becomes the puppet's head when worn on the middle finger. The other three fingers and thumb serve as the legs. Eyes and features may be made from construction paper or markers.

After the activity, ask the children to suggest ways in which these God-given gifts, trees and animals, can be preserved. Discuss how stewardship is an aspect of peacemaking.

Storytelling

PURPOSE:

To compile a shape book on peacemaking at school.

PREPARATION:

Materials
- Paper, white
- Scissors
- Pens or pencils
- Markers
- Stapler
- Staples

Advance Preparation
- Cut a dove-shaped paper for each person.

PROCEDURE:

Invite participants to contribute a page to a class book about peacemaking.

Distribute a dove shaped piece of paper to each person. Make pens or pencils, and markers available. Ask the children to write, on the dove, a few sentences or paragraphs on the subject "I am a peacemaker at school when I...". Suggest that illustrations be drawn, too.

Pass the pages around so that everyone has the opportunity to look at them. Collect and assemble the sheets. Staple them together to form one book. Leave it in the classroom.

Storytelling: Children's Books

PURPOSE:

To consider the peace message in books about school children and school themes.

PREPARATION:

Materials
- Books(s)

PROCEDURE:

Stories about children who have accomplished great things for peace, a unique version of the ABC's, and issues of friendship, as well as fighting, are contained in the suggestions of books dealing with peace in the school.

The Alphabet Tree.[120] Words and sentences that bring hopeful messages are formed on this special tree with the help of two insect friends.

Amos and Boris.[121] At first it seemed like they had nothing in common, however, Amos and Boris, a mouse and a whale, become best friends.

Liar, Liar, Pants on Fire.[122] The new boy in first grade, Alex, was always bragging about something and his classmates continually called him a liar. A special discovery was made at the Christmas party.

Sadako and the Thousand Paper Cranes.[123] Story of Sadako, a Japanese girl, who gets leukemia as a result of the bombing of Hiroshima, and her quest to fold a thousand paper cranes so she may make a wish to regain her health. After her death, her classmates finish folding the cranes and made a wish for world peace.

Samantha Smith: Journey to the Soviet Union.[124] Samantha Smith was the schoolgirl who asked, "Why do the Russians want to blow us up?" and was then invited to visit the Soviet Union. This book, one-hundred-twenty-two pages, is filled with photographs and memories of her trip.

Storytelling:
Folktales

PURPOSE:

To illustrate cooperation by reading and acting out the folktale, The Turnip.

PREPARATION:

Materials
- Folktale, The Turnip.[125]

PROCEDURE:

In The Turnip, a delightful Russian folktale, a grandfather realizes that the vegetable he has grown has become too large for him to pull out of the ground by himself. In order to accomplish the task he invites the cooperation of his wife, grand-daughter, dog and cat. It is only after a mouse (in some stories a beetle), usually an animal considered to be small and insignificant, links onto the rest, that the turnip is pulled up.

After telling the story, assign parts and act it out. Many additional animals may be added after the cat so that every child has an opportunity to participate.

Use this folktale to talk about the importance of each person. Also explore ways in which everyone in a class can cooperate to resolve conflicts that arise at school.

[98] Justice/Peace Education Council. Infusion Curriculum Training Workshop. New York: Justice/Peace Education Council, 1981, 18.

[99] Office on Global Education for Church World Service [McFadden, Sandra L., Phyllis Vos Wezeman, Tom Hampson, and Loretta Whalen]. Make a World of Difference: Creative Activities for Global Learning. Baltimore: Office on Global Education, National Council of Churches, 1989, 39. Adapted with permission.

[100] Justice/Peace Education Council. Infusion Curriculum Training Workshop. New York: Justice/Peace Education Council, 1981, 14-16.

[101] Comic Relief: Drawings from the Cartoonists' Thanksgiving Day Hunger Project. New York: Henry Holt, 1986.

[102] A Day in the Life of the Soviet Union. New York: Collins Publishers, Inc., 1987, 23, 32-37, 68-73, 88-89, 132, 148, 162- 165, 170, 194.

[103] Dixon, Dorothy Arnett. Teaching Children to Care: 80 Circle Time Activities for Primary Grades. Mystic, CT: Twenty- Third Publications, 1981, #35.

[104] Longacre, Doris Janzen. More with Less Cookbook. Scottdale, PA: Herald Press, 1977, 50-51.

[105] Dwyer, Paulinus, and Carole MacKenthun. Peace: A Christian Activity Book with Reproducible Pages. Carthage, IL: Shining Star Publications, 1986, 5.

[106] Woollcombe, David. Peace Child. David Gordon, composer. Fairfax, VA: Peace Child Foundation, 1981. Available from: Peace Child Foundation, 3977 Chain Bridge Road, Fairfax, VA 22030. (703) 385-4494. Also available: Study Guide with script, score and production hints, audio and video cassettes and newsletter.

[107] Fluegelman, Andrew, ed. The New Games Book: Play Hard, Play Fair, Nobody Hurt. San Francisco: The Headlands Press, 1976.

[108] Fluegelman, Andrew, ed. More New Games and Playful Ideas from the New Games Foundation. San Francisco: The Headlands Press, Inc., 1981.

[109] Orlick, Tom. The Cooperative Sports and Games Book. New York: Pantheon Books, 1978.

[110] Weinstein, Matt, and Goodman, Joel. Play Fair: Everybody's Guide to Noncompetitive Play. San Luis Obispo, CA: Impact Publishers, 1980.

[111] Hopkins, Susan, Jeff Winters, and Laurie Winters, eds. Learning to be Peaceful Together to Build a Better World. Fullerton, CA: Concerned Educators Allied for a Safe Environment, n.d., 15.

[112] Krehbiel, Jude, and Doug Krehbiel. I Can Make Peace. Scottdale, PA: Herald Press and Mennonite Central Committee, 1983.

[113] Grammer, Red. Teaching Peace. Peekskill, NY: Smilin' Atcha, n.d.

[114] Weiss, Evelyn, ed. Children's Songs for a Friendly Planet. Burnsville, NC: World Around Songs, 1986, 14.

[115] Ibid., 95.

[116] Ibid., 42.

[117] Hawkes, Mary, and Paul Hamill, eds. Sing to God: Songs and Hymns for Christian Education. New York: United Church Press, 1984, 157.

[118] Drum, Jan, and George Otero. "Teachable Moments." Muscatine, IA: The Stanley Foundation, Dec. 1987. Adapted with permission.

[119] Buster and Me: Getting Active. KRON-TV, 1983. Available from: Church World Service, P.O. Box 968, Elkhart, IN 46515- 0968.

[120] Lionni, Leo. The Alphabet Tree. New York: Pantheon, 1968.

[121] Steig, William. Amos and Boris. New York: Farrar, Straus and Giroux, 1971.

[122] Cohen, Miriam. Liar, Liar, Pants on Fire. New York: Greenwillow Books, 1985.

[123] Coerr, Eleanor. Sadako and the Thousand Paper Cranes. New York: Dell Publishing, 1977.

[124] Smith, Samantha. Samantha Smith: Journey to the Soviet Union. Boston: Little, Brown and Co., 1985.

[125] Parkinson, Kathy. The Turnip. Niles, IL: Albert Whitman, 1986.

CHAPTER SIX

PEACE IN THE NEIGHBORHOOD

Introduction

Suggestions for six ways to prevent conflict in a family are offered in the book, Peacemaking for Little Friends.[126] They are suitable for establishing peaceful relationships in a neighborhood as well.

1. "Give each child some special time each day." As children in the neighborhood walk to and from school, play games, or do yard work, make a point to greet them with a friendly smile or a happy "hello." A special treat, or even a party, would be appropriate and appreciated.

2. "Teach children to ask for attention constructively." Encourage positive methods of getting attention, such as praising the accomplishment of riding a bike or mastering a pair of skates. This will discourage means of getting attention in negative ways.

3. "Recognize children as individuals." Learn the names of children in the area. Acknowledge the special and unique qualities of each person.

4. "Teach children how to negotiate with others." Encourage children to explore alternatives and to learn non-violent methods of resolving conflicts.

5. "Structure the environment to reduce conflict." Reduce temptation by putting bikes and yard equipment away. Work towards improving playgrounds and sports facilities.

6. "Visualize children as competent and caring." Children often act as people think they will. Expect them to be successful.

The activities for the theme "peace in the neighborhood" stress methods to help children understand the basic peace concept, human dignity. They emphasize respect for people and property.

Architecture

PURPOSE:

To learn about the work of Habitat for Humanity.

PREPARATION:

Materials
- Information on Habitat for Humanity.

Advance Preparation
- Invite a speaker from Habitat for Humanity.

PROCEDURE:

Habitat for Humanity is an international organization, with many local chapters, which rehabilitates older houses and builds new homes for people who cannot afford adequate housing.

Invite a speaker to describe Habitat's program and to challenge participants to become involved in a local, neighborhood project.

Art

PURPOSE:

To explain the significance of the origami peace crane and to provide an opportunity to make them.

PREPARATION:

Materials
- Origami paper
- Instructions
- Thread, string or yarn
- Needles
- Book, Sadako and the Thousand Paper Cranes[127]

Advance Preparation
- Duplicate instructions
- Fold sample cranes

PROCEDURE:

Origami is the Japanese art of paper folding. The origami paper crane has become a symbol of peace. It is often associated with the story of Sadako, a young Japanese girl who became ill after the bomb was dropped on Hiroshima. Knowing the legend that if a person folds one thousand paper cranes and makes a wish, the wish will come true, Sadako folded cranes and wished for health. After folding six hundred forty four, she died. Her classmates folded the three hundred sixty six needed to reach one thousand, and made a wish for peace.

Show the children a paper crane and invite them to make one or several. Provide origami paper and instructions. Although directions are available in many books and from many sources, the illustrations by Megumi Yanada of Miyazaki, Japan, are especially clear and concise.[128] Guide the children through each step of the process. Offer assistance where needed.

Suggest that the children start a neighborhood project involving peace cranes. They could string several together and use them to decorate trees and bushes. Display cranes in store windows and public buildings. Neighbors could join together and make one thousand to send to world leaders or to the Hiroshima Peace Tower at the following address: World Friendship Center, 1544 Mirobi-machi, Hiroshima, Japan.

106

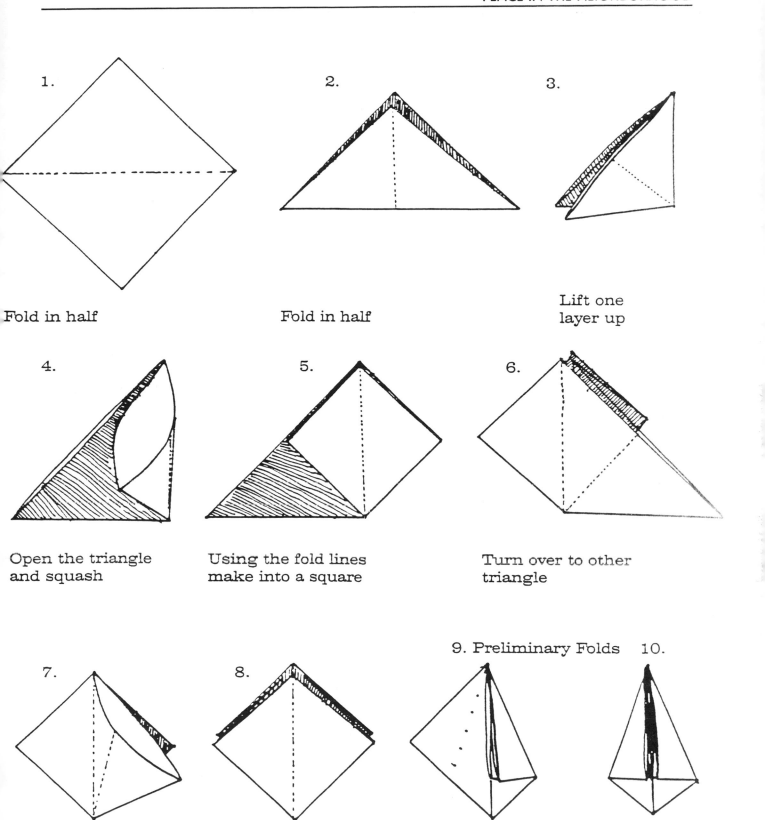

1.

2.

3.

Fold in half

Fold in half

Lift one
layer up

4.

5.

6.

Open the triangle
and squash

Using the fold lines
make into a square

Turn over to other
triangle

7.

8.

9. Preliminary Folds   10.

and squash on fold
lines making a
square

Make sure open
sides of square
are up

Fold open edge
toward center

Fold other
open edge toward
center. Fold
bottom point up

11.

Press folds
tightly

12.

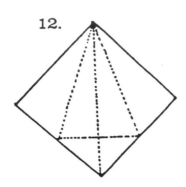

Open to the
square

13.

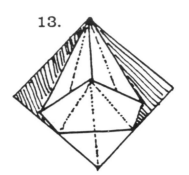

Gradually lift up
first layer only
and press down on
crease

14.

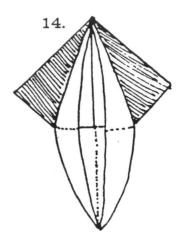

Edges roll in-
ward and meet.
Follow the
diamond. Shape
fold lines.
Press on the
fold lines

15.

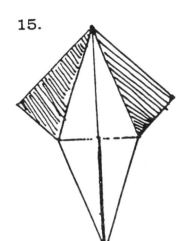

Finish the diamond
shape and press on
the fold lines

16.

Turn over: do
the same as in
#12, #13, & #14

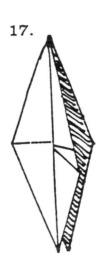

Finished
Double diamond
shape. Top
open

17.

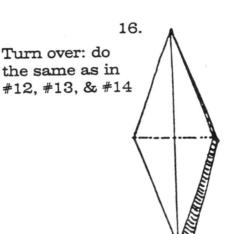

18.

Fold right side
edge to center.
Fold left side
edge to center

19.

Turn over.
Do #17 and #18
to this side

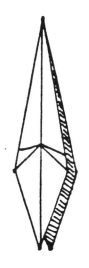

This is the
completed crane
base

20.

Fold on long triangle
inside and reverse
fold under the wing.
Do the same inside
reverse fold on
other side

21.

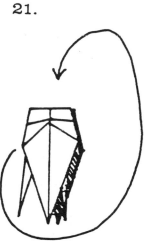

Turn it around
so that the
points are up

22.

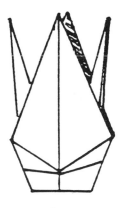

Fold down inside
reverse fold to
make head

23.

Ready to
open

24.

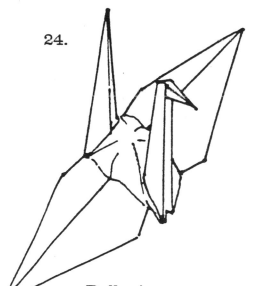

Pull wings apart gently.
Let air in bottom by
pushing up on wings from
underneath with your two
middle fingers.

—Illustrations by
Megumi Yanada
Miyazaki, Japan

Art

PURPOSE:

To demonstrate how each person can be a peace link in the neighborhood.

PREPARATION:

Materials
- Styrofoam sheet, green, 28" x 36" x 1/2"
- Posterboard
- Tempera paint
- Brushes
- Pipe cleaners, multi-colored
- Paper
- Scissors or paper cutter
- Chalkboard or newsprint
- Chalk or marker
- Pens

Advance Preparation
- Design and paint the backdrop for the neighborhood.
- Prepare the styrofoam by painting roads and other neighborhood components onto it.
- Attach the posterboard to the styrofoam base, or hang it on a wall.
- Cut the paper into small strips.

PROCEDURE:

Show the students the neighborhood. Ask them what's missing in it. The answer is people. Emphasize how each person can personally work for peace where he or she lives. Some themes to talk about are cooperating, caring, helping, understanding and listening. Tell the children this activity will stress peace links in a neighborhood. Help the children articulate peace resolutions that can be used in the neighborhood, such as "I will..." or "I will not...". List these on a chalkboard or on newsprint.

Give each pupil a pipe cleaner to use to make a stick figure of himself or herself. Also hand out paper strips which will become the peace links. Using pens or markers, let each child choose a peace resolution to write on the slip. Insert the people into the green styrofoam linked by the peace resolutions or holding hands with the peace messages held by each figure.

To personalize the project even more, have the children bring a picture of themselves to glue to their pipe cleaner person.

Encourage the children to keep the peace resolutions in their own neighborhood.

Art:
Draw Your Dream Of Peace

PURPOSE:

To identify and illustrate ways children in a neighborhood can be peacemakers together.

PREPARATION:

Materials
- "PEACE IN THE NEIGHBORHOOD" coloring sheets
- Crayons or markers
- Paper

Advance Preparation
- Duplicate coloring sheets.

PROCEDURE:

Pass out the "Peace in the Neighborhood" coloring sheets and crayons or markers and tell the students to color them. When they have finished, ask them to draw, write or talk about other ways children in a neighborhood can have fun playing together. Gather and guide ideas on how this helps children be peacemakers.

Art: Draw Your Dream Of Peace

Draw or write other ways children in a neighborhood can have fun playing together.

Talk about how playing together promotes peacemaking.

Banners/Textiles

PURPOSE:

To combine individually produced pieces of fabric art into a powerful peace statement in a neighborhood.

PREPARATION:

Materials
- Muslin, 100% cotton, 2' x 3' piece per person.
- Scissors
- Embroidery thread, liquid paint or permanent markers, optional
- Pins
- Thread
- Sewing machine
- Information on "The Ribbon" project
- Guidelines, optional

Advance Preparation
- Cut a two foot by three foot piece of fabric for each participant.
- Prepare printed guidelines, if desired.

PROCEDURE:

On Hiroshima Day, 1985, the fortieth anniversary of the bombing, thousands of people gathered in Washington, DC and formed a human chain around the Pentagon and several other government buildings. In their hands they held "The Ribbon." This project, originated by Justine Merritt, a mother and grandmother from Denver, Colorado, consisted of numerous two foot by three foot fabric panels which were tied together as an expression of care and concern for the country. The pieces were embroidered, woven, hooked, quilted, needlepointed, appliqued and painted with illustrations of things people cherish most and could not bear to lose in a nuclear war.[129] Details of the project and pictures of the pieces are available in the book The Ribbon: A Celebration of Life.[130]

Adapt this project and use it to bind children, and others, together in a beautiful expression of peace in a neighborhood.

Gather the participants and share information on and pictures of the original ribbon project. Decide around which buildings or areas of the neighborhood the ribbon will be wrapped or displayed. It could be a church, school, city hall, community center, park, playground or store. Individual sections might first be exhibited on homes and later tied together and installed in a public location.

Talk with the young people about designs to create on the sections. These might be family, friends, flowers, fields or forests.

Give guidelines for the project. It would be helpful if these were printed and distributed. Tell each person he or she will receive a piece of fabric which is to be folded double to a finished size of eighteen inches by thirty-six inches. The embroidery may be done on one-half of one thickness and folded over, through both thicknesses, or worked on separate fabric and attached to the muslin. The embroidered, or decorated section, is to be twenty inches by thirty-two inches. Suggest techniques to use such as embroidery, liquid paint or permanent marker. Names may be sewn in the long borders.

Inform the children whether they are to seam the sides or to bring them to one person who will complete the sewing. Announce the date the pieces are due or that they will be displayed.

Distribute the fabric. Encourage the participants to prayerfully and lovingly create their pieces of the ribbon to remind people in their neighborhood that they love the earth and the people on it.

Cartoons

PURPOSE:

To make cartoon strips illustrating ways the children were peacemakers in the neighborhood.

PREPARATION:

Materials
- "A Time I Was A Peacemaker" sheet
- Paper
- Pencils
- Markers
- Duplicating equipment
- Scrapbook or photo album
- Glue or tape

Advance Preparation
- Duplicate cartoon sheets

PROCEDURE:

Brainstorm things the children have seen or done that make peace in a neighborhood. This may include telling the truth, putting peace posters in store windows, sharing toys, including someone in a game and helping a neighbor.

Tell the class they will be drawing cartoons to illustrate a time they were a peacemaker.[131] Assure them it is alright to use stick people. Show them how to make a bubble which is generally used to contain conversation.

Instruct the group to create the cartoon in three parts. The beginning illustrates how the situation started, the middle tells what happened and the end indicates how it was resolved. Titles may be written on the cartoons, too.

Hand out the sheets, pencils and markers. As the students draw a design, talk to them individually about the many ways peacemaking takes place, and thank them for the special things they are doing to promote it.

After the pupils have finished, compile a class book of the cartoons and leave it on display in the room.

A Time I Was a Peacemaker

Beginning

Middle

End

113

Clown/Mime

PURPOSE:

To help children understand the concept of servant-hood as a critical factor in peacemaking.

PREPARATION:

Materials
- Chairs, three
- Rope
- Bucket
- Brushes, various sizes, including a tooth brush
- Rags
- Baby shoe
- Posterboard
- Marker
- Plastic lids
- Aluminum foil
- Hats; man's, woman's, child's cap, and beat-up hat.

Advance Preparation
- Make four coins by wrapping foil around the plastic lids.
- On two coins, write "five cents," on the other two, write "ten cents."

PROCEDURE:

This clown skit, based on the New Testament scripture, John 13:1-17, in which Jesus washed the disciples' feet, is an especially effective way to convey the theme of servanthood which is an underlying concept of both clowning and peacemaking.[132]

If two people play all the roles, Clown One should play the shoe shiner and Clown Two should portray the remaining characters. Otherwise, five different people may present the skit. Involve everyone at the end. It is most effective when done non-verbally.

Script

Clown 1: Enters a bare stage which contains the three chairs. He is carrying a bucket filled with brushes, rags, marker and baby shoe; posterboard; rope. He sets up a shoe shine stand by placing one chair center stage and the remaining two chairs behind it on either side of the stage. The rope is tied around the chair backs. He makes a sign which reads "Shoe Shine - 10 Cents" and hangs it on the rope. When finished, he rests on the chair and waits for the first customer.

Clown 2: Enters wearing man's hat and carrying imaginary briefcase. Gestures that he would like his shoes shined, pays ten cents and sits on chair.

Clown 1: Shines the shoes.

Clown 2: Exits.

Clown 3: Enters wearing woman's hat. Gestures that shoes should be shined, pays ten cents and sits on chair.

Clown 1: Shines the shoes in a delicate way, such as using the toothbrush.

Clown 3: Exits.

Clown 4: Enters wearing child's cap. Gestures for shoes to be shined. Pays five cents.

Clown 1: Points to shoe shine sign and gestures for more money.

Clown 4: Reluctantly pays other nickel. Sits on a chair.

Clown 1: Shines the shoes.

Clown 4: Exits.

Clown 5: Enters wearing tramp hat. Points to shoes.

Clown 1: Requests money.

Clown 5: Gestures that he has no money and begs and pleads to have shoes shined.

Clown 1: Reluctantly gives in and gestures for clown five to sit down.

Clown 5: Sits down.

Clown 1: Shines shoes, but since they are so

dirty, uses exaggerated movements and actions. After trying various brushes, he removes shoes from tramp's feet, scrubs them in the bucket and hangs them on line or sets them on chair to dry.

Clown 5: Waits impatiently for shoes to dry. Pretends feet are very cold.

Clown 1: Since the shoes have not dried, the clown takes off his own shoes (sandals would be good), and places them on the feet of clown five.

Clown 5: Excitedly hugs Clown One and leaves.

Clown 1: Realizes how happy giving of himself for someone else has made him and changes sign to read "Shoe Shine - Free" rather that "10 cents." At this point he begins to take people from the audience and clean their shoes. He can also supply them with brushes and rags and send them through the group to "wash" other people's feet.

After the skit, apply the concept of servanthood to the theme, "Peace In The Neighborhood." Ask the children to cite ways in which they can be servants. Examples could include shoveling snow for an elderly neighbor, playing with a small child to give the parent a break, or baking bread and delivering it as a gift.

Creative Writing

PURPOSE:

To make and send telegrams that promote peace in the neighborhood.

PREPARATION:

Materials
- Telegram
- Construction paper
- Markers

PROCEDURE:

Show the children an actual telegram, if one is available. Ask the group if they know what makes a telegram unique. It contains a brief, to the point message, and it often carries unexpected news. Suggest to the children that the telegram idea can be used to promote peace in the neighborhood. It could be called a "Peacegram."

Brainstorm messages to write and people to whom they might be sent, like "I won't walk on your grass anymore." for the neighbor who just re-seeded his lawn, or "You're invited to play ball at 4:00 p.m." to the girl who just moved into the next block.

Pass out construction paper and markers and instruct the learners to write "Peacegram" in large letters across the top of the page. Tell the participants to address the communication to someone specific, to write a message, and to sign it. Encourage them to deliver the "peacegram," and to follow through on what they wrote.

Creative Writing: Poetry

PURPOSE:

To identify common, ordinary people who promote peace in a neighborhood, and to write Cinquain poetry about them.

PREPARATION:

Materials
- Pictures of community helpers, optional
- Paper
- Pens
- Stationary

PROCEDURE:

Ask the students to name various people who live and work in a neighborhood. The list may include parents, teachers, fire fighters, crossing guards and doctors. Show the children pictures of community helpers, if desired. Request examples of ways in which each of these people are peacemakers.

Invite each pupil to think specifically of one person and to write a poem about a way, or ways, in which he or she has observed that person being a peacemaker.

Demonstrate how a Cinquain poem is written. Show the children that it contains five lines and is based on the following formula:

Line One: A one-word noun.
Line Two: Two adjectives that describe the noun.
Line Three: Three "-ing" words that describe the noun.
Line Four: Four words that express a feeling about the noun.
Line Five: One word that is a synonym for the noun.

For example:

John
Painter, Repairer
Sharing, Caring, Giving
Helping those in need
Peacemaker.

Ask the children to read their poems to the rest of the group. Use these creative expressions to celebrate the excitement of the variety of ways there are to be peacemakers.

Continue the project by allowing each child to choose a piece of stationery or special paper. Ask each "poet" to copy his or her Cinquain onto the paper and to deliver it to the person about whom the poem was written.

Culinary Arts

PURPOSE:

To grow a neighborhood garden and to share the yield.

PREPARATION:

Materials
- Seeds
- Plants
- Gardening tools and equipment

PROCEDURE:

Growing a neighborhood garden is a project much like peacemaking. It requires cooperation and commitment. Besides yielding great food it can also result in good friendship.

Suggest that the children invite people in their own neighborhood to start a garden. Or, as a group, plant one on the church or school property. Throughout the process of planning, planting and picking, help the children get in touch with the amount of time and energy involved in achieving the product.

When the crop is cultivated, share it with all who have been involved in the project. Prepare a meal from it to eat together. The goods may also be given to people in need or sold and the money distributed to hunger relief organizations.

A children's book on gardening, which emphasizes issues of ecology and world hunger, is <u>Celebrate The Seasons: A Gardening Book for Children Ages 7 and Up</u>.[261]

Dance

PURPOSE:

To use a Native American dance to remind participants of the beauty of self as well as the beauty of people in a neighborhood.

PREPARATION:
Materials
- Drum

PROCEDURE:

The Native American dance, "I Walk In Beauty," will help the participants explore and express the beauty within themselves as well as the beauty of people and places in a neighborhood.

Ask the children to form a circle. Begin the dance with a drum beat and a step to the right. Repeat this procedure for each phrase. Chant a line to the group and accompany it with the appropriate gesture and direct the pupils to echo both back. Movements to use are:

Beauty below me
Reach down in front.

Beauty beside me
Reach to the right.

Beauty inside me
Cross arms in front of chest.

I walk in beauty
Arms raised, elbows bent, palms up.

Beauty outside me
Spread arms to the sides.

Beauty above me
Arms extended over head.

Beauty all around me.[134]
Turn in place.

117

Drama

PURPOSE:

To dramatize ways in which people promote peace in a neighborhood.

PREPARATION:

Materials
- Paper
- Pencils

PROCEDURE:

Use a TV news show format to help the children comprehend peacemaking roles and responsibilities in a neighborhood. Have one or several students be the host or anchor team, and let the others be the people who are interviewed.

Brainstorm a number of neighborhood peacemakers with the students. There could be many: the person who washes the elderly woman's windows, the man who organizes basketball games to give children something to do, the boy who recycles newspaper and the person who shares vegetables from a garden. Stress how all of these people are displaying peacemaking concepts such as regard for human dignity, stewardship of the earth and conflict resolution.

Give the children an opportunity to choose parts, to write short statements and to practice and present the program.

Drama: Plays

PURPOSE:

To provide an opportunity for young people to participate in a dramatic process and production which will identify ways to bring peace to a neighborhood.

PREPARATION:

Materials
- City at Peace[135]

PROCEDURE:

City at Peace is a musical social-inter-action project which is designed to bring diverse groups from conflicting areas of a city together to promote communication, build understanding and create solutions for problems facing a particular area.

The open cast, open stage production has dramatic roles, chorus parts and dance numbers. The skeletal script is completed by the cast and, thus, addresses their own particular needs and negotiations.

The unique and creative production enables participants to improve social skills, heighten self-esteem and be empowered to seek solutions to specific problems and to act on them.

118

Games

PURPOSE:

To play a game which encourages an awareness of and an appreciation for differences.

PROCEDURE:

A familiar cooperative game, "Touch Blue," encourages people to discover and affirm differences.

Gather the children in a circle. Tell the participants that a color and an article of wearing apparel will be mentioned. Everyone should gently touch a person wearing the item(s) named. Some suggestions to name for each round are, "Touch someone wearing blue socks, green skirt, red shirt, brown glasses or pink jewelry."

Give everyone in the group an opportunity to suggest a few items. Try to include at least one or two things about every person playing.

After the game, talk about the differences between people who live in the same neighborhood and encourage suggestions of ways these differences can be appreciated.

Music

PURPOSE:

To listen to and record sounds of peace in a neighborhood.

PREPARATION:

Materials
- Tape recorder(s)
- Blank tape(s)

PROCEDURE:

Go on a Sound Scavenger Search. Take a walk through the neighborhood and listen for sounds of peace. Some might be a person shoveling an elderly neighbor's drive-way, a father reading to his son, the chirping of the birds, children laughing together as they wash a car, or boys and girls playing a cooperative game.

Take along a portable tape recorder and make a tape of the sounds. Use one recorder for the entire group or several for individual students or smaller groups. After the walk, play back the tape(s) and talk about the sounds that contribute to peace in the neighborhood.

Music: Song Adaptation

Music: Song Suggestions

PURPOSE:

To write verses for the song "This Little Light of Mine" on the theme peace in the neighborhood.

PURPOSE:

To help children note songs stressing the theme peace in the neighborhood.

PREPARATION:

Materials
- Music, "This Little Light of Mine"
- Accompaniment, optional

PREPARATION:

Materials
- Music
- Accompaniment, optional

PROCEDURE:

Sing the chorus of the song "This Little Light of Mine." As the verse, use the words:

"Let it shine in the neighborhood,
I'm gonna' let it shine.
Let it shine in the neighborhood,
I'm gonna' let it shine,
Let it shine, let it shine, let it shine."

Ask the children to name ways that they can let their lights of peace shine in the neighborhood. Put these ideas into verses, such as:

Help my neighbor rake his leaves,
I'm gonna' let it shine.
Take the baby for a walk,
I'm gonna' let it shine,
Let it shine, let it shine, let it shine.

Remind the children to let their lights shine in all situations in their neighborhoods.

PROCEDURE:

Introduce the topic of peace in the neighborhood by singing:

"All Things Bright and Beautiful"[136]

"How Good It Is and How Pleasant"[137]

"O People, Come and Raise Your Voice"[138]

"There Is Always Something You Can Do"[139]

Photography

PURPOSE:

To photograph a neighborhood renewal project and to share the pictures in a public forum.

PREPARATION:

Materials
- Camera
- Film

Advance Preparation
- Acquire information on several neighborhood renewal projects.

PROCEDURE:

Pick a neighborhood renewal project and take before and after pictures of it. This could range from restoring a home to revitalizing an area, from planting a garden to preparing a playground, or from collecting liter in a park to cleaning a stream of pollution.

Describe several projects to the students and have them select the one they would like to document. Arrange for a time, or several times, to go to the site and to take pictures.

At the conclusion of the work, share the pictures of peacemaking in progress with a local newspaper or city council.

Photography: Media

PURPOSE:

To illustrate the theme peace in the neighborhood through the use of media.

PREPARATION:

Materials
- Film, The Daisy[140]
- Projector
- Screen
- Extension cord

PROCEDURE:

Show the film The Daisy to the children. In it, peace in the neighborhood is disrupted by a single inconsiderate act. This seven minute film shows a man throwing trash over his fence which lands in the yard next door and the retaliation for this act that the neighbor initiates. In a flashback, a flower is thrown over instead, and a totally different and positive interaction takes place between the two people.

Discuss how what is done to a neighbor can have wide reaching consequences.

Puppetry

PURPOSE:

To help children understand that people with differences can live in harmony.

PREPARATION:

Materials
- Paper plates, white
- Craft sticks
- Crepe paper streamers: red, orange, yellow, green, blue, purple
- Markers or crayons
- Stapler
- Staples

Advance Preparation
- Cut paper plates in half.
- Cut crepe paper strips to 12" - 18" lengths.

PROCEDURE:

Make rainbow puppets with the children to help them think about the blend of people in a neighborhood.

Pass out a paper plate half to each person. Provide markers and tell the children to draw a face on the plate. Invite the children to pick up one streamer for each color of the rainbow and to staple them to their plates. Use the rainbow puppets in several ways. Talk about the way the colors harmonize and blend. Parallel this with the importance of each person working towards peace and harmony. Play music and have the children move their puppets to it. Read stories about rainbows and illustrate them with the puppets.

Storytelling

PURPOSE:

To enable children to share stories with older people.

PREPARATION:

Materials
- Paper
- Pens

Advance Preparation
- Obtain the names of elderly people in a congregation, neighborhood, senior center or nursing home.
- Set up a visit.

PROCEDURE:

Involve the children in an adopt-a-grandparent project in a neighborhood. Before the first visit, ask the boys and girls to talk about some of their experiences with grandparents or older relatives, neighbors and church members. Tell the students that they will each have the privilege of visiting and sharing stories with a long lived person and of adopting the man or woman as a friend or grandparent. Suggest conversation starters and questions to use during the visit. Encourage a discussion of the elderly person's fondest childhood memories.

Tell the children that after the visit they will have the opportunity to write the story of their new friend's life. These may be shared with the individual, if desired. It would also be fun to act out the story through drama or puppetry or to draw pictures depicting some of the experiences.

Storytelling: Children's Books

PURPOSE:

To provide an opportunity for children to read books and to consider the theme, Peace in the Neighborhood.

PREPARATION:

Materials
- Book(s)

PROCEDURE:

Conflict resolution is the theme reflected in many books covering the theme of peace in the neighborhood. Try a few of the following to begin a discussion on the subject:

The Hating Book [141] A little girl felt her friend hated her, and finally got up the courage to ask her the reason. They parted friends again. Illustrates the importance of talking through a problem.

Let's Be Enemies [142] Maurice Sendak illustrated this book about the conflict between two boys which results in them becoming "enemies," until they decide they have more fun as friends.

Let's Talk About Fighting [143] Conflict resolution is the theme of this book, which talks about the ways quarrels and fights begin, and explores alternatives to fighting.

The Story of Ferdinand [144] "Ferdinand was chosen to fight in the bull fights of Madrid after he sat on a bumblebee and appeared to be a fierce, fighting bull. What happened when Ferdinand got to the fighting ring makes a happy ending for a bull who loved peace." [145]

That's Not Fair [146] When four friends were playing together on a winter day, a snow ball fight started an argument. Although they all went home angry, they soon became lonely, and made up the next day.

Storytelling: Folktales

PURPOSE:

To explore conflict resolution using the folktale, The Three Billy Goats Gruff, as an example.

PREPARATION:

Materials
- Folktale, The Three Billy Goats Gruff [147]

PROCEDURE:

Ask the children to summarize the familiar Norwegian folktale, The Three Billy Goats Gruff. Have the group identify the basic problem between the goats and the troll. The three billy goats needed to cross the troll's bridge and the troll was hungry and wanted something to eat.

After recalling the story and summarizing the problem, work together to write a new ending that will resolve the conflict. Explore possible ways in which the three goats and the troll might cooperate to meet their needs in a non-violent manner.

Ask the children to think about how people in a neighborhood could work together to make it a peaceful place. Bring up issues such as noise, respect for property and life, assistance for the home bound, and hospitality to newcomers. Just as there are many cooperative ways to resolve the conflict in the folktale, there are numerous non-violent options to use in real life situations too.

[126] Park, Mary Joan. Peacemaking for Little Friends: Tips, Lessons and Resources for Parents and Teachers. Saint Paul, MN: Little Friends for Peace, 1985, 6.

[127] Coerr, Eleanor. Sadako and the Thousand Paper Cranes. New York: Dell Publishing, 1977.

[128] Obold, Ruth. Prepare for Peace: A Peace Study for Children. Part III: Grades 7-8. Newton, KS: Faith and Life Press, 1986, 21-23. Reprinted with permission.

[129] Wollman, Neil, ed. Working for Peace: A Handbook of Practical Psychology and Other Tools. San Luis Obispo, CA: Impact Publishers, 1985, 243.

[130] Philbin, Marianne. The Ribbon: A Celebration of Life. Asheville, NC: Lark Books, 1985.

[131] Hammatt-Kavaloski, Jane, and Maureen Golombowski. Becoming Peacemakers: Peace Education Curriculum Pre-school to Grade 5. Madison, WI: Madison Metropolitan School District, 1985, 23-26.

[132] Based on a skit by the Lovely Lane Clown Troupe of East United Methodist Church, Mishawaka, IN; Kari Mills, Director.

[133] Hunt, Linda, Marianne Frase, and Doris Liebert. Celebrate The Seasons: A Gardening Book For Children Ages 7 and Up. Scottdale, PA: Herald Press, 1983.

[134] Strain, Marie M., ed. Ideas for Celebration of Peace. Concord, MA: National Peace Day Celebrations, 1985, 19. Adapted with permission.

[135] Grossman, Carlo. City at Peace. David Gordon, composer. Fairfax, VA: Peace Child Foundation, 1989. Available from: Peace Child Foundation, 3977 Chain Bridge Road, Fairfax, VA 22030. (703) 385-4494. Also available: Script and score with production notes, newsletter.

[136] Hawkes, Mary, and Paul Hamill, eds. Sing to God: Songs and Hymns for Christian Education. New York: United Church Press, 1984, 34.

[137] Ibid., 125.

[138] Ibid., 160.

[139] Weiss, Evelyn, ed. Children's Songs for a Friendly Planet. Burnsville, NC: World Around Songs, 1986, 48.

[140] The Daisy. Bulgarian State Film Board, 1967. Available from: BFA Educational Media, 2211 Michigan Ave., Santa Monica, CA 90404.

[141] Zolotow, Charlotte. The Hating Book. New York: Harper and Row, 1969.

[142] Udry, Janice. Let's Be Enemies. New York: Harper and Row, 1961.

[143] Berry, Joy Wilt. Let's Talk about Fighting. Chicago: Children's Press, 1984.

[144] Leaf, Munro. The Story of Ferdinand. New York: Ruffin, 1977.

[145] Seitz, Kathryn F., ed. A Working Bibliography of Peace Resources for Children and Youth. Harrisonburg, VA: Education Department, Eastern Mennonite College, 1984, 3.

[146] Fujikawa, Gyo. That's Not Fair. New York: Grosset and Dunlap, 1983.

[147] Asbjornsen, Peter Christian. The Three Billy Goats Gruff. Retold by Paul Galdone. New York: Clarion Books, 1973.

CHAPTER SEVEN

PEACE IN THE
COMMUNITY

Introduction

Many issues, such as homelessness, recycling, domestic violence, drugs and racial tension, come under the theme "peace in the community." Concepts to consider include cooperation, communication, stewardship, and conflict resolution. These themes and topics, as well as others, are addressed in creative ways through the activities included in this section.

Besides helping children explore this theme through activities, however, it is important to teach processes for communicating and cooperating with others which will help them all through life. A design, commonly used in family or classroom meetings, can also be employed in community groups in which young people are involved. A suggested meeting procedure is:

Time: Once a week, every week.

Setting: No interruptions. Should be a comfortable place with participants sitting facing each other.

Length: Fifteen to thirty minutes, depending on the age of the participants.

Agenda: Post ahead of time and include:
1. Gripes and gratitude
2. Problem solving
3. Decision making - calendar, work parties, service projects, fun times.

Leadership: Rotate as much as possible.

Expected Behavior:
1. Everyone has a chance to speak without interruption and criticism.
2. Participants are encouraged to share honest feelings without retaliation.
3. Everyone listens and tries to understand varying points of view.

Decision Making: Adults decide which decisions will be made by the adults or the children after hearing all points of view; other decisions can be made consensually.

Suggested process:
1. Person putting item on agenda explains it and others ask clarifying questions.
2. If appropriate, the person is encouraged to offer a change or solution.
3. Others are asked to add additional solutions or suggestions.
4. Evaluate alternatives suggested.
5. Decide on one and work out a plan to implement it.
6. Set time, if relevant, to evaluate decision.

Architecture

PURPOSE:

To create a cardboard community to emphasize the importance of diversity within a town.

PREPARATION:

Materials
- Appliance boxes, large
- Cartons, various sizes
- Drop cloths
- Newspapers
- Tempera paints
- Brushes
- Matte knives
- Scissors
- Markers
- Tape

PROCEDURE:

Begin with a discussion about the kinds of places people need in a community. Include locations for protection, security, friendship, entertainment, health and so forth. Emphasize the importance of different people offering different things to the community. Also stress that there are many ways to fulfill a need. Food, for example, may come from a convenience store, farmer's market or fast food restaurant.

Tell the children that they will be creating a cardboard community together. Ask each student or group of pupils to pick a place to make. Show the people the supplies and provide each individual or team with a large appliance box. Encourage them to use the materials to construct their buildings. Suggest basics like doors and windows and details such as signs and shingles.

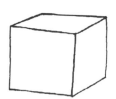

At a designated time, ask everyone to help clean up. Then assemble the box buildings as a community. Invite each architect to share something about his or her building and to name a reason it is important to the community and to peacemaking. Compose individual or group prayers about the buildings and their functions and share them together.

Art

PURPOSE:

To help children realize that the feet of many people have been and can be used for peacemaking purposes.

PREPARATION:

Materials
- Bed sheet, white
- Tape
- Tempera paint, various colors
- Dishpans
- Water
- Liquid soap
- Towels

Advance Preparation
- Spread the bed sheet on the floor and tape down the corners. Pour each color of tempera in a dishpan. Add a small amount of liquid soap to the paint. This will aid clean-up at the conclusion of the activity. Place the dishpans around the sides of the sheet.

PROCEDURE:

For an especially creative activity, try painting a mural of feet. Talk with the children about ways in which feet are used to bring peace in a community. Some ways include volunteering at a homeless shelter or half-way house, walking instead of driving as a way to conserve energy, and participating in a walk for the hungry.

Instruct the children to remove their shoes and socks. Explain the procedure for making the mural. Invite one or two students at a time to choose a color and to carefully step into the dishpan containing it. Direct each person to slowly walk across the sheet. Provide wet paper towels for each pupil as he or she reaches the end. Continue this procedure until everyone has had a turn.

When the activity is completed, talk about the fact that the feet are all going in different directions, yet they all symbolize involvement in peacemaking. Also note that when one color touches another, a change takes place. Comment that when people's feet bring peace, special and wonderful changes take place, too. Cut or draw letters to form the words "Peacemaker's Feet" and place them on the top of the banner or mural. Display it in a prominent location in a classroom, congregation or community building.

Art

PURPOSE:

To involve students in a community art project which depicts peace.

PREPARATION:

Materials
- Varied with project

Advance Preparation
- Arrange for displays, exhibit space and required supplies.

PROCEDURE:

Art exhibits and displays can aid people in thinking about and acting on global and peace issues. Involve the children in one or more of these ideas.

Sponsor a community art exhibit. Select a theme, such as children as peacemakers or community peace projects and invite area artists to submit entries. Provide a button or certificate for all entrants. If prizes are awarded, give something in keeping with the theme of the exhibit.

Display the work of minority and ethnic artists in the Community.

Exhibit art from other countries and cultures. Two groups that specialize in children's art from other countries are:

CONNECT, 4835 Penn Avenue South, Minneapolis, MN 55409. Children's art from the Soviet Union.

PEACE POSTER PROJECT, c/o Michael Kamen, 99 Burlington Street, Lexington, MA 02173. Jewish-Arab Children's Art Project.

Mount displays of art work, such as sculpture and pottery, in empty store front windows and library display cases.

Request permission to paint scenes on the windows of local businesses. Highlight other cultures, ways to help prevent hunger, or an upcoming peace event.

Compile and distribute a directory of area artists who communicate global and justice themes through their media.

Art:
Draw Your
Dream Of Peace

PURPOSE:

To look at hunger in the community in an artistic and active way.

PREPARATION:

Materials
- "PEACE IN THE COMMUNITY" coloring sheets
- Crayons or markers
- Paper

Advance Preparation
- Duplicate coloring sheets.
- Obtain information on hunger relief organizations in the community.

PROCEDURE:

Introduce the topic of hunger in the community by handing out the "Peace in the Community" coloring sheet and crayons or markers. Provide time for the children to complete it.

Talk about specific hunger concerns in the community. Be sure the children are aware that it is not only the homeless or street people who are hungry. Many older people on fixed incomes and many children with parents or caretakers addicted to drugs or alcohol may be hungry too. Give a sheet of paper to each person and ask the boys and girls to divide it into four equal sections. This can easily be done by telling them to fold the paper into quarters and to unfold it again. Instruct the children to draw a picture in each quarter of a way in which they could help hungry people. Invite people to share their drawings.

Choose one or several possibilities and design a project so the children many take action on their art.

Art: Draw Your Dream Of Peace

Divide a piece of paper into four equal parts.

Draw a picture in each section of a way to help hungry people.

Banners/Textiles

PURPOSE:

To make and wear fabric symbols as part of a group's witness for peace.

PREPARATION:

Materials
- Fabric
- Scissors
- Permanent markers or liquid embroidery pens
- Sewing machine
- Thread

Advance Preparation
- Arrange to participate in a community event or project which promotes peace.
- Make a twelve inch bandanna for each person in the group. Plain cotton scarves may be purchased, if desired.

PROCEDURE:

A bandanna or square piece of cloth may serve as a witness to an individual's or group's purpose. Colorful, symbolic bandannas may be worn by persons from a church school class, specific grade, or youth club or group during a hunger walk, community parade or work project. After the event, the pieces can be combined into a banner to serve as a reminder of the group's individual and collective efforts to promote peace.

Before the event, distribute the bandannas to the participants. Instruct them to fold the scarf in half to form a triangular shape. Tell each person to use a permanent marker or liquid embroidery pen to write his or her name on each half. They might also wish to write the date of the event, information about it and the reason they are participating. Symbols, drawings and other decorations may be added.

During the event, participants should wear their scarves.

After the event, on each half of the scarves, have the pupils write feelings or other expressions or impressions elicited by their involvement in the project. If money was collected, the amount raised may be written.

Cut each bandanna in half and finish the rough edges. Give one half to each participant as a keepsake. Sew the other halves together to make a banner or table covering for the church, school or organization.

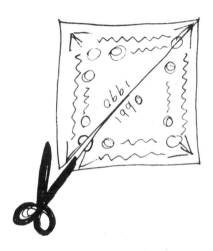

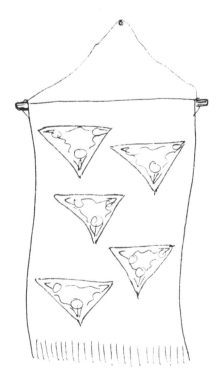

132

Cartoons

PURPOSE:

To make a cooperative cartoon addressing environmental concerns in a community.

PREPARATION:

Materials
- Paper, 8.5" x 11"
- Pens, pencils or markers
- Tape

PROCEDURE:

Addressing issues of environmental concern in a community is a cooperative matter. Make a cooperative, continuous cartoon strip to help the children think about ways they can save the earth and make a difference in their own town.

Tell the group that each person will draw his or her idea on a full sheet of paper. Encourage them to have their work touch the four sides of the paper. Note that the individual "frames" will be joined to make a long cartoon strip. Some of the subjects of the drawings may be planting trees, eliminating styrofoam, recycling newspapers, forming carpools and buying solar powered watches.

Give a piece of paper, recycled if possible, to each person. Let the boys and girls choose if they would like to use pens, pencils or markers.

As the children finish their "frame," tape the section to the wall. When the entire cartoon is completed, ask each child to stand by his or her section. Go down the line and invite the boys and girls to describe what they drew.

Clown/Mime

PURPOSE:

To develop a troupe of clowns for peace to participate in community events.

PREPARATION:

Materials
- Clown white make-up
- Greasepaint: red, blue
- China markers, black
- Mirror(s)
- White socks
- Baby powder
- Brushes, shaving or make-up
- Baby oil
- Paper towels or tissues
- Costumes
- Wigs
- Props

Advance Preparation
- Obtain or make clown costumes and wigs.

PROCEDURE:

Start a troupe of clowns for peace and participate in a community event such as a parade. Demonstrate how to become a white face clown using the following method.

Explain that around the world the white face is the symbol of death. During the application of the white face, the old person is erased, or dies to self.

Be sure the face is thoroughly clean. Tie hair away from the face. A skull cap made from a knotted piece of pantyhose works well for this purpose. If the skin is dry, apply a thin coat of baby oil as a base. Pat dots of clown white make-up to the forehead, cheeks, chin, nose and neck. Smooth it to cover the entire face, including the eyelids and nostrils. Smooth the make-up with the finger tips. If the make-up feels heavy or if it cracks, tissue off the excess and re-smooth. Fill a white sock with baby powder. Pat the powder over the entire white area using the sock. Remove the excess with a shaving or make-up brush. Set the make-up by gently patting it with cold water.

Begin to create the new person by adding color. Select colors that will enhance the personality of the clown character. Only use three colors on the face. To form the mouth, leave the top lip white and apply red to the bottom lip. Experiment with different shapes and sizes. Add eye, cheek or nose decorations. Outline the colored areas with a black china marker. Powder the colored areas carefully, brush off the excess and pat with water.

Help the children get into costume and make-up.

Plan the actions and attitudes that will make the troupe distinctly peacemakers in the community. Talk about places, besides a parade, where the participants could perform. Ideas include nursing homes, children's hospitals, retirement homes, homes for the mentally retarded, special olympics programs, shopping malls, streets, parks, special parties and civic organizations.

Creative Writing

PURPOSE:

To guide children in creative writing opportunities that can be used in every section of the community newspaper.

PREPARATION:

Materials
- Community newspapers
- Paper
- Pens
- Envelopes
- Stamps

PROCEDURE:

Show the children copies of daily and weekly newspapers that are published in the community. Invite them to participate in a creative writing project, or several of them that will encourage the inclusion of peace news in various sections of the papers. Try some of these ideas:

Editorial Page. Write a "Letter to the Editor" or a "Point of View" article on ways in which local residents can work to promote peace and justice.

National News. Encourage the inclusion of positive news of third world developments and national and international stories.

Metro Section. Submit news releases on refugee resettlement programs in the area.

Religion Page. Request a feature on the work of local chapters of world hunger relief organizations.

Culinary/Food Section. Suggest an issue devoted to ethnic dishes, menus or restaurants.

Entertainment Section. Highlight performances by ethnic musicians, drama groups and dance troupes.

Travel Page. Research interesting, little-known places that might be featured.

<u>Women's Page</u>. Create opportunities for interviews with local peacemakers, women representing a variety of cultures, and international guests.

<u>Youth Page</u>. Ask the paper to print children's peace poems or essays.

<u>Sports Page</u>. Supply a story on a community team or athlete playing in another country.

Remember to submit information and articles to church and school newsletters and newspapers as well.

Also, use the newspaper as a resource. Have the youth clip articles that can be used to compile a scrapbook of stories about people working for peace, or to form a peace news bulletin board.

Creative Writing: Poetry

PURPOSE:

To engage children in a poetry event that will help them discover ways in which peace is possible in a community.

PREPARATION:

Materials
- Peace Poetry Guidelines
- Awards

Advance Preparation
- Form Peace Poetry Contest Committee
- Secure judges

PROCEDURE:

Hold a community peace poetry contest for children, or open it to people of all ages. Print and distribute guidelines containing the following information:

Sponsors: List the name(s) of the sponsoring group(s).

Theme: Pick an open-ended theme around which entries can be based, for example, "Peace Is Possible in our community because..."

Age Categories: List grades or ages which may enter.

Format: Name the styles of poetry that are eligible. State how entries are to be submitted, for example, on one side of an 8.5" x 11" paper. Note that name, grade, school or congregation, and phone are to be printed on the back of the page.

Deadline: Include day, date and time.

Submit to: Provide the name of the person or place and the address where the entries may be delivered or mailed.

Judging: Indicate the criteria upon which the entries will be judged, such as imagination, style, content, neatness and so forth. Name categories of judges like teachers, librarians, drama directors. Give specific names, if possible.

Awards: Give a prize, perhaps a button or certificate, to everyone who enters. List first, second and third place prizes. These could be money, t-shirts or books. Note any other type of recognition, such as reading the winning entries at a public function or awarding something special to the school or congregation submitting the most entries.

Other information: Note whether the entries will become the property of the sponsoring group(s) or be returned to the writer. Indicate that the decision of the judges is final.

Contact Persons: List names and phone numbers of people who may be called for questions or information.

After the contest: Mount the entries and display them in public locations. Print the poetry in the newspaper. Compile an anthology of some of the pieces.

Culinary Arts

PURPOSE:

To prepare food and to share it with a community organization.

PREPARATION:

Materials
- Resource material
- Ingredients
- Recipe(s)
- Cooking equipment

Advance Preparation
- Research community projects to which food may be donated.

PROCEDURE:

There are many needs and opportunities for sharing food in a community. These could include soup kitchens, homeless shelters, missions, prisons, group homes and extended care facilities. Enable the children to become aware of some of these through the use of speakers, audio-visual materials, newspaper articles and field trips.

As a group, choose a project and get involved. Some ideas would be to bake bread and bring it to an institution, to prepare and package muffins and share them with other people, or to make soup and serve it at the selected site. Use favorite recipes or some from books at the library.

Emphasize to the students that giving and sharing are two important peacemaking skills. In giving a gift of bread, or any food, <u>Try This</u> suggests "extend the loaf of bread not as a great favor or as a gift but in the sense of sharing: 'We were baking bread today and thought you might enjoy a freshly baked loaf.'"[148]

Dance

PURPOSE:

To express feelings about peace through the language of dance.

PREPARATION:

Materials
- Poetry
- Records or tapes
- Record or tape player
- Tapes, blank
- Paper
- Pens

PROCEDURE:

Use the medium of dance to engage students in exploring their feelings on peace and specifically to express their thoughts on the theme of peace in the community. This may be done in several ways. Try poetry, such as Shel Silverstein's "Hug of War,"[149] and ask the children to interpret it gesturally. Find records and tapes of peace related music and let the pupils add movements to the songs. Have the children write to community leaders addressing peace and justice concerns, tape record the messages and ask each person to interpret his or her letter through dance.

Combine all of these offerings and hold a dance concert for the community.

After the experience, ask the children questions like:

How does dancing peace lead to feeling peace, expressing peace and promoting peace?

How does the way people feel about peace influence what they do about peace?

Drama

PURPOSE:

To use theatre games to stress creativity and cooperation as peacemaking qualities.

PROCEDURE:

Creativity and cooperation are two important qualities of peacemakers. Help the children develop both of these by involving them in a common theatre game called machines.

Tell the boys and girls that they will work together to form one machine. Each person will make an individual sound and a unique movement as part of this process. Everyone's actions and activities are needed to make the machine work.

Ask one person to move to the center of the floor and to begin a movement and make a sound like a machine. Each person, in turn, connects to the previous one and the activity continues until everyone is working together.

After the theatre game, discuss the similarities to peacemaking in the community and suggest ways that people can work together to address this theme.

Drama: Plays

PURPOSE:

To enable children to perform roles that can be acted out in actual community situations.

PREPARATION:

Materials
- The Heart of the Mountain [150]

PROCEDURE:

Many layers of learning are available from the play, The Heart of the Mountain. After children at camp hear a scary story about war, one of the counselors unites them to do something for peace. They make an entry for a community July Fourth celebration which turns a bomb into an instrument for peace. In a parallel plot, one child is struggling with his own father's death in war. This is a play for children to perform with some support from adults.

Games

PURPOSE:

To help students discover international connections in the community.

PREPARATION:

Materials
- Scavenger Hunt lists
- Pens

Advance Preparation
- Prepare Scavenger Hunt lists.

PROCEDURE:

In a scavenger hunt, a popular party game, individuals or teams are given a list of items to find and a designated time and area in which to do it. This popular technique is a good game to use to help children learn more about their community and its international connections.

Sample questions may be:

- Find ten churches that support missionaries in other countries. List the names of the missionaries and the location of their assignment.

- Get the menus from five ethnic restaurants.

- Make a list of five ethnic grocery stores.

- Find what languages are taught in area schools. Get information on five churches with specific ethnic roots.

- Get five area residents who have travelled to another country in the last five years to write a few sentences about the experience and sign it.

- Make a list of three area businesses that are owned by foreign companies.

- List the titles of ten books or magazines in the library that were printed in another country. Write the name of the country, too.

- Find five hymns in the church songbook that were composed by people from other countries.

- Bring samples of five items from grocery stores or bakeries that have international connections.

When the children have finished the scavenger hunt, compare and compile answers so everyone can become more aware of the world in the community.

Music

PURPOSE:

To use music as a method to build community.

PREPARATION:

Materials
- Music
- Accompaniment

PROCEDURE:

Incorporate music into classes and gatherings to build a spirit of community. Ingrid Rogers, in the book Working for Peace, writes "A song at the beginning of a public or private meeting relaxes people and draws the group together. During longer sessions, singing gives a change of pace and raises the mood of participants. A song expressing hope and togetherness is a good way to end an event; it tends to energize people at the closing." [151]

Invite each church school class to pick a favorite peace song. Suggest that all of the selections be combined and that a concert for the community be given. Feature the music of various ethnic and religious groups as well as folk and patriotic songs at this "Singing Together" event. Incorporate opportunities for the audience to participate too.

A black spiritual, "Down By The Riverside," a Jewish blessing, "Shalom Chaverim," Saint Francis' prayer, "Lord, Make Me An Instrument of Your Peace," and a patriotic plea, "Give Me Your Tired, Your Poor" are examples of songs to include in a concert.

Music: Song Adaptation

PURPOSE:

To compose verses for an existing tune on the theme peace in the community.

PREPARATION:

Materials
- Record, "Here We Go Round the Mulberry Bush"
- Record player

PROCEDURE:

Play a recording of "Here We Go Round the Mulberry Bush." Most children will know the tune, but if they do not, teach it to them. Use the tune and write new verses concentrating on children as peacemakers in the community. Start with general statements like "This is the way we work for peace, with children 'round the world," or "This is the way we join our hands, with children 'round the world." Discuss specific ways in which the students in one community can strive to accomplish this. Sing about these ideas, too.

Music: Song Selections

PURPOSE:

To emphasize the theme peace in the community through song.

PREPARATION:

Materials
- Music
- Accompaniment, optional

PROCEDURE:

Sample a selection of music suggesting ways peace can be accomplished in a community. Sing pieces like:

"Little Bit of Light" [152]

"O God of Justice, Hear Our Plea" [153]

"We Shall Overcome" [154]

"When The Poor Ones" ("Cuando El Pobre") [155]

Photography

PURPOSE:

To produce a video on the theme peace in the community.

PREPARATION:

Materials
- Video camera
- Tapes
- VCR
- Monitor
- Resource materials
- Paper
- Pens

PROCEDURE:

Powerful statements on issues that effect peace in the community can be produced as videos. Numerous themes could be addressed including homelessness, pollution, drugs and crime. The finished product can be shared in many ways.

Before the session, obtain a video camera, tapes, VCR and monitor. Be sure the equipment works properly.

Choose a topic with the children. Obtain resources on the selected theme. These could be in the form of speakers, books, films or field trips.

Work together to produce a short video statement on the subject. Suggest creative methods for the presentation such as music, drama or a game show format. Allow time for the group to write the script and to hold a brief rehearsal. If there are a large number of participants, divide them into small groups and have each of them create a scene.

Video tape the segments. Show the finished product(s) to the class. Arrange to have the tapes shown on cable television. Loan them to congregations and schools to use in discussions on the issues.

Photography: Media

PURPOSE:

To show a filmstrip which will introduce children to an issue effecting peace in a community.

PREPARATION:

Materials
- Filmstrip, <u>Charlie Cheddar's Choice</u> [156]
- Projector
- Extension cord

PROCEDURE:

Project <u>Charlie Cheddar's Choice</u>, an informative, motivational and entertaining filmstrip which will introduce children to basic hunger facts. The thirteen minute media experience shows Charlie having a series of dreams which stimulate him to read, think, learn and take action. Encourage the participants to respond to a community hunger concern.

Puppetry

PURPOSE:

To create giant puppets, representing people from around the world, to use at community functions.

PREPARATION:

Materials
- Resource materials, various countries
- Paper
- Pencils
- Aluminum clothesline poles
- Bleach bottles, large
- Hangers
- Duct tape
- Pantyhose
- Paper towel tubes
- Packing material (thin styrofoam-like material from a furniture store)
- Cardboard
- Scissors
- Felt
- Tacky glue
- Fabric
- Plastic bags, colored
- Trims
- Yarn
- Dowel rods, optional

Advance Preparation
- Clean the bottles and remove the labels. Allow the bottles to dry.

PROCEDURE:

Giant puppets, created primarily from recyclable materials, can be an attractive and attention-getting addition to community parades, ethnic festivals and holiday celebrations. They can be made by individuals, classes or groups. A variety of characters, including people representing different countries of the world, are possible.

Provide information on many countries and have each student or group choose one for which they will make a puppet person. It may be helpful to distribute paper and pencils and suggest that a sketch of the puppet be made before the actual work begins.

Distribute the bottles, which will become the puppet's head. Tell the children to turn their bottles up-side-down and to decide if the handle will be used on the front of the face as the nose, or if it will be turned to the back and not seen.

Pass out the aluminum clothes-line poles. The pole is the puppet body. Also give each person a hanger and tell him or her to straighten the hook. Instruct the pupils to insert their pole into the opening of their bottle. Next, direct them to insert the straightened portion of the hanger into the bottle opening on the front side of the pole. Provide duct tape and have each person wrap it around the pole, hanger and bottle to fasten them together.

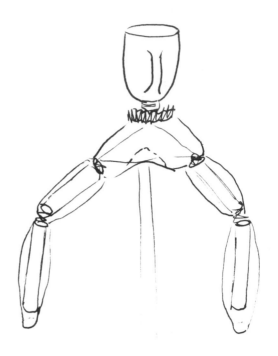

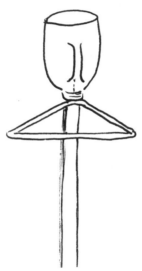

Cut legs from pantyhose and give one to each person to pull over his or her bottle to form the skin. Try to give the children a choice of color to correspond to the skin tones of their "people." Have them gather the pantyhose around the neck, trim the excess and tape it to the pole.

Make felt scraps available and ask the learners to cut facial features, such as eyes, nose, mouth, eyebrows, eyelashes and cheeks and to glue them in place. Be sure the pieces are large enough, even over-sized, to be seen from a distance.

The arms are formed from a full pair of pantyhose and four paper towel tubes. Demonstrate how to do this and then allow time for the children to complete the procedure. Insert a tube into a leg and knot off. Insert the second tube and knot again. Repeat the procedure for the other leg. Pull the pantyhose up over the hanger. Gather and tape it around the neck. Allow the arms to hang from the sides of the hanger. If legs are desired, they may be formed in the same way. Attach them to the center of the puppet body.

Show the young people how to pad the body and to provide an underlining for the costume by wrapping strips or sheets of packing material around the bodice. If the costume is to have a skirt, gather packing material around the waist to provide fullness. Help the children do this part. The students may need to work in pairs so one person can hold a pole while the other one tapes the packing in place. Recycled plastic bags, available in a variety of designs and colors, may be used for the costume. Fabric, if employed, should be lightweight so it doesn't make the puppet too heavy when carried. Packing material, which can be spray painted, may also be utilized. Split the bags at the sides and extend them to their total length. Use them, as well as pieces which have been taped together, to form shirts, blouses, vests, skirts, pants and any other items of clothing. Trim with different textures and materials to create the desired effect.

Pass out cardboard and have each child trace two hands, theirs or a partner's, and cut them out. Poke a hole into the top of each hand, give lengths of yarn, if needed, and tell the children to attach one hand to the bottom of each arm.

Guide the students in making hair from yarn, fibrefil, fake fur or plastic bags, and attaching it to the top of the puppet's head.

To allow for movement and gestures, give each child a dowel rod to attach to one of the hands.

Tell the youngsters to use the aluminum pole as the rod to carry the puppet. It may be carried by one person and a second person may work the arm. [157]

Storytelling

PURPOSE:

To cooperate to tell a story of peace possibilities in a community.

PROCEDURE:

Round Robin is a cooperative method of telling a story. Each participant adds a sentence or statement or a certain number of words.

Invite the children to make up a round robin story to describe ways in which peacemaking takes place in a community. If there are a large number of children, have them add three to five words per person. If only a few people are involved, increase the number of words. Continue until the story seems to be concluded, or until the children run out of ideas.

Following the story, discuss some of the ideas that were presented. If they are real possibilities for peacemaking, challenge the children to make them more than a story!

Storytelling: Children's Books

PURPOSE:

To address the theme of peace in the community through the use of children's literature.

PREPARATION:

Materials
- Books(s)

PROCEDURE:

Peace in a community is a multi-disciplinary issue. Use some of these books to help children consider the various topics.

Duck in the Gun [158] "A general and his men were ready to begin war on a town when they found a duck sitting on a nest in their gun. While they waited for the duck to leave, they became friends with the townspeople. They found that they could not have a battle with people they cared about." [159]

John John Twillinger [160] John John Twilliger lived in Merryall, a town with a fort in the middle of it. The Machine Gun Man ran the town and did not want anyone to be happy or to have fun, that is, until he met John John. After that, the town was changed drastically.

My Friend Jacob [161] Story of the friendship of Jacob and Sam serves as a reminder that although people may be different physically and mentally, everyone is special and needs acceptance.

On the Other Side of the River [162] When the bridge that connected the east side and the west side of the small town of Wynlock-on-the-River collapsed, the people, who usually argued all the time, realized how much they needed each other.

Wolf's Favor [163] Cooperation is stressed in the story of a wolf who does a favor which is eventually returned to him.

Storytelling: Folktales

PURPOSE:

To help participants gain an understanding of the benefits of cooperation through hearing the folktale, Stone Soup.

PREPARATION:

Materials
- Folktale, Stone Soup [164]
- Pot, large
- Rocks
- Markers, permanent

PROCEDURE:

Cooperation is a theme found in the German folktale Stone Soup. When soldiers come into a village proclaiming that they are hungry, the townspeople respond that they have no food to share. As the soldiers begin to make "Stone Soup" from water and a few rocks, the fascinated folk bring contributions, such as potatoes, carrots and meat, which greatly improve the quality and quantity of the product. All share a delicious dinner as well as a new-found friendship.

Compare this cooperative endeavor to ways in which a community can collaborate in addressing issues of hunger, homelessness, recycling, domestic violence and illiteracy. Ask the children to name ingredients that could be put into an imaginary "Stone Soup" to serve to the community. Place a large pan, or soup pot, in the middle of the group. Pass out a stone and a permanent marker to each person. Challenge the children to write the name of an ingredient, such as trust, time, talents, thoughtfulness or tenderness, on their rocks. Take turns placing them into the pot. This may be done in the form of a prayer by having each individual say, "God, I pray for (item written on rock) in our community," as he or she places the stone in the soup. Conclude with a group "Amen."

144

[148] Ecumenical Task Force on Christian Education for World Peace. Try This: Family Adventures Toward Shalom. Nashville: Discipleship Resources, 1979, 48.

[149] Silverstein, Shel. Where the Sidewalk Ends. New York: Harper and Row, 1974, 19.

[150] Hubbard-Brown, Janet. The Heart of the Mountain. Moretown, VT: Parents and Teachers for Social Responsibility, Inc., 1988. Available from: Parents and Teachers for Social Responsibility, Inc., P.O. Box 517, Moretown, VT 05660.

[151] Rogers, Ingrid. "Music as an Instrument of Peace." Working for Peace: A Handbook of Practical Psychology and Other Tools. Neil Wollman, ed. San Luis Obispo, CA: Impact Publishers, 1985, 228.

[152] Weiss, Evelyn, ed. Children's Songs for a Friendly Planet. Burnsville, NC: World Around Songs, 1986, 50.

[153] Huber, Jane Parker. A Singing Faith. Philadelphia: The Westminster Press, 1987, 61.

[154] Sing of Life and Faith. Philadelphia: Pilgrim Press, 1969, 130.

[155] The United Methodist Hymnal. Nashville: The United Methodist Publishing House, 1989, 434.

[156] Charlie Cheddar's Choice. United Presbyterian Health, Education and Welfare Association, 1976. Available from: Church World Service, P.O. Box 968, Elkhart, IN 46515-0968.

[157] Wezeman, Phyllis Vos. "Giant Puppets." Church Educator: Aug. 1989: 9. Adapted with permission.

[158] Cowley, Joy. Duck in the Gun. New York: Doubleday, 1969.

[159] Blaufuss, Deloris, comp. Building a Foundation for Peace: Bibliography of Peace Books for Children and Young Adults. 2nd ed. Burlington, IA: Saint Luke United Church of Christ Peace Fellowship, 1986, 17.

[160] Wondriska, William. John John Twilliger. New York: Holt, Rinehart and Winston, 1966.

[161] Clifton, Lucille. My Friend Jacob. New York: E. P. Dutton, 1980.

[162] Oppenheim, Joanne. On the Other Side of the River. New York: Franklin Watts, Inc., 1972.

[163] Testa, Fulvio. Wolf's Favor. New York: Dial Books for Young Readers, 1986.

[164] Brown, Marcia. Stone Soup. New York: MacMillan, 1947.

CHAPTER EIGHT

PEACE IN THE STATE

Introduction

If all people in a state knew and practiced a simple five-step problem solving technique, the cities and the countryside in many counties might be more peaceful places.

Teach the children this process and help them use it to address state-wide peace issues. It is:

1. Stop. Think. Remain calm.

2. Identify the problem.

3. Generate all of the possible solutions.

4. Evaluate each alternative.

5. Plan one way to solve the problem.

The arts activities not only encourage problem solving on the part of the students, they also enable them to take actions for promoting peace by writing to legislators, networking with pupils in other schools, and learning to appreciate the cultures that make up the population.

Architecture

Art

PURPOSE:

To promote conservation practices and priorities with children.

PREPARATION:

Materials
- Information on historic preservation projects.

PROCEDURE:

In parts of the world, such as Europe, structurally sound buildings are used for centuries. The function may change, but the building is re-cycled again and again. This kind of conservation of resources is becoming more popular in the United States. Still, however, older buildings are often destroyed to erect newer, typically less durable structures. This practice is wasteful of resources and frequently destructive of a rich architectural heritage.

Research what other communities in the state have done with older buildings, including churches. Compare the costs of new building and renovation.

Continue the project by looking around the community for sound buildings which are currently not being used. Direct the student's efforts in speaking to community agencies that are looking for facilities. Try to match needs with existing buildings in terms of size and location. When a match is found, develop a plan to utilize the existing structure.

PURPOSE:

To make buttons which convey peace messages.

PREPARATION:

Materials
- Peace button samples
- Paper
- Pencils
- Supplies will vary with method selected.

Advance Preparation
- Gather samples of peace buttons.

PROCEDURE:

Buttons, created from various techniques, are an effective way to share messages of peace and justice. Show the students buttons from peace groups and movements. Ask the children to make their own peace buttons. The message could focus on the theme of peace in the state. Provide paper and pencils so sample illustrations may be designed and drawn.

Make the buttons using one of the following methods:

- Cut cardboard circles. Create the design with paint or permanent marker. Tape a pin to the back.

- Cut small squares of cardboard and stencil designs on them. Attach pins.

150

- Draw the design on plain name tags. Peel off the backing material and wear them.

- Create a design on small, round plastic lids. Tape on pins.

- Develop and reproduce the design on paper and use a commercial button maker to complete the project.

Encourage the boys and girls to trade and collect the messages of people throughout the state who are working for peace.

Art

PURPOSE:

To produce a mural depicting ways to address statewide issues of peace.

PREPARATION:

Materials
- Shelf paper or newsprint roll, white
- Markers or crayons
- Tape
- Index cards
- Pen

Advance Preparation
- On index cards, write suggested ways in which people can help to promote peace in the state. Write a separate idea on each card. If the ideas are in a particular sequence, number the cards in that order. The number of cards needed will depend on the size of the group and the amount of time available for the activity. Suggestions to write on the card include:

  - Contact state representatives when peace related issues are being addressed.

  - Support peace organizations in the state.

  - Organize a workshop on the topic.

  - Express concern by writing letters.

  - Read newspaper articles, magazines and books on peace themes.

- Spread the roll of paper on a work space such as a long table or the floor. Place markers at appropriate intervals.

PROCEDURE:

Explain to the group that they will be working together to make a mural depicting ways in which people can help to promote peace in a state. Instruct them to work individually or divide them into teams.

Allow each person or team to develop their own idea for the mural, or distribute the suggestion cards which have been prepared in advance. Direct participants to use the markers to illustrate the idea or suggestion on the appropriate part of the mural paper.

Tape the completed mural to the wall and discuss the ideas presented on it.

Art:
Draw Your
Dream Of Peace

PURPOSE:

To stress stewardship of God's creation and creatures.

PREPARATION:

Materials
- "PEACE IN THE STATE" coloring sheets
- Crayons or markers
- Paper

Advance Preparation
- Duplicate coloring sheets.

PROCEDURE:

Stewardship of the earth and all of its inhabitants is an important peacemaking concept. Use the "Peace in the State" coloring sheet as an opportunity to discuss this with the students. Pass out the pictures and talk about ways in which children can be involved in taking care of nature and especially animals. Make crayons or markers available and let the children color the sheets.

Work with the students to gather information on endangered species, wildlife preserves, nature clubs, and parks within the state. Make displays to promote awareness.

If possible, arrange a field trip to a state park to learn more about God's creation and creatures.

Art: Draw Your Dream Of Peace

Draw or write ways to care for God's creatures.

Obtain information on wildlife preservation programs in your state.

Banners/Textiles

PURPOSE:

To add pieces to a weaving representing ways children will work for peace in their state.

PREPARATION:

Materials
- Cardboard, 3' x 5', or large wooden frame.
- Heavy string
- Materials, such as:
  - heavy yarns
  - cloth strips
  - wide ribbon
  - plastic bags
  - paper strips
  - slats, 1' wooden
  - Basket or box
  - Markers
  - Scissors
  - Exacto knife

Advance Preparation
- Prepare the cardboard by cutting one inch slits into the top and bottom of the piece. These should be placed approximately one inch apart. Warp the cardboard by running a continuous piece of heavy string from one side to the other, through each slit.

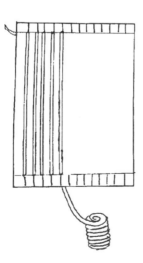

- Cut the materials into strips one inch wide and four to five feet long. Place the pieces in a basket or box.

PROCEDURE:

Weaving is an art form which combines a variety of strands or pieces into a beautiful blend of texture, fabric and design. Create a weaving to help children visualize how their individual contributions can be combined to work for peace in a state. Use the completed piece as a picture or wall hanging.

Show the children the background piece and explain that individually and collectively they will be weaving a new tomorrow in their state.

Ask each participant to pick a piece of material from the basket or box. Distribute permanent markers and ask them to write on the strip one way in which they will work for peace in their state. The ideas could include uniting children to create a peace memorial in the capitol, writing letters to legislators urging a state peace day, and involving themselves in a state- wide anti-drug campaign. Give each person an opportunity to read his or her idea and to weave the piece into the base. Periodically place a wooden slat into the weaving to make it more secure.

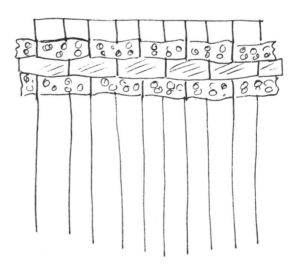

As the weaving is taking place, discuss how this project symbolizes each person's part in weaving a new tomorrow, and how it becomes possible when many people work together on the same cause or issue. Display the piece in a prominent location, or send it to the state legislature or governor with an explanation of the project.[165]

154

Cartoons

PURPOSE:

To give children information about the farm crisis in many states and to draw cartoons suggesting solutions.

PREPARATION:

Materials
- Cartoons depicting rural crisis
- Resources on rural crisis
- Paper
- Scissors
- Pencils
- Markers

Advance Preparation
- Gather resources and cartoons on the farm crisis.
- Prepare a long, narrow strip of paper, 20" x 4", for each participant and draw lines which divide it into eight equal sections.

PROCEDURE:

Many states in America are facing a farm crisis. Explain that family owned farms are going bankrupt at a rapid rate. Farm land is being devalued and production costs are going up. Share the cartoons and resources on this matter. Ask the children to suggest some possible solutions. Give each child a long, narrow strip of paper which has been divided into eight frames. Provide pencils and markers. Ask the students to use the cartoon format to illustrate this problem and to suggest solutions.

Share the results, not only with each other, but also with political and agricultural leaders in the state.

Clown/Mime

PURPOSE:

To develop skits around the theme of working together.

PREPARATION:

Materials
- Chalkboard or newsprint
- Chalk or marker
- Tape

Advance Preparation
- Make a list of "Working Together" situations such as:
  - Grocery clerk and customer
  - Magician and assistant
  - Doctor and patient
  - Parent teaching child to cook
  - Bank teller and customer
  - Boss and secretary
  - Cowboy and wild horse
  - Carpenter and helper
  - Director and actor

PROCEDURE:

The book Send In His Clowns [166] suggests mime exercises that emphasize working together. Help the children concentrate on the theme peace in the state by using some of these activities.

Form pairs and have each team choose a mime skit from the list that was prepared in advance and posted in the room. Allow time for the children to practice their presentations. Take turns sharing the short, silent pantomime pieces with the group.

At the conclusion, ask the students to name ways in which people in a state need to work together to promote peace.

Creative Writing

PURPOSE:

To develop a proclamation declaring an official day to celebrate peace in the state.

PREPARATION:

Materials
- Paper
- Pens
- Envelope
- Stamp

Advance Preparation
- Obtain the Governor's address

PROCEDURE:

Develop a proclamation, a public or official statement, with the children, declaring a certain date as a day to celebrate peace in the state. Write a series of "Whereas" statements citing reasons why a peace day should be observed.

Form small groups to write the phrases or sentences. Assign each group a particular theme to develop, such as self, family, congregation, school, neighborhood, community, state, nation and world, and have them come up with a few lines stating a reason a special day celebrating peace should be held. Conclude the proclamation with a "Therefore" statement declaring the date and the action that will be taken.

Write a final draft of the document and send it to the Governor or state legislature asking that positive action be taken to adopt the proclamation and to observe the day.

Creative Writing: Poetry

PURPOSE:

To challenge students to imagine ways in which their actions can contribute to peace in their state.

PREPARATION:

Materials
- Newsprint
- Markers
- Tape

PROCEDURE:

Challenge the students to imagine what a world at peace would be like. Tell them to close their eyes and to dream of a way in which this could begin in their own state, and more specifically, through their own actions. Pose questions like:

- Would it begin if people of different races began to trust each other?

- Could it happen if people conserved more resources and used only what they needed?

- Might it be possible if children and adults learned positive ways of resolving conflict?

Give the pupils an opportunity to put their mental thoughts and pictures into words. Tell them that they will be writing an acrostic poem expressing ways in which they will promote peace in their state. Form groups of four to six participants. Pick a word to be used, for example, "state," "peace" or "justice," or a phrase such as "Peace in My State." Distribute sheets of newsprint and markers and instruct each group to write the word(s) vertically down the left side of their papers. Model how to do the first line. Ask the students to think of a word or phrase which begins with the first letter of the chosen word. For example, for the "P" of peace, it could be the word "Pray" or the phrase "Promote Understanding." Guide the groups as they complete their acrostics. When finished, each poem can be taped to the wall and read to the total group.

A simple acrostic is:

J *ust use what I need*
U *se less, so others will have more*
S *upport hunger organizations*
T *ithe and donate income*
I *t starts with me*
C *onsume less energy*
E *ncourage others*

If time allows, make the exercise extremely personal by having each learner write an acrostic using the letters of his or her first name to express the chosen theme and actions.

Culinary Arts

PURPOSE:

To taste the cuisine of nationalities represented in a state and to develop an appreciation for people from various backgrounds.

PREPARATION:

Materials
- Cookbooks
- Ingredients
- Equipment

Advance Preparation
- Obtain information on ethnic areas and festivals throughout a state.

PROCEDURE:

Tasting the cuisine of various countries may encourage an appreciation for and an understanding of the people who live there. Ask the children to think about people throughout their state and to name some of their countries of origin. In advance, obtain information on ethnic neighborhoods or festivals in several large or nearby cities to share with the group.

Hold an international smorgasbord and allow the pupils to taste the foods from various places. Center the menu on the dishes of one country, or for more variety, serve samples of items from all over the world.

If the learners are to be involved in the preparation, an excellent cookbook for children to use is Loaves and Fishes.[167] It contains many easy to make ethnic recipes.

Invite guests from the countries represented by the foods to share the meal as well as to bring information that may help the youngsters gain insight on those nations and their peoples.

Dance

PURPOSE:

To use a Native American ritual, involving movement, for reflection on people in a state from North, South, East and West.

PREPARATION:

Materials
- Drum

PROCEDURE:

Native Americans respected the wholeness of the earth before the word "ecology" was known. Today the colors, red, yellow, black and white, honor the four races which are represented by the population in a state.

Ask the participants to move to one of the four corners of the room, representative, if possible, of their origins, for quite meditation and reflection on North, South, East and West. Some examples include:

North: cold, star, white, winter

South: sun, green, laughter, summer

East: dawn, yellow, fire, spring

West: sunset, browns, earth, fall

At a signal, such as a drum beat, ask people to gather in the center of the space to share their thoughts. Highlight ideas that promote peace and justice.[168]

Drama

PURPOSE:

To improvise current event situations as a way to explore state-wide peace themes.

PREPARATION:

Materials
- Newspapers
- Magazines

PROCEDURE:

Arrange the participants into small groups. Provide each team with a stack of current newspapers and magazines.

Invite each group to find and to agree on one article which pertains to a peace and justice issue facing a state. Explain that the groups will improvise and act out the situations. Each child must have a part to play.

Give the groups ten to fifteen minutes to find the articles and to prepare the skits.

Have the children take turns presenting their dramas for the entire group. After everyone has shared their improvisations, discuss the scenes and the peacemaking concerns and concepts they illustrated. The groups may then dramatize possible solutions.

Drama: Plays

PURPOSE:

To use drama as a method to explore creative ways to resolve conflict.

PREPARATION:

Materials
- OPQRS, ETC. [169]

PROCEDURE:

Use the play OPQRS, ETC. to help children discover new and non-violent conflict resolution methods.

Six characters act in this fantasy which takes place in front of a public building. Otto, the official, controls the community and limits it to the use of his favorite color, orange. Only his girlfriend dares to attempt to search for independence, although her efforts are not supported by others. A wandering artist resolves the conflict in a clever and non-violent way and releases the people, even Otto, from their limited way of seeing themselves and their surroundings.

Games

PURPOSE:

To experience peace as cooperative behavior.

PREPARATION:

Materials
- Posterboard
- Ruler
- Pencil
- Scissors
- Marker
- Envelopes, five per game

Advance Preparation
- Cut five six inch posterboard squares for each group of five players. Rule each square into the pattern provided.

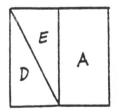 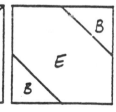

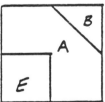 

- Make the measurements as accurate as possible. Mark each shape with the appropriate letter. Cut out the shapes and sort them into sets of the same letter. Put each set into an envelope marked with that letter.

PROCEDURE:

Start the game by forming a group or groups of five. Give each child in the group a different envelope. Explain that each person has in his or her envelope pieces to a square, but no one will be able to complete a square with just these pieces. All five squares can be completed only when people cooperate to accomplish the task. Note that the exercise will continue until each person has a complete square. A person may pass a puzzle piece to another player, but no one may reach out and take a piece. No talking or any other kind of communication is allowed.

After the five squares have been assembled, talk about the cooperation that was required during the process. Ask the students to name ways in which cooperative efforts are needed in a state to put the pieces of peace together.

Music

PURPOSE:

To make rhythm instruments from recyclable materials.

PREPARATION:

Materials
- Aluminum pie plates
- Bells
- Pipe cleaners
- Plastic bottles
- Pebbles
- Wood blocks
- Egg cartons
- Sandpaper
- Coffee cans with lids
- Dowel rods
- Nails
- String
- Hangers
- Paper punch
- Glue
- Scissors
- Tapes, music of various cultures
- Tape player

PROCEDURE:

Stress the need for recycling in a state by creating rhythm instruments from throw-away objects. Provide a variety of materials for the students to use and demonstrate a number of methods to make the items. Design a tambourine by punching holes around the edge of an aluminum pie plate and attaching bells to the holes with pipe cleaners. Fill empty plastic laundry bottles with pebbles to create shakers. Cover blocks of wood, or egg cartons, with sandpaper and rub two of them together as scrapers. Form drums from coffee cans with plastic lids. Use dowel rods as the sticks. Tie nails on various lengths of string, attach the strings to a coat hanger, and strike the nails with a larger nail to devise chimes.

Tell the class to choose materials and to make at least one rhythm instrument to use with the activity that follows. As the children work, circulate through the room and encourage them to think about other ways in which items may be recycled.

Explain that people throughout a state are from many different ethnic backgrounds. Then play music from some of these cultures. Invite the students to keep time to the music with the rhythm instruments they have made.

Music: Song Adaptation

PURPOSE:

To write songs about recycling responsibilities.

PREPARATION:

Materials
- Newsprint
- Markers

Advance Preparation
- Write sample recycling verses on newsprint.

PROCEDURE:

Write a song about recycling using the tune "Row, Row, Row Your Boat." Sing through the song one or two times and then show the students new words, such as:

Save, save, save your trash
Think of things you can do
With plastic bottles and paper tubes,
It will be fun for you.

or:

Re-cycle paper, glass and cans,
The earth needs everyone's care.
Pick up litter on the street,
We all can do our share.

Divide the students into groups of four, provide newsprint and markers and instruct them to use the same tune to write a new verse on the theme of recycling. Have each group share a song with the other students. Invite everyone to sing them together.

The messages may be extended by "compiling" songbooks and sending them to other children in the state.

Music: Song Suggestions

PURPOSE:

To acquaint children with music that will help them think about ways to make peace in the state.

PREPARATION:

Materials
- Music
- Accompaniment, optional

PROCEDURE:

Many people are needed to promote peace and justice concerns in a state. The words of these songs can help children understand some ways in which they can be involved.

"God of Justice, God of Mercy" [170]

"Love Grows One By One" [171]

"O God, to Whom We Sing" [172]

Photography

PURPOSE:

To enable pupils to participate in a program that will promote peace in the state.

PREPARATION:

Materials
- Materials on project
- Bulletin board or posterboard
- Tacks or tape
- School supplies
- Camera
- Film

Advance Preparation
- Obtain information and materials on a state project to support.

PROCEDURE:

Use photographs as a way to introduce the children to people in another part of the state. In advance, decide on a project. This might be acquiring school supplies for a day care center for the children of refugees or migrant farm workers, or collecting books for a community literacy program. Contact representatives of the project and ask them to send pictures of the children, the center and the city. Make a display and call attention to it when explaining the situation and the needs in the targeted area.

Invite the children to name items they could collect and contribute. Possibilities are crayons, pencils, pens, glue, rulers, tape, paper and so forth. Ask each child to supply his or her picture or take a photo of the class and include it with the goods. Send the materials together with the request that the leaders of the day care or community center send pictures of the children using the new supplies.

Photography: Media

PURPOSE:

To reflect on a peace in the state theme through the use of media.

PREPARATION:

Materials
- Filmstrip, Once Upon A Rainy Day [173]
- Projector
- Screen
- Extension Cord

PROCEDURE:

Show the ten minute filmstrip Once Upon A Rainy Day. When Wally the Water Wizard drops in, an adventure including riding on a cloud and journeying into the future begins for two children who learn the importance of water. Stress how valuable and essential this resource is throughout the state.

Puppetry

PURPOSE:

To make tube puppets and to use them to explore the theme of peace in the state.

PREPARATION:

Materials
- Felt
- Yarn or fake fur
- Fabric scraps
- Scissors
- Glue
- Craft sticks
- Paper towel tubes

PROCEDURE:

Turn paper towel tubes, of various sizes, into puppets and use them to help the children think about common, ordinary people who work for peace everyday. These are people who are better known by profession than by name. Ask the children to suggest some of these people. Guide the discussion to include ministers, counselors, teachers, nurses and legislators. To be more specific, add re-cycling workers, homeless center coordinators and health department employees. Help the boys and girls become aware that every job has peacemaking potential. Ask them to focus on a certain one for the puppet project.

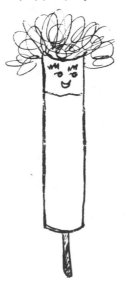

Distribute a tube to each participant and place the other materials within sharing distance of the children. Have them form the puppet face by cutting a piece of felt and gluing it to the top one-third of the tube. Tell the group to cut facial features from felt scraps and to glue them in place. Yarn or fake fur becomes hair and should be attached to the top of the tube.

Instruct the students to glue a piece of felt around the remainder of the tube to serve as the undergarment. Layers of fabric in contrasting or complementary colors can be added as overgarments.

Make arms from strips of cloth or felt and glue them to the sides of the tube.

Help each child apply a craft stick to the inside back of his or her tube to serve as the rod by which the puppet is operated.

If felt is not available, use construction paper instead. The facial features may be drawn on with marker. Substitute tissue paper for fabric to form the outer garments.

When the puppets are completed, take turns having the children use them to tell stories of everyday peacemakers.

Storytelling

PURPOSE:

To use a story to remind children that they have a role in peacemaking.

PREPARATION:

Materials
- Story, "The Weight of a Snowflake"
- Map of state
- Paper, white
- Scissors
- Markers
- Tape

PROCEDURE:

Read the children the charming, yet challenging, story "The Weight of a Snowflake."[174] Let it serve to remind them that everyone has a role in and a responsibility for peacemaking.

The Weight Of A Snowflake

"'Tell me the weight of a snowflake,' a coal-mouse asked a dove.

"'Nothing more than nothing,' was the answer.

"'In that case I must tell you a marvelous story,' the coal-mouse said. 'I sat on the branch of a fir, close to its trunk, when it began to snow, not heavily, not in a raging blizzard, no, just like in a dream, without any violence. Since I didn't have anything better to do, I counted the snowflakes settling on twigs and needles of my branch. Their number was exactly 3,741,952. When the next snowflake dropped on to the branch - nothing more than nothing, as you say - the branch broke off.'

"Having said that, the coal-mouse flew away.

"The dove, since Noah's time an authority on the matter, thought about the story for a while and finally said to herself: 'Perhaps there is one person's voice still needed for peace to come about in the world.'"

After the reading, hang a map of the state in the room. Talk about ways in which the students can be peacemakers on a state-wide level. This may be writ-

ing to legislators, adopting a day care center in another city, or networking with other pupils on an important project.

Pass out white paper, scissors and markers and ask each person to cut out a snowflake. Have them write their name and one personal action for peace on it. Provide tape and help each child attach his or her snowflake to the map.

Storytelling: Children's Books

PURPOSE:

To help children, through the use of books, consider peace issues that are common throughout a state.

PREPARATION:

Materials
- Book(s)

PROCEDURE:

The possibilities presented for pursuing the theme, peace in the state, promote concepts of acceptance and openmindedness.

The Indians on the Bonnet.[175] Accepting people from different races and cultures is a state-wide challenge. The story of a boy and his grandmother who befriend an Indian family, amidst opposition from the townspeople, will help children consider this theme.

A Look at Prejudice and Understanding.[176] Photographs and text explore prejudice and its causes. The book serves to remind children that people who isolate themselves from other types of people are the "losers" since they are not open to new experiences and growth.

The Story of Johnny Appleseed. [177] Johnny Appleseed spread a message of peace wherever he went as he traveled around with a bag full of apple seeds on his back and a cooking pan on his head. Johnny's story serves to remind children to spread peace in their state in many ways.

The Sun and The Wind. [178] Re-telling of an Aesop fable which exemplifies that love and non-violence are stronger than force and violence.

What Color Are You? [179] Despite differences in color, people are basically the same and have the same needs. This book explains this through words and pictures.

Storytelling: Folktales

PURPOSE:

To use the story of Henny Penny [180] to stress the importance of having elected officials who are committed to peace and justice.

PREPARATION:

Materials
- Folktale, Henny Penny

PROCEDURE:

When Henny Penny, the title character in an old English tale, declares that the sky is falling, she sets out to tell the king. Along the way she informs several other barnyard birds of the impending disaster, and, without questioning the validity of the claim, they all join her on the journey. Unfortunately, because of their innocence and ignorance, all but Henny Penny fall prey to the cunning fox.

Ask for a volunteer to read the story to the group. This story offers an opportunity to stress the importance of the children being Christian citizens who are informed about state and federal leaders. Ask them to express ways in which their representatives' and senators' decisions might contribute to peace.

Read some of the Gospel accounts of the kind and compassionate ways in which Jesus led his followers.

165 Wezeman, Phyllis Vos, and Jude Dennis Fournier. Counting the Days: Twenty-five Ways. Brea, CA: Educational Ministries, Inc. 1989, 51. Adapted with permission.

166 Perrone, Stephen P., and James P. Spata. Send In His Clowns. Colorado Springs: Meriwether Publishing, 1985, 35.

167 Hunt, Linda, Marianne Frase, and Doris Liebert. Loaves and Fishes: A Love Your Neighbor Cookbook. Scottdale, PA: Herald Press, 1980.

168 Strain, Marie M., ed. Ideas for Celebration of Peace. Concord, MA: National Peace Day Celebrations, 1985, 20. Adapted with permission.

169 Miller, Madge. OPQRS, ETC. New Orleans: Anchorage Press, 1984. Available from: Anchorage Press, P.O. Box 8067, New Orleans, LA 70182.

170 Huber, Jane Parker. A Singing Faith. Philadelphia: The Westminster Press, 1987, 63.

171 Weiss, Evelyn, ed. Children's Songs for a Friendly Planet. Burnsville, NC: World Around Songs, 1986, 39.

172 Huber, Jane Parker. A Singing Faith. Philadelphia: The Westminster Press, 1987, 60.

173 Once Upon a Rainy Day. Church World Service, 1981. Available from: Church World Service, P.O. Box 968, Elkhart, IN 46515-0968.

174 Office on Global Education for Church World Service [McFadden, Sandra L., Phyllis Vos Wezeman, Tom Hampson, and Loretta Whalen]. Make a World of Difference: Creative Activities for Global Learning. Baltimore: Office on Global Education, National Council of Churches, 1989, 199.

175 Ladd, Elizabeth. The Indians on the Bonnet. New York: William Morrow and Co., 1971.

176 Anders, Rebecca. A Look at Prejudice and Understanding. Minneapolis: Lerner Publications Co., Inc., 1976.

177 Aliki. The Story of Johnny Appleseed. Englewood Cliffs, NJ: Prentice-Hall, Inc., 1963.

178 Lehn, Cornelia. The Sun and the Wind. Newton, KS: Faith and Life Press, 1983.

179 Walton, Darwin. What Color Are You? Chicago: Johnson Publishing Co., Inc., 1973.

180 Martignoni, Margaret E., ed. "Henny Penny." The Illustrated Treasury of Children's Literature. New York: Grosset and Dunlap, 1955, 66-68.

CHAPTER NINE

PEACE IN THE NATION

Introduction

In order to promote peace in the nation, as well as in the world, author and educator Betty Reardon of Columbia Teachers College, suggests seven categories of "peace" education which should be taught to children. They are:

1. International Education. Emphasizes an understanding of systems.

2. Global Education. Explores problems shared by all people of the earth.

3. Multi-cultural Education. Stresses social systems, respect for diversity and area studies.

4. Conflict Resolution. Promotes mediation skills.

5. Nuclear Education. Explains the problems, technical aspects and consequences, and challenges the capacity to struggle for alternatives.

6. Nuclear Age Education. Broadens nuclear education and global education and underscores community building skills.

7. Peace Education. Contains elements of the other six categories and deals with problems of violence at all levels of life. [181]

The activities in this chapter touch on all seven areas, and should be used to empower children with the information and insights they need to advance peace in the nation.

Architecture

PURPOSE:

To envision the design of a national peace monument.

PREPARATION:

Materials
- Pictures of models of national monuments
- Paper
- Pencils
- Blocks
- Cardboard
- Toothpicks
- Glue
- Markers

PROCEDURE:

Show the children pictures or models of several well-known national monuments. Include places like the Statue of Liberty, the Lincoln Memorial and the Viet Nam War Memorial. Spend time talking about the history and circumstances associated with each of them. Ask the pupils to discuss the peaceful and unpeaceful aspects of these situations.

Distribute paper and pencils, or materials like blocks, cardboard or toothpicks, and challenge the children to design a national peace memorial. Talk about the concepts the architecture of such a monument should convey. This could be an individual or a group project.

Send the model or sketch to a government agency and encourage the establishment of a national peace memorial.

Art

PURPOSE:

To acquaint children with the purpose and programs of national peace groups.

PREPARATION:

Materials
- Paper
- Pens
- Envelopes
- Stamps
- Posterboard
- Bulletin Board
- Scissors
- Glue
- Tape
- Tacks

PROCEDURE:

A collage, or collection of pictures or information, can address a variety of peacemaking themes. Use this method to acquaint the children with the large number of peacemaking groups in their nation, as well as in other countries. This art activity will help students discover and discuss some of the ways in which the groups promote peace and justice concerns. A list of organizations is provided at the back of the book and many additional names are available from other sources. The Peace Catalog [182] contains seventy-seven pages listing peace groups. Pass out paper and pens and ask each child to write to a different group requesting information on its purpose and programs. Provide envelopes and stamps and mail the letters.

When the materials arrive, invite the participants to make collages to tell the story of the groups. One large group collage, made on a bulletin board or a piece of posterboard, may also be made to help the children learn about the diversity and direction of national peace organizations.

Art

PURPOSE:

To support the idea that each person can work for peace and that each peace act is important.

PREPARATION:

Materials
- Map of the United States
- Bulletin Board
- Tacks
- Construction paper
- Scissors
- Markers
- Straight pins

Advance Preparation
- Cut construction paper into quarters.

PROCEDURE:

This activity will help children understand that everyone in a nation can work for peace and that each person's contribution is important.

Begin by mounting a map of the United States on the bulletin board. Give each child a construction paper square, markers and a scissors. Tell them to cut the figure of a person out of the rectangle and to personalize and decorate it. Ask each learner to write or draw on the figure something that he or she will do to promote peace in the nation. Emphasize that these can be simple acts such as smiling instead of staring or hugging rather than hitting.

Ask the children to pin their figures to the map, forming a long row across the United States. Suggest that this symbolizes the united stand people need to take to bring peace to a nation.

Art:
Draw Your Dream Of Peace

PURPOSE:

To envision bridges of peace that are needed in a nation.

PREPARATION:

Materials
- "PEACE IN THE NATION" coloring sheets
- Crayons or markers
- Pencils
- Paper
- Tape or tacks

Advance Preparation
- Duplicate coloring sheets.

PROCEDURE:

Distribute the coloring sheets, crayons or markers, and pencils. Talk with the children about the bridges of peace that are needed in a nation. Ask them to write their ideas in the gap between the two sides of the bridge. Encourage general concepts like trust, communication and cooperation, as well as specific actions such as reduction of military spending, equal pay for women and better refugee resettlement programs. Tell the students to finish coloring the sheets. Tape or tack them around the room.

Art: Draw Your Dream Of Peace

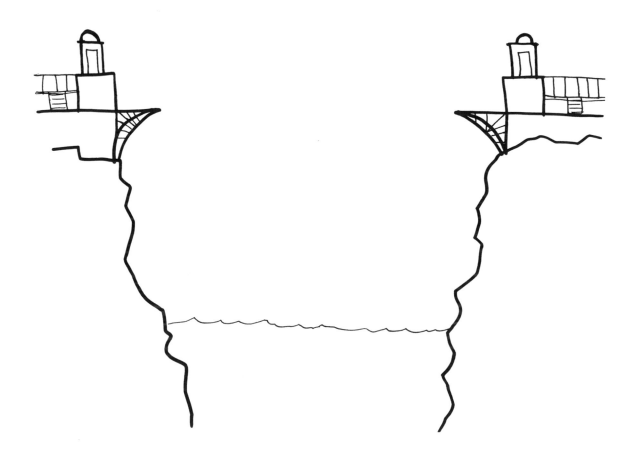

What bridges of peace are needed in the nation?

Write your ideas in the gap between the two sides.

Banners/Textiles

PURPOSE:

To make batik windsocks with symbols and slogans that promote peace in the nation.

PREPARATION:

Materials
- Muslin, 100% cotton
- Pencils
- Rulers
- Permanent markers, various colors, or fabric paints
- Meltex beeswax
- Paraffin
- Coffee can for heating waxes
- Paint brushes
- Container, wide, for dye
- Dye
- Water
- Brown paper or grocery bags
- Scissors
- Iron
- Pan or tray for hot iron
- Hot plate or electric skillet with temperature controls
- Newspaper
- Clothesline or cord
- Clip clothespins
- Posterboard, lightweight
- Yarn or string
- Fabric glue or stapler and staples
- Fabric or ribbon strips for streamers
- Patterns for symbols or diagrams, optional

Advance Preparation
- Cut a sixteen inch by nineteen inch rectangle of muslin for each person.

PROCEDURE:

Batik is an Indonesian method of layering wax and dyes to create works of art. In this fabric technique, fibers respond to the process and the cloth is changed. This activity gives students the opportunity to design symbols and slogans which promote peace in the nation. Note that people who see them may also respond and grow in their interest and involvement in peacemaking.

Think with the pupils of symbols and slogans which promote peace. For instance, prayer could be symbolized by folded hands, a hunger drive by a basket of food, and a letter writing campaign by a piece of paper and a pencil or pen.

Tell the students they will be making windsocks containing symbols or slogans for peace. Invite each person to think of one or more symbols to use for the project.

Distribute a piece of muslin to each learner. Provide pencils and instruct them to sketch their symbols or designs onto the horizontal portion, or width, of the material. The symbols should be placed two to three inches apart. The same symbol may be repeated, or several may be used. Pass out permanent markers or fabric paints and have the young people use them to color their entire drawings.

Ask the youngsters to set aside their fabric pieces and to watch carefully as the rest of the procedure is demonstrated.

Mix one-half Meltex beeswax and one-half paraffin in the coffee can, and heat it on the hot plate or in the electric skillet. Controlling the heat is easier when using an electric skillet with various temperature settings. When melting beeswax and paraffin, be extremely cautious to use low heat as wax is flammable at high temperatures.

173

Use a brush to paint the wax mixture over the entire surface of the sample windsock. Allow it to harden. Wrinkle the piece into a ball shape until the wax begins to crack slightly, then carefully open the cloth.

Gently slide the cloth into a wide container of cold water dye bath or warm tap water dye bath. A dye solution requiring boiling water will cause the wax to melt and should be avoided. After totally saturating the cloth with dye, remove it and clip it to the clothesline to air dry. Do not wring the cloth. Newspaper should cover the floor in this area.

Allow time for the children to apply the wax and dye to their windsocks. Carefully supervise this procedure.

While the cloths are drying, re-gather the group and explain the next step of the process to them. Place the dry sample cloth between sheets of brown paper or split grocery bags. Iron the paper with a warm iron until the wax on the cloth is absorbed into the paper. Remove the brown paper.

When the children's cloths have dried, help them complete this step of the project. Depending on the age of the participants, the ironing should be done, or carefully supervised by an adult. Use these few minutes with each individual child as a time to talk about the meaning of his or her symbol(s).

Cut two sixteen inch long and one inch wide strips of posterboard for each windsock. These are used to stabilize the top and bottom of the cloth. Distribute two to each person. Also pass out glue or staplers which are needed for this step of the activity. Instruct the students to place their windsocks in front of them with the design side facing down. Demonstrate how to place a strip one inch below the top edge and to fold the material over it.

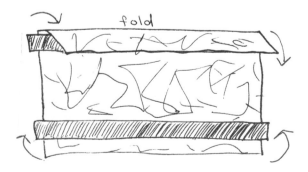

Help the students glue or staple the fabric and posterboard together. Repeat the procedure on the remaining side. Guide the children as they curve their cloth and posterboard around to form a cylinder. Glue or staple to close the overlapped seams.

Allow the children to choose streamers, made from ribbon or cloth, and to glue or staple them to the bottom of the windsocks. Pass out pieces of string. Help the youngsters attach them to the top of the cylinder at three or four points and tie them together in the center.

Hang the completed windsocks in the room and provide an opportunity for each child to share a story about his or her symbols. Challenge the children to respond in faith to God's challenge to be peacemakers in the nation.

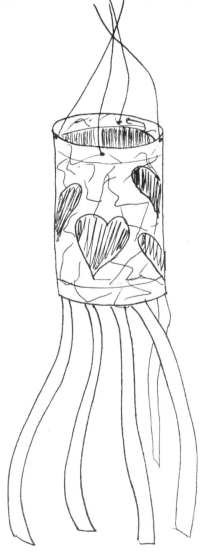

Cartoons

PURPOSE:

To help children analyze cartoons dealing with national issues.

PREPARATION:

Materials
- Magazines
- Newspapers
- Scissors
- Paper, optional
- Pens, optional

Advance Preparation
- Start a cartoon collection. Cut cartoons which deal with national issues from newspapers and magazines. Try to obtain cartoons from other countries, too.

PROCEDURE:

Issues of national scope are communicated to children via the media. Daily radio, television and newspaper reports involve relations with other countries, national security and trade. Use cartoons to help children explore, and thus deal with some of these issues. There are various ways to do this.

Form small groups and pass out several cartoons to each of them. Guide the activity by asking the participants to discuss which cartoon has the most impact and why, to talk about the meaning of a cartoon, or to write new captions.

Clown/Mime

PURPOSE:

To involve children in a modern day version of the Good Samaritan story.

PREPARATION:

Materials
- Bible
- Clown costumes
- Clown make-up
- Elastic bandage
- Tennis shoes
- Paper, optional
- Duplicating equipment, optional

Advance Preparation
- Duplicate copies of script, optional.

PROCEDURE:

Read the story of the Good Samaritan from Luke 10:25-37. Invite the children to dress as clowns and to act out a modern day version of it, "Here Comes Sam!"[183] Assign the parts of Pam, Sam, and the Storyteller. Pam should wear sneakers and Sam should not wear blue jeans. Form three groups, the basketball team, high school band, and back up rhythm group, from the remaining participants. Provide a copy of the script for each person for practice purposes, if desired. Explain that the lines of the story are repeated by various groups as the action takes place.

"HERE COMES SAM!"

Storyteller: "This is a story that Jesus told his friends: Once upon a time there was a man who was going on a trip down the road. But some people came and beat him, robbed him, took his clothes, and left him by the curb. Along came a Pharisee on his motorcycle, who saw him, but went on by with his nose in the air. Along came a Levite in his custom van, but said "yeelch" and went by in the other lane. But then a Samaritan came by who stopped when he saw the man, put him in his car, took him to the nearest motel, gave the clerk his credit card, and said to take good care of him until next Tuesday when he could return with more money. Now wasn't that a good Samaritan?

Team: What's a Fricassee? Isn't that chicken?

Band: What's a Levite? Isn't that something you wear?

Back-up: And what's a Samaritan?

Storyteller: You don't understand. Those are kind of old-fashioned words, but let me try and explain. A Pharisee was somebody very important. Everybody wanted to be a Pharisee. They were famous, kind of like a basketball team today.

(Team bows)

And the Levites, well, they were famous too. They were special and got to wear special uniforms, kind of like a high school band today. Everybody wishes that they could look like that.

(Band bows)

And the person going down the road? We see joggers everyday. Maybe it was a jogger.

(Pam bows)

And the Samaritan? Nobody liked them; they were real turkeys. Who would they be today? Let's find out.

(With the Team on one side, the Band on the other, and the Back-up in the center preferably on a higher level, the tempo should be jazzy and finger-snappy. The storyteller says the lines, and the designated group echoes the repeat lines.)

Once there was a jogger whose name was Pam.
(Back-up repeat; Pam bows)

She liked to run as fast as she can.
(Back-up repeat; Pam jogs)

She practiced for the day of the great big race,
(Back-up repeat)

But she ran into trouble and fell on her face.
(Back-up repeat)

Her sneakers got taken and so did her pride,
(Team and Band repeat while Back-up runs out, knocks her down, takes shoes)

And she lay by the side of the road and cried.
(Team and Band repeat while Back-up returns)

The basketball team came running by.
(Team repeat)

They were strong and fast and tall — so high!
(Team repeat)

All: Here comes the team, here comes the team, here comes the team...

They were running so fast that Pam was a blur.
(Back-up repeat while Team circles Pam, tossing imaginary ball)

They didn't think to stop and try to - help her.
(Back-up repeat with a jazz step at the hyphen)

The high school band came marching by,
(Band repeat)

Playing so loud that it filled the sky.
(Band repeat)

All: Here comes the band, here comes the band, here comes the band...

They were playing so loud Pam couldn't be heard.
(Back-up repeat while band circles Pam playing imaginary instruments)

They went right by is the — latest word.
(Back-up repeat with jazz step)

Into our story comes a funny little guy.
(All repeat)

Sam's the name; let's all say Hi!
(All: "Hi, Sam!")
Sentence not repeated.

Can't dribble a ball or swing a bat.
(Team repeat)

Sports is definitely not where he's at.
(Team repeat)

Can't carry a tune or play on key,
(Band repeat)

So he's not in the band; what good is he?
(Band repeat)

He likes to study and to eat string beans,
(All repeat with slower tempo making faces)

And he doesn't even own a pair of faded blue jeans!
(All repeat)

Well, he's walking with a book down past the track,
(Back-up repeat, picking up tempo again)

He had a chance to not look back;
(Back-up repeat)

But he stopped and said:
(Sam: "Hey, you need a hand?") No repeat.

He helped her up and they brushed her off,
(Back-up repeat)

And took her to the nurse, Mrs. Cover-your-mouth-when-you-cough,
(All cough) No repeat.

They put on a bandaid and they chased the blues,
(Back-up repeat, Sam wrap Pam with elastic bandage)

And he let her borrow his own gym shoes.
(Back-up repeat, Sam give Pam shoes from his pocket)

Well, we don't care who won the race!
(All repeat loudly)

If people aren't helpful, that's a disgrace!
(All repeat)

When last we left our new-found friends,
(Back-up repeat)

They were sharing popcorn, and that's how it ends.
(Back-up repeat)

All: Here comes the end, here comes the end, here comes the end... TA-DA!
(All bow)

After the skit, talk about ways in which Good Samaritans are needed in the nation today. Ask the children who the Good Samaritans are? Also ask them to name some people who might need help. Talk about ways to get involved and to not pass by people with problems and needs.

Creative Writing

PURPOSE:

To sponsor an essay contest to help young people form concrete ideas about ways to work for peace in the nation.

PREPARATION:

Materials
- Essay Guidelines
- Paper
- Pens or pencils
- Resource materials
- Awards

Advance Preparation
- Form essay contest committee.
- Secure judges.
- Prepare guidelines.

PROCEDURE:

Hold an essay contest and use this creative writing technique to help children plan actions they can take to bring about peace in the nation. Give the youth a specific theme, like "Peace is possible in the nation because..." Distribute guidelines for the activity which contain information on the sponsor(s), theme, age categories, format, deadline, entry location, judging criteria, judges, awards and contact person. When the essays are completed, make arrangements to have some of the participants read their written work in public locations. Submit a sampling of the entries to a national publication. Send the essays to children in other cities in the United States and invite them to send their ideas back.

Creative Writing: Poetry

PURPOSE:

To guide pupils in a discussion of national issues and to suggest solutions through a poetry project.

PREPARATION:

Materials
- Newspapers
- Magazines
- Scissors
- Construction paper
- Markers

PROCEDURE:

Gather current newspapers and magazines which contain pictures of events of national interest. Distribute them to the students and tell each pupil to chose a photograph which depicts a situation that needs to be addressed in order to have peace in the nation. Scenes could range from pictures of domestic violence or pollution to homelessness or hunger. Allow each student to show and describe his or her picture.

Inspire the children to come up with creative solutions to some of these issues by involving them in a poetry project. Challenge them to imagine that they are in a time machine and are experiencing a future period in which many of these problems have been solved and the United States is at peace. Use a five line diamond shaped poem to engage the learners in this process. The formula is as follows:

Line One: One word which is an opposite of line five.

Line Two: Two words which describe line one.

Line Three: Three words which resolve the conflict.

Line Four: Two words which describe line five.

Line Five: One word which is an opposite of line one.

For example:

> Litter
> Garbage everywhere
> New uses found.
> Gather. Collect.
> Recycle.

Distribute construction paper and markers and guide the students as they write their poems about possible solutions to national issues.

Submit the poetry to a church or school newsletter and share the children's ideas with other people.

Culinary Arts

PURPOSE:

To aid children in making healthy and helpful food choices.

PREPARATION:

Materials
- Newsprint or butcher paper
- Tape
- Magazines
- Newspapers
- Scissors
- Glue

PROCEDURE:

This activity can help children discover ways in which their food selections not only help themselves but also benefit others. Invite the class to create a mural which will show healthy and junk food choices.

Tape newsprint or butcher paper to the wall. Provide magazines, newspapers, scissors and glue. Divide the class into two groups and instruct one team to find pictures of nutritious foods and to attach them to the mural. Tell the other group to do the same with junk food illustrations.

Choose a specific product such as sugar. Talk about the way it is often grown in places such as Central America as a crop to bring cash to wealthy land-owners. Using the earth for this purpose may deprive people of that particular nation of the food they need to grow for their own survival.

Also point out that the purchase of certain national brands contributes to life for others. For example, one company that makes ice cream gives a percentage of their profit specifically to peace causes.

Dance

PURPOSE:

To use gestural interpretation to help children understand Martin Luther King, Jr.'s "I Have A Dream Speech."

PREPARATION:

Materials
- I Have A Dream Speech
- Plastic lids; small, colored
- Bells
- Hole punch
- Ribbon

PROCEDURE:

Obtain a copy of Martin Luther King, Jr.'s "I Have A Dream" speech and use this gestural interpretation[184] to help the children understand the meaning of the words. This movement and mime piece requires a narrator and twelve participants. If more learners are involved, an even number is suggested.

Note that this interpretation is based on twelve participants, who work as a total group, as well as in pairs and individually. The pairs will be referred to as letters of the alphabet, and the individuals are assigned numbers as follows:

```
A
1 2
B
3 4
C
5 6
D
7 8
E
9 10
F
11 12
```

In advance, or as a student project, make rhythm instruments from small colored plastic lids. Tennis ball can or margarine tub container lids are ideal.

Punch a hole in the lid wherever a bell is desired. Two bells per lid should be sufficient. Thread ribbon through the holes in the lid and the hole in the bell to join the two together. Tie securely.

Prepare the narrator to slowly and deliberately read the speech as the action takes place. Direct the mimes to change movements on the following key words or phrases:

Entrance. Enter in a single file line. Stand in a semi-circle, with back to audience.

I have a dream. Turn to audience. Working in pairs, kneel on the inside knee. The person on the left kneels on the right knee, and the person on the right kneels on the left knee. Extend the outside arm across the knee. The inside arm should remain at the side.

Rise up. Stand. Left arms to waist. Extend hands with palm up.

All men. Partners join inside hands.

Created equal. Entire group joins hands.

Red hills. Pair A moves to center stage. Join hands and raise them to form hills. Return to group.

Slave...slave owners. Pair F moves to center stage. Number eleven, the slave, kneels and mimes lifting an object from left to right. Number twelve, the slave owner, stands over number eleven, with arms folded.

Table of brotherhood. Number twelve, the slave owner, reaches down, helps up number eleven, and they shake hands. Return to group.

State of Mississippi...sweltering. Remain in line. Extend right arm over face.

Transformed. Swing arms at sides. Extend arms over head. Cross arms with the next person.

Justice. Relax arms at side.

I have...four little children. Groups C and D step forward and act afraid. Remainder of group points and laughs at them and pretends to sneer and ridicule.

Not be judged. Pointers stop, shake their head no, step forward and place their hands on the shoulders of the "four children".

Character. Reassemble as group in semi-circle.

State of Alabama. Turn back to audience. Stand with arms at sides.

Interposition. Clench right fist.

Nullification. Clench left fist.

Transformed. Release fists. Turn to partner. Join hands. Walk to the right and circle back to starting position.

I have...valley...exalted. Pair B moves to center stage and kneels. Join hands, right to left. Stand. Raise hands over head to form mountain peaks. Return to group.

Mountain made low. Pair E moves to center stage. Join hands, right to left. Lift hands over head to form mountains. On word "low," lower hands and kneel. Remain through plains. Return to group.

Crooked places. Pair C moves to center stage. Bend and twist in strange shapes. On word straight, untangle self and stand straight and tall. Return to group.

Glory of the Lord. Group, in semicircle, joins hands and raises them.

This is our hope. Group forms circle, holding hands over heads, to form mountain.

How out. Pair D steps out of group and walks around the mountain. Returns to group.

With this faith. Relax arms at side. Re-form semi-circle.

With this faith...work together. Pair A steps forward. Number one kneels next to number two and mimes handing an object back and forth. Continue action.

Pray together. Pair B steps forward. Number three kneels and number four stands. Each places palms together in a gesture of prayer. Continue action.

Struggle together. Pairs C and D step forward. Pair C forms as bridge, around pair D. They struggle together. Continue action.

Jail together. Pairs E and F step forward. Numbers nine, ten and eleven encircle number twelve. Continue.

Stand up for freedom. All stop. Re-form semi-circle.

Free one day. Sit Indian style. Hold hands and begin to sway from side to side very slowly.

And if America. Stop swaying movement.

Prodigious hilltops of New Hampshire. Pair A jumps up, joins and lifts hands to form mountains.

Mighty mountains of New York. Pair F jumps up, joins and lifts hands to form mountains.

Heightening Alleghenies of Pennsylvania. Pair B jumps up, joins and lifts hands to form mountains.

Snowcapped Rockies of Colorado. Pair E jumps up, joins and lifts hands to form mountains.

Curvaceous peaks of California. Pair C jumps up, joins and lifts hands to form mountains.

Stone Mountain of Georgia. Pair D jumps up, joins and lifts hands to form mountains.

Lookout Mountain of Tennessee. Pairs A and B join to form mountain. Pairs C and D, as well as Pairs E and F do likewise.

Hill and molehill of Mississippi. Entire group joins to form one mountain.

When we let. Re-form semi-circle. As speech continues, number one and number twelve walk to center stage, each picks up a bell or tambourine and begins to shake it while moving down the center aisle to return to the middle of the semi-circle. Number two and number eleven, number three and number ten, number four and number nine, number five and number eight, and number six and number seven do likewise until everyone has a bell and all have re-formed a semi-circle.

Free at last. Raise arms over head, continuing to shake bells.

Thank God. With arms extended, share and shake bells in joyful movements.

Exit. Relax arms at sides. Exit.

Drama

PURPOSE:

To re-tell the stories of nationally known peacemakers by using various dramatic methods.

PREPARATION:

Materials
- Varied with chosen method

PROCEDURE:

Re-tell the stories of nationally known peacemakers, from the United States and other countries, by using various drama methods. Try some of these ideas:

Formal Drama. Perform a full scale production with memorized parts, costumes, lighting, sets, and so forth.

Play Reading. Use a script, of any length, without memorizing the parts. Have the students read it as a learning activity.

Reader's Theatre. Performance read from scripts or told informally according to a pre-arranged plan. Props, sets and costumes are usually not used.

Tableau. Dramatic scene which is both silent and motionless. The players freeze, like statues, in an interesting pose which interprets or illustrates a reading.

First Person. Tell the character's story as if the speaker were the person.

Masks. Use masks to represent characters in a story. They may be made from paper plates, posterboard or another material.

Stories of people of peace may be found in many sources. The book, Teaching Children to Care[185] sections forty-five through fifty-five, contains short stories on Jane Addams, Clara Barton, Mary McLeod Bethune, Dr. Tom Dooley, Toyohiko Kagawa, Martin Luther King, Jr., Cardinal Paul-Emile Leger, Nellie McClurg, Florence Nightengale, Dr. Albert Schweitzer and Mother Theresa. A full page illustration of each person's face, suitable for a mask, is included with each biography.

Prepare For Peace, Part III,[186] contains a reader's theatre script, plus a one paragraph biography, on King Asoka of ancient India, Saint Francis of Assisi, William Penn, Elizabeth Fry, Jane Addams, Gandhi, Muriel Lester, Sadako Sasaki, Martin Luther King, Jr., Mother Teresa, Corrie ten Boom and Bishop Desmond Tutu.

Select one dramatic method for the entire group to use, or enable the students to experiment with many techniques to tell the stories of these great teachers of peace.

Drama: Plays

PURPOSE:

To act out a story which addresses the national issue of nuclear power.

PREPARATION:

Materials
- Alice in Blunderland [187]

PROCEDURE:

Alice in Blunderland is a musical satire which addresses the nuclear issue. It requires a cast of thirteen speaking roles plus a chorus. The characters and setting are based on the story Alice in Wonderland. For example, the Cheshire Cat is a journalist who directs Alice's search for the truth about "fairy dust". Tweedledum and Tweedledee are two superpowers who stockpile "fairy dust" and argue about treaties. The lyrics are creative and clever. Older children are needed for the speaking roles, but all ages are appropriate for the chorus.

Games

the contributions they have made to society. It is designed especially with non-readers in mind.

PURPOSE:

To design and play a game to help children learn about the contributions of all races.

PREPARATION:

Materials
- Pictures of minority and ethnic people who have made contributions to society, ten duplicate sets
- Scissors
- Glue
- Posterboard
- Marker
- Contact paper, clear

Advance Preparation
- To make a game board for each child or each two children, select ten pictures of minority and ethnic people. Since this is a matching activity, each of these must have a duplicate. Glue each of the cut-out pictures to posterboard or construction paper to make them firm. The background pieces should all be the same size. For durability, cover the pictures with clear contact paper.
- To prepare the game board, take a piece of posterboard large enough to hold all twenty pieces, allowing for spaces in between them. With a marker, outline spaces for all twenty pictures. Use four rows of five. On the second and fourth rows, glue one set of ten pictures.

PROCEDURE:

Various ethnic and racial groups within a nation can often be in opposition to each other. This tension can be very evident in the lives of children who are involved directly or indirectly in these struggles. Finding ways to appreciate people in these groups as individuals rather than as labels contributes greatly to reducing these stresses and to promoting peace. This activity encourages children to concentrate on the strengths of various minority and ethnic people and

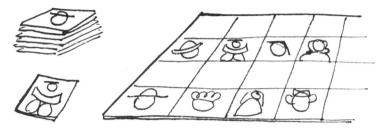

For one player, stack the individual picture cards in front of the person and ask him or her to match them with the cards glued on the board. For two players, make two game boards for five pictures each. Stack the ten matching cards face down between the players. Each, in turn, looks at a picture. If the picture matches one on his or her board, it goes in the appropriate space. If it belongs to the other, it is turned over beside the stack. Play continues until both players have matched all the spaces of their boards. To increase learning, let each player tell the other what is going on in the pictures as they are matched.

Music

PURPOSE:

To use the song "We Shall Overcome" to help participants identify with oppressed people.

PREPARATION:

Materials
- Music, "We Shall Overcome"
- Accompaniment, optional
- Record or tape, optional
- Record or tape player, optional

PROCEDURE:

"We Shall Overcome" has been a song associated with many freedom movements throughout the nation. The words express the hope and belief of people in oppressive situations. The application exercises in the study guide, Christ Is Our Peace: Biblical Foundations for Peacemaking,[188] suggest a unique way to use the song with a group.

If the children do not know the song, sing it to them or play it for them. After they are familiar with it, use the song to help the students identify with different groups of people who are still oppressed. Sing the song together and ask the pupils to imagine themselves as slaves in the brickyards of Egypt. Sing the song again and tell the group to imagine themselves as black slaves on a plantation before the Civil War.

Before singing the piece the third time, talk with the boys and girls about people who are living in oppressive conditions and circumstances in the United States. Ask them to picture senior citizens living below the poverty level, homeless children living in cars or bus terminals and runaway teens who have become entrapped to drugs. As the song is sung for the last time, ask the participants to picture themselves as one of these people.

Follow this musical introduction to oppression with a study or speaker on what can be done to alleviate these problems.

Music:
Song Adaptation

PURPOSE:

To re-write national television jingles to slogans with peace messages.

PREPARATION:

Materials
- Paper
- Pens
- Envelopes
- Stamps

Advance Preparation
- Find the addresses of national corporations, television networks and schools in various parts of the nation to which letters may be sent.

PROCEDURE:

Pick several commercial jingles that are or have been aired on national television and re-write them as peace slogans. For example, change "Oh, what a feeling, Toyota" to "Oh, what a feeling, Peace is!" Or, modify the Alka Seltzer commercial, "Plop, plop, fizz, fizz, oh, what a relief it is," to "Trust, hope, love, share; then peace will be everywhere."

Pass out paper and pens and allow time for the children to think of and to write down several jingles. This may be done individually, in small groups, or as a total group.

Suggest that the jingles be sent to a school in another part of the United States with the request that they send some back. They may also be mailed to national television networks, news programs and corporations with a cover letter explaining the project and asking them to do all that they can to promote peace in the country.

Music: Song Suggestions

PURPOSE:

To emphasize the theme peace in the nation through song.

PREPARATION:

Materials
- Music
- Accompaniment, optional

PROCEDURE:

Acquaint the children with music that can help them concentrate on the theme, peace in the nation. This includes:

"God Is Our Strength" [189]

"If I Had A Hammer" [190]

"Step by Step" [191]

"This Is My Song" [192]

Photography

PURPOSE:

To help children develop an appreciation of and an empathy for people who pursue peace in various ways.

PREPARATION:

Materials
- Book(s)
- Camera
- Slide film
- Tape recorder
- Tape
- Costumes
- Props
- Projector
- Screen

PROCEDURE:

Make a slide show to tell the story of a nationally known peacemaker. Choose a book, such as The Tall Man [193] or Ted Studebaker: A Man Who Loved Peace, [194] to use. Works on people like Martin Luther King, Jr., Rosa Parks, Harriet Tubman, Jane Pittman, Jane Addams or Cesar Chevez, are readily available in libraries. Divide the story into scenes, choose props and costumes and assign and practice parts.

Tape record the story while the students read it. Play back the recording and have the costumed children take their poses. Snap pictures of each scene.

Get the slides developed and assemble the presentation. At the next session, set up the projector and screen and show the visualized story to the children. Present it for other groups as well.

Photography: Media

PURPOSE:

To view, through the use of a film produced by young people, children's outlooks on peace in the nation.

PREPARATION:

Materials
- Film, <u>Bombs Will Make The Rainbow Break</u> [195]
- Projector
- Screen
- Extension cord

PROCEDURE:

Shown <u>Bombs Will Make The Rainbow Break</u> to the participants. Children's art work and narration are used to emphasize the confusion they feel over the issue of nuclear war. This visualization provides a good way to start a discussion on the arms build-up in the nation.

Puppetry

PURPOSE:

To make puppets representing people who have worked for peace and justice and to tell their stories using these tools.

PREPARATION:

Materials
- Bottles, laundry or dish washing detergent type
- Felt
- Fabric scraps
- Yarn or fake fur
- Scissors
- Glue
- Paper towel tubes
- Duct tape
- Trims
- Biographical information on peacemakers

Advance Preparation
- Clean and de-label bottles.

PROCEDURE:

Used bottles, in various shapes and sizes, can be re-cycled into puppets by adding low-cost or no-cost materials. Make each puppet a person who has worked to promote peace and justice in the nation. Include people like Rosa Parks, Martin Luther King, Jr., Jane Addams, Clara Barton, Tom Dooley and Sojourner Truth.

Provide biographical information and ask each youngster to pick a person to research and to report his or her story by using the puppet.

Have the boys and girls pick their bottles. Tell them to turn the bottles upside down and to decide if the side with the handle will form the front or the back of the face. If it is to be the front, the handle becomes the puppet's nose.

Hand out paper towel tubes and tell each child to place one on the pouring spout of the bottle. It will become the rod by which the puppet is operated. Use duct tape to secure the two pieces together.

Make felt scraps available, as well as scissors, and give the learners an opportunity to form the face. Ask them to cut eyes and a mouth and to glue them in place. Eyebrows, eyelashes and cheeks may also be added.

Show the group how to make hair from yarn, fake fur or fibrefil. Guide them in this process and help them glue it to the top of the puppet heads.

Invite the children to choose a large square of fabric for the costume. Tell them to cut a small hole in the center of the material and to slide their paper towel tube through it. The fabric is taped to the neck of the puppet. Contrasting pieces and trims may complete the costume.

Give each child a turn to tell the story of his or her person of peace. Conclude the activity by asking each pupil to share how he or she will help to promote peace in the nation and to end injustice.

Storytelling

PURPOSE:

To use a storytelling method involving bags, baskets or boxes to help children explore the lives of national peacemakers.

PREPARATION:

Materials
- Resource materials on national peacemakers
- Objects related to the peacemaker
- Bags, boxes or baskets

PROCEDURE:

Share the stories of people who promoted peace in the nation. Use a method involving bags, boxes or baskets for this activity. For example, to tell the story of Martin Luther King, Jr., place a toy bus in one container, a picture of a drinking fountain in another, and a model of the Washington Monument in the third. Distribute the bags to three different children. Ask each person, one at a time, to remove the object inside. Invite the boys and girls to guess who's life story will be shared.

Another method would be to place all the objects in one box. Remove each of them at the appropriate point in the story to serve as visual aids.

Challenge the children to research peacemakers and to tell their stories using one of these methods.

Storytelling: Children's Books

PURPOSE:

To portray role models for children by telling the stories of people who have worked for peace in the nation.

PREPARATION:

Materials
- Book(s)

PROCEDURE:

Books to browse for the peace in the nation theme have a central focus on people who spent their lives working for peace and justice. Many additional resources on role-models are readily available.

Armed With Courage. [196] Short stories about seven people who spent their lives working for peace and justice. Biographies include: Florence Nightingale, Father Damien, George Washington Carver, Jane Addams, Winfred Grenfell, Mahatma Gandhi and Albert Schweitzer.

Don't Ride the Bus on Monday. [197] Rosa Parks' courage and conviction is evident in the story of her refusal to give up her seat on the bus. Her non-violent protest sparked a campaign to end discrimination in the United States.

Immigrant Kids. [198] The theme of acceptance is addressed in a book about people, especially children, who have immigrated to the United States.

Quanah Parker: Indian Warrior for Peace. [199] A true account, based on the life of an Indian warrior who had an Indian father and a white mother, that all people in a nation must unite for peace.

Value of Friendship. [200] Emphasis is placed on friendship in the story of Jane Addams' work with the poor.

Storytelling: Folktales

PURPOSE:

To consider stewardship of God's gifts after re-telling the folktale, The Fisherman and His Wife. [201]

PREPARATION:

Materials
- Folktale, The Fisherman and His Wife

PROCEDURE:

The Brothers Grimm, from Germany, wrote a classic tale which can help children focus on ways in which the greed of some may contribute to problems for others. The Fisherman and His Wife is a story of one woman's excessive demands and desires and her attempts to accumulate possessions and power.

Play a tape, show a video, or read the folktale to the youngsters. Use this story to consider ways in which the pupils are stewards of God's gifts. Does the greed of some people in this nation contribute to the poverty of others? Do the ways in which natural resources are used for the pursuit of possessions and pleasure harm the environment? Ask the youth to name substances, such as plastics, throw-away bottles and cans, and aluminum foil, that effect the environment. Talk about recycling opportunities. Lead the group in thinking about specific things they can do to care for God's creation.

[181] Lecture by Betty Reardon, Saturday, May 13, 1989, Midwest Peacemaking Conference, University of Notre Dame, Notre Dame, IN.

[182] Sweeney, Duane, ed. The Peace Catalog. Seattle: Press for Peace, 1984, D1-D77.

[183] Brown, Margie. "Here Comes Sam." The Good News Caravan. Dayton, OH: Clownibrations, 1979, 24-31. Available from: Margie Brown, 2140 Shatluck Ave., #2112, Berkeley, CA 94704. Used by permission.

[184] Based on choreography by Frances Ann Barna for the January 1983 Martin Luther King, Jr. Community Celebration in South Bend, IN.

[185] Dixon, Dorothy Arnett. Teaching Children to Care: 80 Circle Time Activities for Primary Grades. Mystic, CT: Twenty-Third Publications, 1981.

[186] Obold, Ruth. Prepare for Peace: A Peace Study for Children. Part III: Grades 7-8. Newton, KS: Faith and Life Press, 1986.

[187] DeFrange, Tim, and Tom DeFrange. Alice in Blunderland. Stow, OH: Legacy, Inc., 1983. Available from: Legacy, Inc., 1275 Goldfinch Trail, Stow, OH 44224.

[188] Boss-Koopman, Gayle, Steven D. Hoogerwerf, and Robert A. White. Christ is Our Peace: Biblical Foundations for Peacemaking. Lansing, IL: Reformed Church Press, 1982, 19.

[189] Illinois Chapter United Church of Christ Fellowship in the Arts. Songs of Hope and Peace. New York: Pilgrim Press, 1988, 13.

[190] Sing of Life and Faith. Philadelphia: Pilgrim Press, 1969, 103.

[191] Weiss, Evelyn, ed. Children's Songs for a Friendly Planet. Burnsville, NC: World Around Songs, 1986, 72.

[192] The United Methodist Hymnal. Nashville: The United Methodist Publishing House, 1989, 437.

[193] Davis, Carl, and Dorothy Brandt Davis. The Tall Man. Elgin, IL: Brethren Press, 1963.

[194] Moore, Joy Hofacker. Ted Studebaker: A Man Who Loved Peace. Scottdale, PA: Herald Press, 1987.

[195] Bombs Will Make the Rainbow Break. Zahm-Hurwitz, 1983. Available from: Films, Incorporated, 5547 North Ravenswood Ave., Chicago, IL 60640.

[196] McNeer, May, and Lynda Ward. Armed With Courage. Nashville: Abingdon Press, 1957.

[197] Meriweather, Louise. Don't Ride the Bus on Monday. Englewood Cliffs, NJ: Prentice-Hall, 1973.

[198] Freedman, Russell. Immigrant Kids. New York: E. P. Dutton, 1980.

[199] Anderson, LaVere. Quanah Parker: Indian Warrior for Peace. Champaign, IL: Garrard Publishing Co., 1970.

[200] Johnson, Anna. Value of Friendship. La Jolla, CA: Value Communications, Inc., 1979.

[201] Grimm, Jakob Ludwig, and Wilhelm Grimm. The Fisherman and His Wife. Trans. Elizabeth Shub. Illus. Monika Laimgruber. New York: Greenwillow Books, 1978.

CHAPTER TEN

PEACE IN THE
WORLD

Introduction

In the book, <u>Despair and Personal Power in the Nuclear Age</u>,[202] author and educator Joanna Rogers Macy suggests twelve ways that parents and teachers can responsibly and supportively address children's concerns about living in a nuclear world. In summary, they are:

1. Know your own feelings.

2. Invite children to share their feelings about the world.

3. Give your complete attention.

4. Let yourself listen.

5. Help children define their feelings.

6. Let them know they are not alone in these feelings.

7. Acknowledge what you don't know.

8. Don't feel you must relieve your children of their painful feelings.

9. Let children make choices.

10. With your children, take joy in life.

11. Show them you care enough about your world and about them to engage in actions to promote peace.

12. Support children in taking action in their own right.

Use these guidelines, together with the activities suggested in this chapter, to help children become people who foster world peace.

Architecture

PURPOSE:

To contrast the architecture of the public and the poor sides of a city.

PREPARATION:

Materials
- National Geographic magazines
- Cardboard
- Scissors
- Glue
- Clear contact paper, optional
- Marker

Advance Preparation
- Cut pictures from magazines, such as National Geographic, of the most elaborate buildings in a given city and also pictures of homes in the poorest areas. Repeat for several cities. Glue the pictures to cardboard that has been cut to fit. Number the pictures,

being careful to avoid a pattern that can be easily detected by the players. Record the numbers to form an answer key. Cover each picture with clear contact paper, if desired, to provide durability. Arrange the pictures on a table before the students arrive.

PROCEDURE:

This exercise provides an opportunity for people to contrast the architectural magnificence of the public side of a city with the architectural realities of the poorer portions.

When the participants arrive, or at an appropriate time during a class, ask the pupils to match the photographs from the same cities. After everyone has finished, read the correct answers. Ask the group to discuss what strikes them about this exercise.[203]

Art

PURPOSE:

To incorporate peace symbols into a woodworking project.

PREPARATION:

Materials
- Wood blocks, 5" x 7"
- Sandpaper
- Finishing nails, 1/2"
- Hammers, small, tack-type
- Markers

Advance Preparation
- Obtain scrap lumber and cut the blocks to a five inch by seven inch size.

PROCEDURE:

Ask the children to name several world-wide peace symbols. Some are a dove, crane, olive branch, broken bomb and peace sign. Have each person choose a symbol or word to use in a woodworking project.

Ask each student to pick a piece of wood. The edges of the board may need to be sanded. Provide markers and ask the boys and girls to draw the design on the board they have prepared. Direct the children to outline their symbols with nails. Pass out as many nails as needed. While giving assistance in hammering or straightening nails, use the opportunity to discuss the peace symbol.

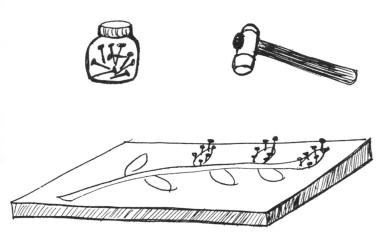

Display the finished products at a community event.

For an exciting project, mount a large piece of plywood containing an outline of a peace symbol. Make hammers and nails available and invite many people to contribute to the finished product. Talk with the group about ways in which many people can work to achieve world peace.

Art

PURPOSE:

To use crafts to introduce children to cultures and countries of the world.

PREPARATION:

Materials
• Varied with projects selected

PROCEDURE:

Hold a crafts festival to introduce children to the cultures and countries of the world. This may be done in several ways. Choose one of these formats to use.

Invite each student or small group to research a particular country and to report on it or to bring examples of its crafts to share with the group.

Introduce a new craft, from a different country, each week.

Ask each participant to bring the supplies and instructions for making a simple craft and to demonstrate the project for the class.

Set up a learning center for each continent and have examples of crafts as well as materials and methods for making them available for the students to explore. If possible, ask a guest from that country to come to share stories with the children. The book, Art From Many Hands,[204] contains chapters on the arts of West Africa, the Middle East, Europe, Asia, Central and South America, the Caribbean Islands, the United States and Canada. Several activities are provided and complete instructions, as well as photographs and diagrams, are included. There is also a bibliography, by country, of art resources. Many additional books are also available.

Art:
Draw Your
Dream Of Peace

PURPOSE:

To draw a design of children as peacemakers.

PREPARATION:

Materials
- "PEACE IN THE WORLD" coloring sheets
- Crayons or markers
- Paper
- Resource materials on flags of the world

Advance Preparation
- Duplicate coloring sheets

PROCEDURE:

Distribute the "Peace in the World" coloring sheets and crayons or markers. Provide resource material, such as encyclopedias, on the flags of the world. Ask the children to complete their pictures by drawing in the design of a different flag for each child represented on the sheet. Tell them to write the name of the country under the child. Indicate that the participants may color the activity sheets as they choose.

Following the coloring, lead a discussion on ways children can be world peacemakers. Ask each boy and girl to silently reflect on one thing he or she will commit to doing for world peace.

Art: Draw Your Dream Of Peace

What can children do for world peace?

What will you do?

Banners/Textiles

PURPOSE:

To teach children to write peace in many languages and to pray for the people who live in these countries.

PREPARATION:

Materials
- Ribbon, one inch wide or wider
- Pole or rod
- Tacks or duct tape
- Permanent markers
- Basket or box
- World map, optional
- "Peace" words list

Advance Preparation
- Cut a piece of ribbon, for each day of the month, to the desired length. Place the strips in a basket or box.
- Hang the world map, if one is to be used.
- Duplicate a copy of the peace words list for each participant.

PROCEDURE:

World peace is the prayer of many people around the globe. Although the word "Peace" means the same thing in many languages, it is written and pronounced differently in most of them. Combine various ways to write the word into a ribbon banner activity.[205] As each ribbon is added, remember the people in that country in prayer.

Pass out and review the peace in many languages list with the students. Find more to add to the list, if needed. Explain the project.

Have the students take turns picking one language a day and, using a permanent marker, ask them to write "peace" on a ribbon. Tape or tack the ribbon to the rod or pole. Ask the group to try to pronounce the word together. If desired, have the boys and girls find the location of the country on the world map. Offer a prayer for the people in the country.

Allow the ribbons to flow freely, or attach another pole across the bottom to make them more secure. When the banner is completed, display it in a prominent place or install it in a permanent location. Encourage the children to re-commit to working to end injustice and to bringing the news of the inner peace that God provides for the people of the world.

SUGGESTED WORDS

Arabic
سلام
Pronunciation: Sah-laahm

Chinese
和平
Pronunciation: Ho-P'ing

French
Paix
Pronunciation: Peh

German
Friede
Pronunciation: Free-duh

Greek
ειρήνη
Pronunciation: Ih-Ray-Nay

Hebrew
שלום
Pronunciation: Shah-lohm

Hindi
शांति
Pronunciation: Shan-tee

Hungarian
Beke
Pronunciation: Bayh-kuh

Indonesian
Perdamaian
Pronunciation: Pear-dah-my-ahn

Irish
Siochain
Pronunciation: See-uh-kawn

Italian
Pace
Pronunciation: Pah-chay

Japanese
平和
Pronunciation: Hay-uah

Laotian
ສັນຕິພາບ
Pronunciation: San-tee-fat

Nepalese
शान्ति
Pronunciation: Shan-tee

Persian
صلح
Pronunciation: Sohl'h

Philipino
Kapayapaan
Pronunciation: Kah-pye-yah-oah-ahn

Polish
Pokoj
Pronunciation: Poh-koy

Portuguese
Paz
Pronunciation: Rhymes with Roz

Russian
Мир
Pronunciation: Mir

Spanish
Paz
Pronunciation: Pah th

Srilankan
සාමය
Pronunciation: Sah-ahm-ah-yuh

Swahili
Amani
Pronunciation: Ah-mah-nee

Swedish, Danish and Norwegian
Fred
Pronunciation: Like man's name

Thai
สันติภาพ
Pronunciation: San-tee-pop

Vietnamese
Hoa-binh
Pronunciation: Hwa-bean

Cartoons

PURPOSE:

To consider an international peace concern depicted in a cartoon.

PREPARATION:

Materials
- Cartoon
- Paper
- Pens

PROCEDURE:

Choose a cartoon which addresses an issue of world peace. It may depict political changes in Eastern European countries or the drug crisis in Central and South America. Display the cartoon in the room or duplicate a copy for each participant.

Individually or in small groups, ask the boys and girls to illustrate the theme of the cartoon by acting it out, writing a story about it, or composing a song. Allow time for the children to consider and create. Share the results together.

Clown/Mime

PURPOSE:

To demonstrate that each person has the power and ability to do away with the barriers that separate people, and to build positive pathways or bridges between people.

PREPARATION:

Materials
- Cardboard bricks, shoe boxes or cartons
- Newsprint, brown grocery bags or poster paints
- Tape or glue
- Brushes
- Markers or crayons
- Wood blocks, various sizes

PROCEDURE:

Use this activity, based on Ephesians 2:14, as a clown skit to help children think about values that promote peace in the world.

Through group discussion, make a list of negative values that build walls and positive values that create bridges between people. Write each list on a piece of newsprint. Negative values may be violence, doubt, greed, fear, selfishness, hate, prejudice, hurt, anger, and jealousy. Some positive values are love, openness, acceptance, kindness, cooperation, joy, sharing, caring and gentleness.

Tell the students they will be making a wall of negative attitudes and also a bridge to peace.

Distribute the bricks, boxes or cartons. Provide materials, such as paper, paints, tape, glue and brushes. Have each child choose a positive and a negative value and print them on opposite sides of his or her brick.

After the brick construction, build a wall with negative values. Knock down the wall, either in-

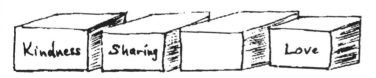

dividually or as a group. Individually, have each person take a turn building up negatively, knocking down and building again positively. This emphasizes the role

Following the activity, lead a discussion using questions like:

How did you feel about the wall?

What word bothered you the most?

What did it feel like to build the wall?

Did you feel "closed in"?

How did you feel as you knocked down the wall?

What word or value would you most like to get rid of?

What was it like to build a bridge to peace?

Which word on the pathway was your favorite?

Have you been more like a wall or a bridge in the past?

If wall-like, what one thing can you do to change that?

Think about a recent time you added a brick to the wall by something you did or said? How did it feel?

Describe a time when you helped to build a bridge. How did it feel?

Close the activity with a prayer in which each child asks God to help him or her be a bridge to peace.

each individual plays in peacemaking. As a group, pretend the wall is very strong and it takes everyone to knock it down. Work together to complete the task. This emphasizes peacemaking as a cooperative effort which requires everyone working together.

After knocking down the wall, take the scattered bricks and build a pathway or bridge with the positive values facing up. Invite the group to walk through the pathway. After the children cross the bridge, have them pick a piece of wood and a marker and write "Build A Bridge to Peace" on one side and a positive value on the other. Let the children keep these pieces as reminders to work towards peace in the world.

Creative Writing

PURPOSE:

To initiate an opportunity for learners to write letters promoting world peace.

PREPARATION:

Materials
- Paper
- Pens
- Envelopes
- Stamps
- Chalkboard or newsprint
- Chalk or marker

Advance Preparation
- Addresses of persons/organizations to whom letters will be sent.

PROCEDURE:

Invite the children to write letters to world leaders urging them to work for peace. Brainstorm a list of people to whom the notes could be sent. It might include:

The President of the United States
The White House
1600 Pennsylvania Avenue N.W.
Washington, DC 20500

The President of the Soviet Union
c/o The Embassy of the U.S.S.R.
1125 16th Street, N.W.
Washington, DC 20036

Others to contact would be congressional representatives or the Secretary General of the United Nations.

Distribute paper, pens and envelopes. Ask the children to write or draw a message to the people they have chosen to contact. Suggest sample messages, or write them on a chalkboard or a piece of newsprint. Some possibilities are:

"Be at peace as you work for peace."

"I believe that peace is possible. I will do all I can to achieve it, and I hope you will too."

"I will work for peace in my family and community as you work for peace within our world family and community."

Encourage the children to share some of their letters. After envelopes are passed out, help the boys and girls address them, place their letters inside, put stamps in the corners, and mail the messages.

As an additional, or alternate, letter writing activity, begin a Pen Pal program with children in another part of the world. In these letters suggest that the children include name, address and age, as well as information on family, school and hobbies.

Send the letters to an organization that arranges Pen Pal exchanges between children of the world. Some are:

International Friendship League
22 Battery March Street
Boston, MA 02109

International Pen Friends
P.O. Box 14126 B.O. Station
San Juan, PR 00915 USA

League of Friendship
P.O. Box 509
Mt. Vernon, OH 53050

Student Letter Exchange
910 4th Street SE
Austin, MN 44912

World Pen Pals
1690 Como Avenue
St. Paul, MN 55108.

Letters that are sent directly to the Soviet Union may be addressed:

Pioneer Palace
International Friendship Club
Moscow (or name of another city)
U.S.S.R.

For information on a Pen Pal project and unique "Peace" stationary to go with it, contact:

Pen Pals for Peace
c/o Crafters Link
59999 Myrtle Road
South Bend, IN 46614

Creative Writing: Poetry

PURPOSE:

To engage students in an activity that will enable them to gain a deeper appreciation for the gifts, as well as the feelings, of people around the world.

PREPARATION:

Materials
- Collections of poetry from around the world
- Construction paper
- Scissors
- Markers

PROCEDURE:

Collect poetry, or invite the pupils to bring poems which were written by men, women and children in other countries. These may be found in international collections or anthologies, such as:

Miracles: Poems by Children of the English-Speaking World. [206]

or

Zero Makes Me Happy. [207]

Distribute the writings to individuals or to small groups and ask the learners to read them. Take time to share some of the favorites with the entire class.

Help the group respond to the feelings that were stirred after reading the thoughts of someone from another land by writing individual poems in a Japanese style, Haiku. According to Ross Snyder, "A haiku is a Japanese poem of three lines. Since the Japanese language, on the whole, consists of short words, you learn under haiku discipline to suggest a lot with just a few sounds. This forces you to meditate and meditate and meditate on what the essential 'gist' is that you want to say. Everything non-essential has to be left out. To be sure, a haiku does not have to

rhyme, and that frees us to write honestly. But it must be poetry - you have to have a kind of picture in your mind that you're expressing." [208]

Point out that the format for a Haiku consists of three lines and seventeen syllables. Line one has five beats, line two seven and line three five. Share an illustration on the theme of peace in the world, like:

People everywhere
Sharing, caring and loving
Friendships form and grow.

Pass out construction paper, markers and scissors. Tell each pupil to write his or her haiku and then to cut the paper into a shape to fit the words on it. Arrange the writings on a bulletin board in the classroom and allow time for the students to read each others' work.

Culinary Arts

PURPOSE:

To help children acknowledge a worldwide need for peace.

PREPARATION:

Materials
- Pictures
- Globe
- Posterboard
- Marker
- Cupcakes, undecorated
- Frosting, various colors
- Knives
- Cake decorating equipment, if available
- Napkins

Advance Preparation
- Prepare cupcakes and frostings.
- Make peace words poster.

PROCEDURE:

An Irish custom involving cupcakes can be used to help children recognize and appreciate a worldwide need for peace. It can also encourage a positive concept of peace all over the earth.

Begin by showing the young people pictures of people, especially children, from various countries. Ask them to guess where they might live. Provide a globe or world map and help the learners locate some of these places on it. Discuss ways in which these children also want peace.

Explain an Irish custom of giving a cupcake to someone with whom you would like to make peace. Show the children a poster with the word "peace" written in many languages. Some words to include are:

French: <u>Paix</u>

German: <u>Frieden</u>

Hungarian: <u>Beke</u>

Irish: <u>Siochain</u>

Italian: <u>Pace</u>

Polish: <u>Pokoj</u>

Russian: <u>Mir</u>

Spanish: <u>Paz</u>

Swahili: <u>Amani</u>

Swedish, Danish and Norwegian: <u>Fred</u>.

Guide each pupil in choosing a word to use in a special activity.

Surprise the children with undecorated cupcakes and several colors of frosting. Give each person a cupcake and assist him or her in writing "peace" on it in the language selected. Invite the group to give the cupcakes to someone as an offering of peace. Better yet, have each student make two: one to eat and one to share.

Dance

PURPOSE:

To build community, as well as hope for the world, among participants through the use of folk dance.

PREPARATION:

Materials
- "Peace Prayer" music[209]
- Accompaniment, optional

PROCEDURE:

"Folk dances, like folk songs, have grown from the experiences and needs of ordinary people. Through the ages, they have been an outlet for personal exuberance and communal celebration. A joyous experience in sensing the oneness of a group that is moving together can do very much to build unity and hope in people. People need to hope together."[210]

The "Peace Prayer" is a chant-dance based on Isaiah 2:4. Its message, promoting world peace, is that people shall hammer their swords into plowshares, their spears into sickles, and war shall not be taught. The book, A Dancing People, suggests a traditional folk dance grapevine step to accompany the words and music.

Gather the participants in a circle, in concentric circles, or in a line, and instruct them to move to the left. Tell the children to extend their hands along the adjoining person's arms, gripping wrists or elbows, or to extend their hands to opposite shoulders.

Begin the music and the movements slowly and speed up as the dance progresses. The following movements are suggested:

Nation shall not: Cross right foot behind left foot and bend knees. Step sideward on left foot.

Lift sword: Cross right foot in front of left foot.

Against nation: Step sideward on left foot.[211]

Continue the pattern throughout the rest of the dance.

To end the dance, draw the group into a spiral and lead a prayer or benediction.

Drama

PURPOSE:

To use costumes and dramatize stories of people around the world.

PREPARATION:

Materials
- Costume pieces representing various countries:
  - Clothing
  - Shoes
  - Hats
  - Accessories
- Box

PROCEDURE:

Dramatize stories of people from various countries. Provide a box of simple costume pieces, including clothes, shoes, hats and different accessories.

Choose one topic, like the reaction of the children in East and West Germany to the breaking down of the wall, and have the group improvise a story about it. Individual skits may be prepared in which each person chooses a situation to portray. Suggest a child receiving his or her first textbook in Africa, a young person working on a farm in Central America, or a youth arriving in a new land for the first time. Tell the children to choose one or two costume pieces which are in keeping with the character they will portray. Take turns presenting the scenes. After the short dramas, converse with the students about the lives and situations of people around the world.

Drama: Plays

PURPOSE:

To have children experience the concept of peace in the world through participation in a dramatic production.

PREPARATION:

Materials
- Play, Square Pegs, Round Holes [212]

PROCEDURE:

Square Pegs, Round Holes is a play based on the premise that peace will come when individuals stop looking at each other as enemies and get to know each other as people. In this imaginative play, requiring two adults and two children, the Rounds and the Squares live on opposite sides and each group claims to be right about everything. Just before the big contest for power, Little Square sees Little Round playing and becomes interested in his toy. They forget their differences and become friends, however the adults do not know this. In the contest, the boys are put on opposite sides, and as they see the pegs being stockpiled each child runs to the opposite side with the hope that the adults will not throw pegs at their own children. This is a good play to perform for younger and older children.

206

Games

PURPOSE:

To prepare and play games containing facts on global topics.

PREPARATION:

Materials
- Posterboard
- Index cards
- Paper
- Pencils
- Markers
- Resource materials

PROCEDURE:

Ask the children to name things they would like to know about other countries and their people. Challenge them to find the answers to some of these questions and to make games to help other students learn them.[213] Working as individuals or as small groups, invite every person or team to pick either a different game format or a different topic to incorporate into the project.

Make reference books available and tell the learners to use them to find their facts. These could be inventors, musicians, world sports records, currency of countries, endangered species or capital cities. Have the children put this information into the form of a game like Concentration, Twenty Questions or Jeopardy. For example, for the answer "Rubles," the Jeopardy question would be "What is the currency of the Soviet Union?"

Provide an opportunity for the participants to play each other's games and to learn more about the world in the process.

Music

PURPOSE:

To provide a creative way for children to sing songs from other countries and those which speak of peace.

PREPARATION:

Materials
- Magazines
- Posterboard or manila folders
- Scissors
- Markers
- Glue

Advance Preparation
- Prepare puzzle pieces.

PROCEDURE:

Piece it together in a fun, creative way using songs from other countries and those which speak of peace.

In advance, select large, colorful pictures which show positive images of local, national and international people and places. Choose one picture for each group of five children. Cut a piece of posterboard or manila file folder to fit the picture and glue the photo to it to add strength and rigidity. Cut each picture into five puzzle pieces. On the back of the five pieces from one picture, write the name of a familiar ethnic or peace song. Some suggestions include "Kum Ba Ya," "Jesus Loves the Little Children," "For God So Loved the World' and "We Are the World." Repeat this process with a different song for each picture. Mix up all the puzzle pieces.

Randomly distribute one puzzle piece to each student. Inform the participants that they will be singing the songs written on their puzzle pieces while moving around the room trying to locate others who are singing the same song. If a child does not know the song, instruct him or her to say the title while looking for the other partners. When the five children find each other, have them form a group and complete the puzzle. If the students do not know each other, each should introduce him or herself. Request that the group begins singing and searching. After all the groups are formed, sing or learn the songs together as a way of celebrating the people of the world.[214]

Music:
Song Adaptation

PURPOSE:

To sing "He's Got the Whole World in His Hands" and to compose new verses which will make the children more aware of places in the world.

PREPARATION:

Materials
- Music, "He's Got the Whole World in His Hands"
- Accompaniment, optional
- Globe, optional

PROCEDURE:

Sing the chorus "He's Got the Whole World in His Hands." Compose new verses which focus on various countries and continents. Make special mention of places where the church supports missionaries. Pass around a globe while the song is being sung and encourage the children to find these locations on it.

Sign language is a way of communicating with many hearing impaired people throughout the world. Find and teach the signs for the key words in the song: He (God), world and hands. Sign and sing this beautiful musical message.

Music:
Song Suggestions

PURPOSE:

To introduce children to the range of songs available on the theme peace in the world.

PREPARATION:

Materials
- Music
- Accompaniment, optional

PROCEDURE:

Peace in the world is a common theme in music. Some of the more unfamiliar songs to sing with children are:

"A Plea for One World" [215]

"Grand and Glorious" [216]

"Red, White and Blue" [217]

"The World of Tomorrow" [218]

Photography

PURPOSE:

To use photographs to help children explore the world and the people in it.

PREPARATION:

Materials
- Photographs
- Magazines
- Newspapers
- Paper
- Pens

PROCEDURE:

Photographs can provide a source of information and a stimulus to inquiry. Gather a collection of pictures of people and places around the world. These may be found in magazines, newspapers and calendars and can be used in many ways.

Form small groups of students and pass out several pictures to each of them. Tell the children to concentrate on one person in a picture and to imagine what his or her life might be like. Feelings, family, school, work, friends, income, and many other things could be considered.

Pass out paper and pens and propose that the students write a short story about this person. These may be shared within the small groups.

Also suggest that the children talk about problems that may be shown in the pictures and that they discuss actions that could be taken to relieve them in the short term and to alleviate the causes in the long term.

Photography: Media

PURPOSE:

To depict the stories and situations of children around the world through the use of media.

PREPARATION:

Materials
- Video or film, Remember Me [219]
- VCR or projector
- Monitor or screen

PROCEDURE:

Show Remember Me, a challenging video or film which portrays the ways in which the environment shapes the lives of several impoverished children in many countries of the world. It runs seventeen minutes.

Puppetry

PURPOSE:

To present a non-verbal puppet demonstration to illustrate the maldistribution of the world's resources.

PREPARATION:

Materials
- Card tables, three
- Tablecloths, three different colors
- Paper cups, one hundred
- Posterboard or construction paper
- Marker
- Scissors
- Life cereal, three boxes
- Puppet, wearing a chef's hat

Advance Preparation
- Set up the tables in a row and spread a tablecloth on each of them.
- Distribute the cups in the following way: Place seventy-two cups on the first table to represent seventy-two percent of the world's population. This includes Africa, Asia and South America, commonly called the "third world." Place twenty-two cups on the second table to represent the twenty-two percent of the world's population living in the "First World," or the Western capitalistic countries and the "Second World," including the Soviet Union and the Eastern European countries. The third table represents just the United States, with six percent of the world's population. Place six cups on it.
- Make a sign for each table. The placard for table one should read "72 Hungry People," for table two, "22 Hungry People," and for table three, "6 Hungry People."

PROCEDURE:

Use this silent puppet presentation to visually illustrate the reality of the maldistribution of the world's resources. In this simulation, food is the specific example. The cereal is poured into the cups to represent all the basic resources of the earth. Roughly seventy-two percent of the world's population has access to only about twenty-two percent of the world's resources, while the United States, with only six percent of the world's population, consumes about forty percent of the world's resources. Following the exercise, participants may interpret the demonstration and identify ways to change the global injustice.

Arrange the children on the floor or on chairs so they can see the presentation. Explain that if any cereal falls on the floor it is to be left there, and that all of the materials will be re-used for similar demonstrations.

Use the puppet and begin the demonstration. Pour the first box of cereal primarily into the seventy-two cups on the "Third World" table, but also pour some into the cups on the second table. Set the empty box on the "Third World" table. Pour the second box mostly into the cups on the second table, with some also going into a few of the "U.S." cups. Set the empty box on the second table. Pour the contents of the third box completely into the six cups on the "U.S." table, causing the cereal to overflow these cups and to spill all over the table. Set the box on this table. To reflect even more accurately the maldistribution of resources, the realities of hunger within the United States and the wealth of a few in the Third World, have the puppet pour most of the cereal from at least one of the six U.S. cups into a few of the other five cups on this table. Pour cereal from a few of the seventy-two cups into a few of the others, so that some of the Third World cups overflow.

After the skit, ask the group to explain what the cups, the cereal and the tables represent and what the puppet was doing in each step. Provide clues and guide the discussion. Continue the dialogue by asking what can be done to change this situation. [220]

Storytelling

PURPOSE:

To help children read and remember stories from around the world.

PREPARATION:

Materials
- Stories from other countries

Advance Preparation
- Arrange for people from various countries to speak.

PROCEDURE:

Hold an "Around the World Storytelling Festival" to help the children learn more about people from other countries and cultures. Provide resources containing collections of stories from various places. Ask each child to pick a book, and a story from it, to share with the class.

Also invite people from other countries, or those who have traveled to different areas, to speak to the class about the place and its people.

Talk about ways in which knowing more about others promotes peacemaking.

Storytelling: Children's Books

PURPOSE:

To use children's books to concentrate young people's attention on the theme peace in the world.

PREPARATION:

Materials
- Book(s)

PROCEDURE:

A small sample of the many selections available under the theme, peace in the world, are listed below. Because so many books fall within this category, ten, rather than five descriptions are provided.

The Butter Battle Book. [221] A disagreement over whether bread should be buttered on the top or on the bottom causes a war between the Yooks and the Zooks. They build bigger and bigger weapons to destroy each other and the book concludes with the question, "Who will drop their weapon first?"

Children Everywhere. [222] Interesting, informative book about children around the world and the way they live.

Fifty-seven Reasons Not to Have a Nuclear War. [223] Fifty-seven drawings that illustrate reasons for having peace rather than war.

The General. [224] While riding through the field, the general is thrown off of his horse and lands in the grass. For the first time he notices the wonders of nature. That night, he envisions his soldiers marching all over the beautiful flowers, and he puts an end to the army to save the earth and the world.

The Peace Book. [225] The story of a little boy who declares "I want to live" and sets out on a mission to declare the dangers of nuclear warheads. He meets with world leaders, unites children as well as adults, and devises an exchange program which brings peace to the world.

People. [226] Highly Illustrated book with the theme of individual uniqueness and respect for all people of the world.

Potatoes, Potatoes. [227] Two brothers in opposing armies meet at their mother's home with their troops. They are hungry and ask her for potatoes from her field, but she will not feed them until they promise to put down their weapons and stop fighting.

The Search for Delicious. [228] When the King's messenger conducts a search to determine the most delicious food in the kingdom, the results are chaos and the possibility of war. Children will learn that wars may start for reasons that are ridiculous.

Tistou of the Green Thumbs. [229] The message children receive after reading Tistou's story is to look at world problems in a new light.

Two Silly Kings. [230] Two kings decide to go into battle and in the process of preparing for the confrontation, forget why they are fighting. A young boy playing a flute changes the situation to a scene of joy.

Storytelling: Folktales

PURPOSE:

To focus on the role of perception in peacemaking after hearing the folktale, The Blind Men and the Elephant.

PREPARATION:

Materials
- Folktale, The Blind Men and the Elephant [231]

PROCEDURE:

When six blind men attempt to discover what an elephant is like, each person forms a different impression. The man who only touched the ear thought an elephant resembled a fan and the one who felt the trunk thought it must look like a snake. Memorize and recite the tale of The Blind Men and the Elephant, a classic from India.

Help the children realize that the ways people perceive things often influences the way they react or respond to a situation. People bring their own "experiences, needs, values and feelings" to the occurrence. [232]

Follow the story by asking questions like:

Do people in the approximately 170 countries of the world perceive each other differently?

Are decisions related to world peace based on partial or incomplete information, facts and details?

What can be done about it?

[202] Macy, Joanna Rogers. Despair and Personal Power in the Nuclear Age. Baltimore: New Society Publishers, 1983, 52-54.

[203] Office on Global Education for Church World Service [McFadden, Sandra L., Phyllis Vos Wezeman, Tom Hampson, and Loretta Whalen]. Make a World of Difference: Creative Activities for Global Learning. Baltimore: Office on Global Education, National Council of Churches, 1989, 103. Adapted with permission.

[204] Schuman, Jo Miles. Art From Many Hands: Multi-cultural Art Projects. Worcester, MA: Davis Publications, Inc. 1984.

[205] Wezeman, Phyllis Vos, and Jude Dennis Fournier. Counting the Days: Twenty-five Ways. Brea, CA: Educational Ministries, Inc. 1989, 9-10. Used with permission.

[206] Lewis, Richard, ed. Miracles: Poems by Children of the English-Speaking World. New York: Simon and Schuster, 1966.

[207] Lueder, Edward, and Primus St. John. Zero Makes Me Happy. New York: Lothrop, Lee and Shepard, 1976.

[208] Snyder, Ross. Young People and Their Culture. Nashville: Abingdon, 1969, 80-81.

[209] Ortegal, Adelaide. A Dancing People. West Lafayette, IN: The Center for Contemporary Celebration, 1976, 130.

[210] Ibid., 129.

[211] Ibid., 130. Adapted with permission.

[212] Surface, Mary Hall. Square Pegs, Round Holes. Washington: Mary Hall Surface, 1987. Available from: Mary Hall Surface, 229 Connecticut Avenue, N.W. #3706, Washington, DC 20008.

[213] Elder, Pamela, and Mary Ann Carr. Worldways: Bringing the World Into the Classroom. Menlo Park, CA: Addison-Wesley Publishing Co., 1987, 35.

[214] Office on Global Education for Church World Service [McFadden, Sandra L., Phyllis Vos Wezeman, Tom Hampson, and Loretta Whalen]. Make a World of Difference: Creative Activities for Global Learning.

Baltimore: Office on Global Education, National Council of Churches, 1989, 37. Adapted with permission.

[215] Sing of Life and Faith. Philadelphia: Pilgrim Press, 1969, 99.

[216] Weiss, Evelyn, ed. Children's Songs for a Friendly Planet. Burnsville, NC: World Around Songs, 1986, 98.

[217] Ibid., 52.

[218] Ibid., 86.

[219] Remember Me. Dick Young Productions for the United Nations, 1980. Available from: Church World Service, P.O. Box 968, Elkhart, IN 46515-0968.

[220] Condon, Camy, and James McGinnis. Helping Kids Care. St. Louis: Institute for Peace and Justice and Meyer Stone Books, 1988, 65-67. Adapted with permission.

[221] Seuss, Dr. The Butter Battle Book. New York: Random House, 1984.

[222] Harrison, David. Children Everywhere. Chicago: Rand McNally and Co., 1973.

[223] Asher, Marty. Fifty-seven Reasons Not to Have a Nuclear War. New York: Warner Books, 1984.

[224] Charters, Janet, and Michael Foreman. The General. New York: E.P. Dutton and Co., Inc., 1961.

[225] Benson, Bernard. The Peace Book. Toronto: Bantam Books, 1982.

[226] Spier, Peter. People. New York: Doubleday and Company, 1980.

[227] Lobel, Anita. Potatoes, Potatoes. New York: Harper and Row, 1967.

[228] Babbitt, N. The Search for Delicious. New York: Farrar, Straus and Giroux, 1969.

[229] Druon, Michael. Tistou of the Green Thumbs. New York: Charles Scribner's Sons, 1958.

[230] Phillips, L., and P. Phillips. Two Silly Kings. Austin, TX: The Steck Co., 1964.

[231] Leach, Maria. "The Blind Men and the Elephant." Noodles, Nitwits and Numskulls. Cleveland, OH: William Collins, 1961.

[232] Abrams, Grace Contrino Peace Education Foundation. Peace Pages. May 1988.

BIBLIOGRAPHY

General Resources

A Day in the Life of the Soviet Union. New York: Collins Publishers, Inc., 1987. Photo essay on life in the fifteen republics of the Soviet Union, taken on one day, by one hundred of the world's greatest photographers.

Berger, Gilda. Religion: A Reference First Book. New York: Franklin Watts, 1983. Alphabetical listing of the world's religions with information on each of them. Material is suitable for grades four through eight.

Blaufuss, Deloris, comp. Building a Foundation for Peace: Bibliography of Peace Books for Children and Young Adults. 2nd ed. Burlington, IA: Saint Luke United Church of Christ Peace Fellowship, 1986. Extensive annotated bibliography of books for children and youth that promote peace concepts. Titles are categorized according to reader age: lower elementary, upper elementary, middle school and high school.

Brenner, Avis. Helping Children Cope with Stress. Lexington, MA: Lexington Books, 1984. A book for professionals which identifies natural stresses of family life as well as the trauma caused by abuse, divorce, death, etc. and provides suggestions for helping children learn to cope.

Brooke, Joel Memorial Committee. First Steps to Peace: A Resource Guide. 2nd ed. New York: Fund for Peace, 1985. A thorough, sixty-three page, annotated list of introductory resources for people working for peace at the grass roots level. Includes information on pamphlets, books, media, speakers and groups.

Burton, M. Garlinda. "Peace From A Black Perspective." Church School Today. Winter 1987-88: 39-41. Interviews with black bishops of several denominations indicating that blacks, as well as other ethnic groups, need to commit to supporting peace and justice causes so that funds can be diverted from military spending to meeting human needs.

Channing L. Bete Company, Inc. About Peace. South Deerfield, MA: Channing L. Bete Company, 1973. Booklet emphasizing God's plan for peace and Christians' responsibility to seek and promote it in their own lives.

Channing L. Bete Company, Inc. About Social Justice. South Deerfield, MA: Channing L. Bete Company, 1986. Booklet containing information and ideas on ways in which people can promote social change. It emphasizes the Christian's mission to serve as Jesus served.

Church World Service. About World Hunger. South Deerfield, MA: Channing L. Bete Company, 1987. A fifteen page booklet containing information on hunger, myths associated with the issue, causes and actions that can be taken to produce short and long term solutions.

Cloud, Kate, et al. Watermelons Not War! A Support Book for Parenting in the Nuclear Age. Santa Cruz, CA: New Society Publishers, 1984. A book for parents who strive to pass on peace values to their children. Covers all aspects of the nuclear issue. One-hundred-fifty-seven pages with many resource listings.

"Curriculum Resources on Peace and Justice." Church School Today. Winter 1987-88: 46-47. Annotated list of resources on peacemaking for adults and children published by the United Methodist Church.

Donaghy, John, ed. To Proclaim Peace: Religious Communities Speak Out on the Arms Race. Nyack, NY: Fellowship Publications, 1983. A fifty-three page compilation of statements addressing issues of peace and disarmament by a broad range of religious groups in the United States.

Greiner, Rosemary. Peace Education: A Bibliography Focusing on Young Children. Santa Cruz, CA: Rosemary Greiner, 1984. Comprehensive bibliography based on six elements of peace education: self-concept, community, problem-solving, environment, multi-cultural and creative arts.

Hawkes, Glenn W. What About the Children? The Threat of Nuclear War and Our Responsibility to Preserve This Planet for Future Generations. Moretown, VT: Parents and Teachers for Social Responsibility, Inc., 1983. Information on the nuclear issue and suggestions on what to do about it with the purpose of stimulating global activity that will help young people to prevent nuclear war.

Hinton, Pat C. Images of Peace. Minneapolis: Winston Press, 1984. Forty personal devotions on peace with art, poems, stories and scripture passages.

Hodge, Sandy, and Mike Hodge. "What Is Peace?" Church School Today. Winter 1987-88: 26-28. Discussion of shalom, translated as "peace with justice," being God's vision of wholeness for the whole earth and its peoples.

Jampolsky, Gerald G., ed. Children As Teachers of Peace, By Our Children. Berkeley, CA: Celestial Arts, 1982. Collection of children's poems, drawings, stories and sayings which reveal their hopes and fears about peace, as well as their suggested solutions.

Justice/Peace Education Council. Infusion Curriculum Training Workshop. New York: Justice/Peace Education Council, 1981. Forty-six page handbook containing a model for incorporating peace and justice education into the existing curriculum. Contains a list of basic peace concepts and explains how to infuse them into classroom content.

Keyes, Ken, Jr. The Hundredth Monkey. Coors Bay, OR: Vision Books, 1982. Research on the Hundredth Monkey phenomenon on the island of Koshima is paralleled with the need for every human being to work to rid the world of nuclear war. The one-hundred-seventy-six pages contain statistics, research and information on nuclear war, as well as suggestions on working on and changing the basic "me vs. you" mentality of the population to a "me and you" attitude.

Lappe, Frances Moore, and Joseph Collins. World Hunger: Twelve Myths. San Francisco: Food First, Institute for Food and Development Policy, 1986. Answers for twelve myths commonly associated with hunger.

Larson, Jeanne, and Madge Micheels-Cyrus, eds. Seeds of Peace: A Catalogue of Quotations. Philadelphia: New Society Publishers, 1987. Twenty-nine chapters, five sections and sixteen-hundred quotes on peace.

Lehn, Cornelia. Peace Be With You. Newton, KS: Faith and Life Press, 1980. Collection of stories on the lives of many people who have pursued peace through the centuries.

Longacre, Doris Janzen. Living More with Less. Scottdale, PA: Herald Press, 1980. Practical suggestions in chapters on money, clothing, homes, home keeping, transportation, travel, celebrations, recreation, meetinghouses, eating together and strengthening each other.

Macy, Joanna Rogers. Despair and Personal Power in the Nuclear Age. Baltimore: New Society Publishers, 1983. A guide to despair and empowerment work related to the nuclear issue. Includes a chapter on helping children and youth deal with the threat.

Mc Cracken, Barbara. "Teaching Peace, Teaching Justice: An Educator's Guide. National Catholic Reporter. 23 Sept. 1988. Newspaper supplement containing annotations and ordering information on educational materials pertaining to peace and justice.

Mc Ginnis, Kathleen, and James Mc Ginnis. Parenting for Peace and Justice. Maryknoll, NY: Orbis Books, 1981. Christian perspective on parenting skills that promote peacemaking.

New Global Yellow Pages. New York: Global Perspectives in Education, 1986. Listing of organizations and projects stressing global education in schools.

Nuclear Information and Resource Service. Growing up in a Nuclear Age: A Resource Guide for Elementary School Teachers. Washington: Nuclear Information and Resource Service, 1983. Annotated list of resources on nuclear issues including books for teachers and students, organizations, audio visuals and classroom materials.

Peck, M. Scott. The Different Drum: Community Making and Peace. New York: Simon and Schuster, 1987. Discussion of the ways in which groups become communities.

Reardon, Betty A. Comprehensive Peace Education: Educating for Global Responsibility. Hagerstown, MD: Teachers College Press, 1988. Explanation of peace education: what it is now, has been and should be. Annotated bibliography.

Redding, Earl, and Helen Redding. "Resource Tools for Teaching Peace to Children. Quaker Life. July-August, 1982: 17. Resource suggestions to correspond to several points of Peachey's book, How To Teach Peace To Children.

Seitz, Kathryn F., ed. A Working Bibliography of Peace Resources for Children and Youth. Harrisonburg, VA: Education Department, Eastern Mennonite College, 1984. Resources for educators for teaching peace themes to children. Categories covered include books for various age levels, parent/teacher materials, media, games and catalogs.

Selim, M. A. Annotated Bibliography of Teaching Materials for Global Economics (Grades K-12). St. Paul, MN: College of St. Thomas, Center for Economic Education, 1983. Six sub-topics listing media, organizations, curricula, materials, bibliographies, newsletters and catalogs. Grade levels are indicated.

Sider, Ronald. Rich Christians in an Age of Hunger. New York: Paulist Press, 1976. Discussion of the problem of hunger and suggestions for a Christian response.

Simon, Arthur. Bread for the World. New York: Paulist Press, 1975. A classic introduction to world hunger by the founder of the organization, Bread for the World.

Sweeney, Duane, ed. The Peace Catalog. Seattle: Press for Peace, 1984. Two hundred eighty eight pages of articles and essays on nuclear war written by leading authors, scientists and statespersons. These contain information on the problem, suggested solutions and ideas for using personal power to effect change. The fourteen sections, with several articles in each of them, have themes ranging from U.S. prevention of nuclear war to military spending and non-violent action. A "Where Do We Go From Here" page follows each section and lists further reading and groups to contact. The rest of the book, seventy-seven pages, is a directory of national, local, regional and international peace groups. Resource listings, all geared to nuclear war issues, include books, directories, periodicals, media, film catalogs and resource centers.

Weiss, Evelyn. Peace Teaching and Children: Resources for Teachers and Parents, K-Grade 6. New York: The Riverside Church Disarmament Program, 1983. Annotated bibliography of resources and information on where to find them.

Wezeman, Phyllis Vos. Peace Is Possible: Guidelines for a Community Peace Festival. Elkhart, IN: New Call to Peacemaking, 1987. Complete guidelines for planning, preparing and presenting a positive, creative community peace festival.

Wollman, Neil, ed. Working for Peace: A Handbook of Practical Psychology and Other Tools. San Luis Obispo, CA: Impact Publishers, 1985. Thirty-five chapters written by psychologists and educators, with practical, yet professional, suggestions for peace workers and peace groups. Contains six especially helpful chapters: "Adding Peace to the Curriculum" (21), by Linden Nelson, "The Arts in Peacemaking" (29), by Ingrid Rogers, "Music as an Instrument of Peace" (30), by Marianne Philbin, "Teaching Peace Through Drama" (31), by Lauren Friesen, "Creative Arts Projects and Organizations" (32), by Marianne Philbin, and "Humor for Peace" (33),

by Gary A. Zimmerman.

World Resource Institute and International Institute for Environment and Development. World Resources. New York: Basic Books, Inc., 1988-89. Statistics and information on various countries of the world.

Activities/Curricula

Abrams, Grace, and Fran Schmidt. Learning Peace. Philadelphia: Jane Addams Peace Association, 1972. Early work of Abrams and Schmidt, leaders in educational materials on non-violent conflict resolution for children.

Abrams, Grace, and Fran Schmidt. Peace Is In Our Hands. Philadelphia: Jane Addams Peace Association, 1974. Out of print resource containing information and ideas to help children learn non-violent methods of resolving conflict. Material has been updated and implemented into new resources from the Grace Contrino Abrams Peace Education Foundation.

Abrams, Grace Contrino Peace Education Foundation. Peace Pages. May 1988. A four page newsletter filled with activities and ideas for use in classrooms.

Beem, Cecile. "Workshop for Peace." Church School Today. Winter 1987-88: 42-45. Model for a workshop to help people understand that peace and justice are interconnected in God's plan, and to address personal, interpersonal and societal actions that can and should be taken to achieve them.

Berman, Shelly. Perspectives: A Teaching Guide. New York: Educators for Social Responsibility, 1983. A wide range of peacemaking themes for use with students in grades K-12 with suggestions, activities, resource lists and bibliographies.

Boss-Koopman, Gayle, Steven D. Hoogerwerf, and Robert A. White. Christ is Our Peace: Biblical Foundations for Peacemaking. Lansing, IL: Reformed Church Press, 1982. Adult study material written to help Christians discover and deepen their understanding of God's plan for peace and the biblical resources for peacemaking. The six chapters contain commentary, reflection questions and application exercises.

Buland, Donna Miller. "Living The Good News of God's Peace." New York: Presbyterian Peacemaking Program, 1987. Packet of children's materials to use in conjunction with the annual offering for peacemaking. Includes four short stories, art ideas and a daily calendar of scripture suggestions for a year.

Camp Fire. A Gift of Peace. Kansas City, MO: Camp Fire, Inc., 1985. Camp Fire program containing twenty-six activities designed to teach first through sixth graders about peace.

Camp Fire. In Pursuit of Peace. Kansas City, MO: Camp Fire, Inc., 1985. Camp Fire program exploring five topics from self peace to world peace in twenty-nine activities.

Carlsson-Paige, Nancy, and Diane E. Levin. Helping Young Children Understand Peace, War, and the Nuclear Threat. Washington: National Association for the Education of Young Children, 1985. Fifty-page resource to help parents and teachers address the issue of helping young children resolve conflicts in non-violent ways.

Channing L. Bete Company, Inc. About World Hunger: A Coloring and Activities Book. South Deerfield, MA: Channing L. Bete Company, 1986. Coloring and activity book to help elementary school children learn about and address the hunger issue.

Channing L. Bete Company, Inc. Let's Learn About World Hunger: An Information & Activities Book. South Deerfield, MA: Channing L. Bete Company, 1986. Activity book for pre-teens to explain world hunger and to encourage action to address the issue.

Children's Defense Fund. In Celebration of Children: An Interfaith Religious Action Kit. Washington: Children's Defense Fund, n.d. Celebration is the theme of the seven sections and many chapters of this book which covers children's sabbath, Sunday school, family, holidays, youth, children's activities and resources.

Church World Service/Office on Global Education with Center for Teaching International Relations, University of Denver. World Food Day Curriculum, K-3. Baltimore: Office on Global Education, 1986. One-hour session on world hunger for K-3 students.

Church World Service/Office on Global Education with Center for Teaching International Relations, University of Denver. World Food Day Curriculum, 4-7. Baltimore: Office on Global Education, 1986. Lesson plans for grades 4-7 on hunger themes.

Church World Service/Office on Global Education with Center for Teaching International Relations, University of Denver. World Food Day Curriculum, 8-12. Baltimore: Office on Global Education, 1986. Curriculum for introducing grades 8-12 to world hunger issues.

Cole, Ann, et al. Children Are Children Are Children: An Activity Approach to Exploring Brazil, France, Iran, Japan, Nigeria and the U.S.S.R.. Boston: Little, Brown & Co., 1978. Over two hundred pages of activities and experiences to help children explore life in the six countries listed in the title. Topics include customs, festivals, arts, crafts, foods, sports, toys, clothing and much more.

Crary, Elizabeth. Kids Can Cooperate: A Practical Guide for Teaching Problem Solving. Seattle: Parenting Press, 1985. Resource and activities for teaching children a five step program of conflict resolution and problem solving.

Crouch, Timothy J., and Ralph E. Dessem. The Hunger Workbook. Lima, OH: C.S.S. Publishing, 1977. One hundred ideas for presenting problems of world hunger.

Damonte, Roy. "Advocating Peace Through the Sunday School." Church School Today. Winter, 1987-88: 31-33. Information on the peace advocates program in a congregation in California. Suggests networking with peace groups in the community, holding a festival, buying books for the library and inviting speakers from other countries.

Date, Barbara, Boyd Lien, and George Parsons. A Vision of the Caring Community. Eugene, OR: Date, Lien & Parsons, 1982. Vacation Church School curriculum for grades one through six stressing helpfulness, caring and cooperation.

Dixon, Dorothy Arnett. Teaching Children to Care: 80 Circle Time Activities for Primary Grades. Mystic, CT: Twenty- Third Publications, 1981. Eighty lesson plans designed to foster self-esteem, develop empathy and promote caring behavior in pre-school and primary children.

Dorn, Lois, and Penni Eldredge-Martin. Peace In The Family: A Workbook of Ideas and Actions. New York: Pantheon Books, 1983. Book to help parents and children relate happily with a realistic approach to family living. The resource emphasizes interrelatedness and stresses affirmation, communication, patience, love and acceptance. Part Two moves from ideas to actions and exercises.

Drum, Jan, and George Otero. "Teachable Moments." Muscatine, IA: The Stanley Foundation, Dec. 1987. Monthly newsletter which gives suggestions for incorporating global awareness themes into ordinary classroom activities.

Drew, Naomi. Learning the Skills of Peacemaking: An Activity Guide for Elementary-Age Children on Communicating. Cooperating. Resolving Conflict. Rolling Hills Estates: Jalmar Press, 1987. Resource for teachers and students, grades one through six, on self-esteem, communication skills, conflict resolution and multi-cultural themes.

Dwyer, Paulinus, and Carole MacKenthun. Peace: A Christian Activity Book with Reproducible Pages. Carthage, IL: Shining Star Publications, 1986. An activity book containing work sheets, games, songs, puzzles and a prayer service to motivate children to learn about "the God of peace, peace brought to the world by others, and the peace experienced in their daily lives."

Ecumenical Task Force on Christian Education for World Peace. Try This: Family Adventures Toward Shalom. Nashville: Discipleship Resources, 1979. Joint project of several denominations to help people of all ages understand the biblical vision of shalom, value all people, use conflict creatively, participate in creative change of institutions and systems, care for and share world resources and choose to live joyously toward the shalom vision.

Eisenhart, Elizabeth. Peace: The Good News: Grades 3-6. n.p.: Church of the Brethren Peace and Service Committee, n.d. Thirteen lesson plans on peace themes and Brethren peacemakers for use in Sunday School.

Elder, Pamela, and Mary Ann Carr. Worldways: Bringing the World Into the Classroom. Menlo Park, CA: Addison-Wesley Publishing Co., 1987. Rich two-hundred-fifty-one page resource for incorporating global education into all curriculum areas for grades four through nine. Seventy-six activities, many focusing on the arts, reproducible masters, extensive annotated bibliography in numerous categories and appendix of reference materials.

Fellers, Pat. Peace-ing It Together: Peace and Justice

Activities for Youth. Minneapolis: Winston Press, 1984. Worksheets and activities for peace education.

Fletcher, Ruth. Teaching Peace: Skills For Living In A Global Society. San Francisco: Harper and Row, 1986. Fifty-seven lessons on the broad themes of conflict management and non-violence, cooperation, whole earth system, and peace and the threat of nuclear war.

Friesen, Delores Histand. Living More With Less: Study/Action Guide. Scottdale, PA: Herald Press, 1981. Study guide offering projects, questions, goals and resources for the fifteen chapters in the book Living More With Less.

Fry-Miller, Kathleen, and Judith Myers-Walls. Young Peacemakers Project Book. Elgin, IL: Brethren Press, 1988. Projects designed to help children understand issues related to peace, to build their self-esteem, to promote creation and cooperation as fun, and to introduce the language, concepts and characters of peace.

Fry-Miller, Kathleen, Judith Myers-Walls, and Janet Domer-Shank. Peace Works: Young Peacemakers Project Book II. Elgin, IL: Brethren Press, 1989. Instructions for a variety of projects that promote peace and concern for the environment.

Gerrard, Pat, and Tany Alexander. One World on Your Doorstep: Planners' Handbook for One World Week and Other Events. London: One World Week, 1986. Handbook of information and activities for churches and communities aimed at promoting an awareness of the interdependence of the world's people and the factors which create and sustain injustice. Specific material, "Listen for a Change," for celebrating One World Week in 1986.

Haessly, Jacqueline. Peacemaking: Family Activities for Justice and Peace. New York: Paulist Press, 1980. Book which provides families with information and activities to consider the call to peacemaking in the family as well as in the broader family of God, the world.

Halverson, Delia. "A Festival of Friends." Church School Teacher. Winter 1987-88: 34-36. Information on a three day program, "Festival of Friends," in which children learned about four ethnic groups represented in the United States: Hispanic, Asian, Black and Native American.

Hammatt-Kavaloski, Jane, and Maureen Golombowski. Becoming Peacemakers: Peace Education Curriculum Pre-school to Grade 5.

221

Madison, WI: Madison Metropolitan School District, 1985. Four part, fifty-six page, curriculum to engage children in a study of the concept of peace, the themes of peacemaking, the skills of non-violence and to involve them in actions that promote peacemaking.

Hasbrouck, Ellen. "Teaching Peace" Instructor. November/December 1988: 108. Six suggestions for incorporating peace themes into the classroom during the holiday season.

Heckman, Shirley J. Peace Is Possible: A Study/Action Process Guide on Peacemaking. New York: United Church Press, 1982. Eight sessions, aimed at adults or older youth, which focus on the nuclear issue. Uses awareness-analysis-action- reflection method and "activities" are readings or reflections on the topic or projects in which to get involved after the study.

Hodge, Sandy. "Learning Centers on Peacemaking." Church School Today. Winter 1987-88: 29-30. Description of learning centers on peacemaking set up as a summer Sunday school program. The centers were: Make a Mobile, Listen and Sing, Weapons of Jesus, Peacemakers Mural, Building the House of Peace, Make a Computer, and Heroes and Heroines of Peace.

Hope, Dorothy. Family Ideas for Building Hope and Peace. Melbourne, Australia: Joint Board of Christian Education, 1986. Collection of activities under the themes following the Prince of Peace, and peacemaking in our family.

Hopkins, Susan, Jeff Winters, and Laurie Winters, eds. Learning to be Peaceful Together to Build a Better World. Fullerton, CA: Concerned Educators Allied for a Safe Environment, n.d. Handbook of peace education philosophy and curriculum for teachers of young children. Themes include self awareness, awareness of others, peaceful conflict resolution, global awareness, celebrations of peace, and resources. Lesson charts for introducing preschoolers to several countries of the world.

Judson, Stephanie, ed. A Manual on Nonviolence and Children. Philadelphia: New Society Publishers, 1984. Classic collection of educational philosophy, teaching suggestions and cooperative games.

King, Edith W. The World: Context for Teaching in the Elementary School. Dubuque, IA: William C. Brown, 1971. Resource for teaching a global perspective through art and music and for introducing global themes into other subject areas.

Kochtitzky, Bob, et al. The Alternatives Celebration Catalog. Bloomington, IN: Alternatives, 1978. Wealth of information on alternative celebrations that promote a more simple lifestyle and responsible stewardship of God's gifts.

Kownacki, Mary Lou, and Carol Clark. Let Peace Begin With Me: Teacher Manual. Chicago: International Catholic Movement for Peace, n.d. Curriculum developed for use in Catholic schools to educate for peace.

Kriedler, William. Creative Conflict Resolution. Glenview, IL: Scott, Foresman and Company, 1984. Over two hundred activities for use with K-6 to resolve conflict in the classroom.

Leegan-Hillenbrand, Pat. "Youth Activity Calendar." New York: National Week for Peace with Justice, 1986. Suggestions for four grade levels to use during Peace with Justice Week.

Lersch, Phil, Jean Lersch, and Bonnie Munson. Hunger Activities for Children. St. Petersburg, FL: Brethren House, 1978. Active activities to raise children's awareness of hunger issues. One-hundred-twenty-one pages of ideas and plans for addressing many concepts.

Lersch, Phil, Jean Lersch, and Bonnie Munson. Peacemaking Activities for Children. St. Petersburg, FL: Brethren House, 1982. Twenty-eight pages of learning activities on peacemaking covered in four themes: input, reinforcement, expression and crafts.

Longacre, Paul. Fund-Raising Projects with a World Hunger Emphasis. Scottdale, PA: Herald Press, 1980. Twenty-one projects to raise money for hunger programs and organizations.

Mardock, Joyce. "Teaching Peace to Children." Quaker Life. July-August, 1982: 16. Mission education, which has been taught to children for years, is peace education. Young people need to learn about other cultures. Finding things in common will help them accept the differences.

McCabe, Ellen. Let It Begin With Me. Lancaster, PA: Highland Presbyterian Church, 1987. Lessons and hands-on activities focusing on world, national and community hunger.

McGinnis, James, and Kathleen McGinnis. Christian Parenting for Peace & Justice: Program Guide. Nashville: Discipleship Resources, n.d. Seven sessions, designed for parents and adults, on the biblical vision of shalom.

McGinnis, James, and Kathleen McGinnis. Educating for Peace and Justice: National Dimensions. St. Louis: Institute for Peace and Justice, 1985.

Complete teaching manual covering nonviolent conflict resolution and ten other themes, including ageism, handicapism, racism and sexism.

McGinnis, James, and Kathleen McGinnis. Educating for Peace and Justice: Global Dimensions. St. Louis: Institute for Peace and Justice, 1984. Resource for teachers on hunger, foreign policy, military, war, global poverty and other topics plus resource sections.

McGinnis, James, and Kathleen McGinnis. Educating for Peace and Justice: Religious Dimensions. St. Louis: Institute for Peace and Justice, 1985. Educational manual with lesson material on peacemakers, prophets, justice, peace and service programs.

Miller, JoAnn. Peacemaking for Children. Nashville: Graded Press, 1986. Lesson material on peacemaking for three grade levels: ages three to six, six to eight and eight to twelve, with an additional section on learning centers.

Milne, Teddy. Peace Porridge One: Kids As Peacemakers. Northampton, MA: Pittenbruach Press, 1987. Two-hundred- ninety-one pages filled with activities to help children catch the excitement of working for peace. Major sections include First Steps, Things to Do, Thoughts and Projects, and Resources and Groups.

Milne, Teddy. Peace Porridge Two: Russia, to Begin With. Northampton, MA: Pittenbrauch Press, 1987. A book dealing with activities and attitudes related to the Soviet Union. Contents of the one-hundred-ninety-five page volume deal with what American visitors say, other contacts, easy language lessons and resources and groups.

Milwaukee Peace Education Resource Center. "Peacemaking for Children." Milwaukee Peace Education Resource Center Newsletter. Winter, 1986. Four page newsletter with peacemaking articles and activities for children.

Minnesota Peace Child. The Peace Child Doll: Activity Book for Children and Parents. Minneapolis: Minnesota Peace Child, 1985. Simple activities and familiar projects for use by an individual child, several children, families and groups in connection with or separate from the Peace Child doll. Includes a one page bibliography of children's books.

Mueller, Jeanne, and Judy Wood. Called to be Peacemakers. Hinton, WV: First Presbyterian Church, 1985. Five session Vacation Bible School program, including brief lesson plans and activity instructions, on the themes: getting to know you, peacemakers love, peacemakers share, peacemakers forgive and peace begins with me.

Munson-Benson, Tunie. Blessed Are The Peacemakers. Minneapolis: Augsburg, 1985. Two-part resource including a book of curricula material containing stories, games and drama for use with children, and a leader's guide for planning and presenting the lessons.

Neale, Judy. "Spreading the Good News of God's Peace." New York: Presbyterian Church (U.S.A.), 1988. Packet of activities and patterns for a corresponding banner to use in conjunction with the 1988 Presbyterian Offering for Peacemaking.

Obold, Ruth. Prepare for Peace: A Peace Study for Children. Part I: Grades 1-3. Newton, KS: Faith and Life Press, 1986. An eight session curriculum designed to incorporate a children's story, scripture and activities to illustrate and develop peace concepts.

Obold, Ruth. Prepare for Peace: A Peace Study for Children. Part II: Grades 4-6. Newton, KS: Faith and Life Press, 1986. For intermediate grades, eight sessions are provided which offer alternatives to hate, violence and war. A TV format is used in each of them, as well as a brief story, which is provided, and a few activities.

Obold, Ruth. Prepare for Peace: A Peace Study for Children. Part III: Grades 7-8. Newton, KS: Faith and Life Press, 1986. Curriculum emphasizing the nurturing of peacemaking skills through the methods of a peace journal, bulletin board of peace happenings, peacemakers to research and a story in each of the eight sessions.

Office of Social Witness/General Program Council, Division of Christian Discipleship. Children Making Peace: A Resource Packet. New York: Reformed Church Press, 1982. Peacemaking packet for teachers containing songs, liturgies, sermon topics, book and film suggestions, cooperative games and ideas for peacemaking at home.

Office on Global Education for Church World Service (McFadden, Sandra L., Phyllis Vos Wezeman, Tom Hampson, and Loretta Whalen). Make a World of Difference: Creative Activities for Global Learning. Baltimore: Office on Global Education, National Council of Churches, 1989. A hefty handbook of creative activities and approaches to involve people in exploring and experiencing hunger and global issues.

Park, Mary Joan. Creating a Peace Experience: Peace Camp Curriculum and Resources. Mount Rainier, MD: Little Friends for Peace, 1988. Guidelines for running a peace camp for children ages four to ten, complete with curriculum suggestions and games.

Park, Mary Joan. Peacemaking for Little Friends: Tips, Lessons and Resources for Parents and Teachers. Saint Paul, MN: Little Friends for Peace, 1985. Twelve lesson plans on themes such as hunger, conflict resolution and cooperation, with practical, usable ideas. Information in the beginning, ie., family meetings, is reprinted from other sources. Extensive bibliography, partially annotated, on resources, children's books, support groups and media.

Peachey, J. Lorne. How to Teach Peace to Children. Scottdale, PA: Herald Press, 1981. A resource for parents and families who want to build peacemaking lifestyles into their homes and communities. Twenty suggestions for teaching peace to children are developed.

Phillips, Patti. "Children Become Fully Involved in Themes of Peace and Peacemaking." Church Teachers. March-April-May, 1986: 135-137. Skeletal outlines for six centers, involving games, stories, projects and more, to help children understand that peace is more than the absence of war.

Pickering, Nancy. Sparklers, Too. Philadelphia: Friends General Conference, 1989. Pre-school curriculum which helps children explore themes of family, peacemaking, non-violent cooperation and natural world.

Pickering, Nancy, and Sally Farneth. Sparklers: Pre-school Curriculum. Philadelphia: Friends General Conference, 1982. Curriculum for young children which uses trade books and activities to help children understand Quaker peace themes.

Polon, Linda, and Aileen Contwell. The Whole Earth Holiday Book. Glenview, IL: Scott, Foresman & Co., 1983. Information on fifty world festivals with reproducible worksheets.

Presbyterian Church (U.S.A.) Division of Mission Promotion. "For Doing Peacemaking At Home." New York: Presbyterian Church (U.S.A.), n.d., n.p. Family peacemaking activities for four themes: learning to care, learning to resolve conflict, learning to make enemies into friends and learning to be stewards of God's earth.

Presbyterian Peacemaking Program. The Things That Make for Peace Begin with the Children. New York: Presbyterian Church (U.S.A.), n.d. Lesson material and activities on learning to care, to resolve conflicts, to make enemies into friends and to be stewards of God's earth.

Prutzman, Priscilla, et al. The Friendly Classroom for a Small Planet. Wayne, NJ: Avery Publishing, 1978. Suggestions for developing communication and conflict management skills in children. The handbook is the text of the Children's Creative Response to Conflict Program.

Schmidt, Fran, et al. Fight Fair: Dr. Martin Luther King, Jr. For Kids. Miami: Grace Contrino Abrams Peace Education Foundation, 1986. Book of information for teachers and activities and worksheets for students, poster and an eighteen minute video based on Martin Luther King, Jr.'s methods of non-violence and their application to everyday situations.

Schmidt, Fran, et al. Peacemaking Skills for Little Kids. Miami: Grace Contrino Abrams Peace Education Foundation, 1988. Resource kit, including book, poster, hand puppet and audio cassette, for use in kindergarten through third grade. The material is intended to heighten self esteem and introduce peacemaking skills.

Schmidt, Fran, and Alice Friedman. Creative Conflict Solving for Kids. Miami: Grace Contrino Abrams Peace Education Foundation, 1983. Kit for grades 4-8 using creative methods for resolving conflict.

Schmidt, Fran, and Alice Friedman. Fighting Fair For Families. Miami: Grace Contrino Abrams Peace Education Foundation, 1989. Resource and activity book to help families develop problem solving and conflict resolution skills.

Scott, O. J. "Community Peace Celebrations." Church School Today. Winter 1987-88: 37,38. Three models for celebrating peace in a community including a day of activities in a park, an event in the capitol building and a dance.

Sider, Ronald J., ed. Cry Justice: The Bible on Hunger and Poverty. New York: Paulist Press, 1980. A study guide on biblical texts pertaining to hunger, justice and the poor. Six sections cover many topics and include commentary, references and reflection questions.

Sprinkle, Patricia Houck. Hunger: Understanding the Crisis through Games, Dramas and Songs. Atlanta: John Knox Press, 1980. Games, skits and songs to help all ages consider hunger issues.

Activities explore biblical bases for hunger action, teach basic facts, evaluate personal lifestyles, simulate situations that cause hunger and help participants experience what it feels like to be hungry because of circumstances beyond a person's control.

Reardon, Betty A. Educating for Global Responsibility: Teacher Designed Curricula for Peace Education, K-12. Hagerstown, MD: Teachers College Press, 1988. Teacher resource containing effective methods and instructional material on peace themes.

Reford-McCandless International Institute and Canadian Institute of International Affairs with student and teacher participants. Introducing the World: A Guide to Developing International and Global Awareness Programs. Toronto: Reford-McCandless International Institute, 1985. Information on working with groups and activities for introducing global education activities to them.

Rogers, Fred, and Barbara Marsh. Peacemaking in the Family by Mister Rogers: Four Intergenerational Events for Your Church. New York: Presbyterian Peacemaking Program, n.d. Four outlines for congregational intergenerational events on the peacemaking themes of feelings, hard times, celebrations, and living in families and growing as individuals. Background information and a program design with activities are suggested for each topic.

Rogovin, Anne. Dear Parents: Letters to Parents of Young Children. Elizabethtown, PA: The Continental Press, Inc., 1981. Letters written by the author to parents of her pre- school students. Each suggests a way to spend time with a child. All encourage the development of self-esteem.

Rubin, Laurie. The Food First Curriculum. San Francisco: Institute for Food and Development Policy, 1984. Curriculum for fourth through sixth graders, but adaptable for other age groups, which addresses seven hunger themes and stresses positive change.

Shettel, Doris Lee. Life Style Change For Children (and Intergenerational Groups): Leaders Guide and Students Resource. New York: United Presbyterian Program Agency, 1981. Six lessons for children in grades three through six with an emphasis on adopting a personal and group lifestyle more faithful to the gospel.

Strain, Marie M., ed. Ideas for Celebration of Peace. Concord, MA: National Peace Day Celebrations,

1985. Ideas and activities for celebrating National Peace Day, the first Sunday in August. Emphasizes music and dances of the world.

Task Force on Christian Education for World Peace. Teaching Toward a Faithful Vision: Leader's Guide. Nashville: Discipleship Resources, 1979. Leader's guide for a seven week workshop to help participants strive to replace the injustice and violence in the world with God's shalom. Contains planning guide, complete lesson plans and several resource articles.

Task Force on Christian Education for World Peace. Teaching Toward a Faithful Vision: Participant's Manual. Nashville: Discipleship Resources, 1981. Participant's manual, worksheets and resources for a seven week study of shalom.

Van Horn, Harriette. Peace: The Good News: K-2nd Grade. n.p.: Southern Pennsylvania Church of the Brethren Peace and Service Committee, n.d. Sunday School lessons on the meaning of shalom and Brethren peacemakers.

Ward, Elaine M. All About Teaching Peace. Brea, CA: Educational Ministries, Inc., 1989. Suggestions on ways individuals and groups can be involved in peace concerns, as well as several stories to tell and summaries of children's books.

Wezeman, Phyllis Vos. "Let Your Light So Shine: A Martin Luther King, Jr. Commemoration through the Arts." Church Educator. Dec. 1989: 7,8. Suggestions for using the arts to help children explore the life and work of Dr. Martin Luther King, Jr.

Wezeman, Phyllis Vos, and Colleen Aalsburg Wiessner. Hunger and Hope. Grandville, MI: Reformed Church in America, 1988. Packet of information, resources and activities, including an intergenerational event and a puppet show, for a denominational hunger observance.

Wezeman, Phyllis Vos, and Colleen Aalsburg Wiessner. "Life from a Loaf." Church Educator. Sept. 1989: 11-14. Four week activity calendar based on the theme of bread, designed to engage people in a study of hunger issues and to empower them to take action to alleviate the problem.

Wezeman, Phyllis Vos, and Colleen Aalsburg Wiessner. "Ripples of Peace." Church Educator. June 1989: 3,4. Activities based on the ripple effect to help children experience peacemaking themes.

Wezeman, Phyllis Vos, and Colleen Aalsburg Wiessner. "Who Are the Captives? A Bible

Study and Activity Guide for Youth." Church Educator. July 1989: 17,18. Lessons and activities for youth based on the jubilee.

Wezeman, Phyllis Vos, and Colleen Aalsburg Wiessner. Youth and Family Guide: An Activity Calendar. New York: National Week for Peace with Justice, 1987. Family activity calendar written for four age groups, pre-school through senior high, for use during the National Week for Peace with Justice.

Wezeman, Phyllis Vos, and Jude Dennis Fournier. Connections, Choices and Commitments. Elkhart, IN: Church World Service, 1990. Retreat focusing on the theme of connectedness which helps young people make choices and commitments regarding the issue of hunger.

Wezeman, Phyllis Vos, and Jude Dennis Fournier. Counting the Days: Twenty-five Ways. Brea, CA: Educational Ministries, Inc. 1989. Twenty-five creative methods for counting the days from December 1-25, with twenty-five suggestions for using each one. Several of the ideas involve peacemaking themes.

Wilkinson, Anne. It's Not Fair: A Handbook on World Development for Youth Groups. London: Christian Aid, 1985. Handbook of creative arts activities to help youth explore global education themes.

World Studies Project. Learning for Change in World Society: Reflections, Activities and Resources. London: One World Trust, 1983. Information, learning activities and resources to increase global awareness.

Architecture

Eriksen, Aase, and Marjorie Wintermute. Students, Structures, Spaces — Activities in the Built Environment. Menlo Park, CA: Addison-Wesley Publishing Co., 1983. Teacher resource book that focuses on architecture in its broadest sense and the way these structures and spaces frame people's lives.

Hiller, Carl E. Caves to Cathedrals: Architecture of The World's Great Religions. Boston: Little, Brown and Company, 1974. One hundred fifty photographs illustrating how the beliefs of six major world religions have influenced their architectural structures.

Huntington, Lee Pennock. Simple Shelters. New York: Coward, McCann & Geoghegan, 1979. Black and white illustrations of shelters, tools and building techniques in many continents.

Art

Gallivan, Marion F. Fun For Kids: An Index to Children's Craft Books. Metuchen, NJ: Scarecrow Press, 1981. Reference including index of books by author, index by name of project and index by type of material.

Isserow, Susan. "The Posters Say It: 'Peace, Shalom, Sala'am'." Genesis 2. Dec./Jan. 1984/1985: 10. An article describing an art project and traveling exhibit in which children of Jewish and Arab descent in the Boston area imagined and drew pictures of peace between their two peoples.

Rogovin, Mark, Marie Burton, and Holly Highfill. Mural Manual: How to Paint Murals for the Classroom, Community Center, and Street Corner. Boston: Beacon Press, 1973. A complete guide to making murals that speak for a community and its social concerns. Excellent section on involving a classroom in a process and project. Techniques other than painting are discussed.

Schuman, Jo Miles. Art From Many Hands: Multi-cultural Art Projects. Worcester, MA: Davis Publications, Inc. 1984. Activities, photographs, instructions and resource suggestions on art from West Africa, the Middle East, Europe, Asia, Central and South America, the Caribbean Islands, the United States and Canada.

Talocci, Mauro. Guide to the Flags of the World. New York: William Morrow and Company, 1982. Reference, with full color illustrations, on flags of the world.

Zeaman, John. "Young sculptors excel in the art of winning." The Record. 28 Jun. 1987: E1+. Newspaper article about winners of the Cathedral of Saint John the Divine annual sculpture contest. The small animal figures will be added to the church's peace fountain and represent peace and freedom.

Banners/Textiles

Atwood, Cory. Banners for Beginners: A Step-By-Step Approach. Wilton, CT: Morehouse-Barlow, 1986. Color photographs, plus graphs, of banners for various themes. Step-by-step construction procedure.

Knuth, Jill. Banners: Without Words. San Jose, CA: Resource Publications, 1986. Numerous banner designs, with explanations, including several on peace themes.

Litherland, Janet. The Complete Banner Handbook. Colorado Springs: Meriwether Publishing, 1987. Reference and how-to book about banner design and construction.

Ortegel, Adelaide. Banners and Such. Saratoga, CA: Resource Publications, 1980. Book which emphasizes banners as celebration and explains many artistic methods for making them. It includes numerous illustrations and photographs.

Philbin, Marianne. The Ribbon: A Celebration of Life. Asheville, NC: Lark Books, 1985. Photographs and commentary about "The Ribbon," a unique banner which was wrapped around the Pentagon and other public buildings as a plea for peace.

Symbol Patterns: Ideas for Banners, Posters, Bulletin Boards. Minneapolis: Augsburg, 1981. Over thirty symbol patterns, with explanations and suggested banner designs.

Cartoons

Comic Relief: Drawings from the Cartoonists' Thanksgiving Day Hunger Project. New York: Henry Holt, 1986. Syndicated cartoonists' strips on hunger themes.

Munnik, Len. Nothing to Laugh About. New York: Pilgrim Press, 1983. Cartoons on nuclear issues.

Rifos, Leonard. Food First Comic. San Francisco: Food First, 1982. Comic book for upper elementary students explaining causes and solutions for hunger.

Clown/Mime

Brown, Margie. The Good News Caravan. Dayton, OH: Clownibrations, 1979. Scripts of Bible stories specifically adapted for use with clown troupes.

Hamblin, Kay. Mime: A Playbook of Silent Fantasy. New York: Doubleday, 1978. Basic information on the art of mime.

Kipnis, Claude. The Mime Book. New York: Harper & Row, 1974. Classic how-to book on the art of mime.

Litherland, Janet. The Clown Ministry Handbook. Downers Grove, IL: Meriwether Publishing, 1982. Fundamentals of clowning plus details on how to organize a clown troupe for in-church and outreach ministry.

Perrone, Stephen P., and James P. Spata. Send In His Clowns. Colorado Springs: Meriwether Publishing, 1985. Complete workshop manual for training clown ministers.

Robertson, Everett, ed. The Ministry of Clowning. Nashville: Broadman Press, 1983. Basic book on Christian clown ministry.

Shaffer, Floyd. If I Were A Clown. Minneapolis: Augsburg, 1984. Nine chapters which relate the joy and celebration of clowning to every day experiences. Basic how-to clowning information is included.

Shaffer, Floyd and Penne Sewall. Clown Ministry. Loveland, CO: Group, 1984. A how-to manual on clown ministry and skits for service and worship.

Creative Writing

Lewis, Richard, ed. Miracles: Poems by Children of the English-Speaking World. New York: Simon and Schuster, 1966. Poems written by children from around the world.

Lueder, Edward, and Primus St. John. Zero Makes Me Happy. New York: Lothrop, Lee and Shepard, 1976. Poetry representing various ethnic and cultural backgrounds with color graphics.

Mothers Embracing Nuclear Disarmament. Reflections on War and Peace...Children Speak Out. La Jolla, CA: Mothers Embracing Nuclear Disarmament (MEND), 1988. An anthology of children's art and essays on the theme, "When you think of war and peace, what do you see?"

People of St. Vincent de Paul Parish. Peace Poem Anthology. Elkhart, IN: St. Vincent de Paul Parish, 1989. Anthology of peace poetry done by parish members as part of a month of peace and justice activities.

Silverstein, Shel. Where the Sidewalk Ends. New York: Harper and Row, 1974. Popular collection of poetry for children. "The Generals" and "Hug of War" especially promote peacemaking.

Snyder, Ross. Young People and Their Culture. Nashville: Abingdon, 1969. Excellent information on Haiku poetry.

Sutherland, Zena, and May Hill Arbuthnot. "Poetry." Children and Books. 7th ed. Glenview, IL: Scott, Foresman, 1986. A children's literature textbook.

Wezeman, Phyllis Vos, ed. Peace is Possible: Poetry for Peace. South Bend, IN: United Religious Community, 1988. Selected creative writing entries from a community peace poetry contest.

Wezeman, Phyllis Vos. "Peacemaking Creatively...Through Poetry." Church Educator. Oct. 1989: 3+. Suggestions for using poetry as a peacemaking tool for children.

Wezeman, Phyllis Vos. "Peacemaking Creatively...Through Writing." Church Educator. Nov. 1989: 7-8. Creative writing ideas to involve children in peacemaking activities.

Culinary

Hillman, Howard. The Book of World Cuisines. New York: Penguin Books, 1979. Classroom resource on the foods of one-hundred countries.

Hunt, Linda, Marianne Frase, and Doris Liebert. Celebrate The Seasons: A Gardening Book For Children Ages 7 and Up. Scottdale, PA: Herald Press, 1983. Introduction to gardening for children with an emphasis on issues of ecology and world hunger. Includes gift suggestions and recipes.

Hunt, Linda, Marianne Frase, and Doris Liebert. Loaves and Fishes: A Love Your Neighbor Cookbook. Scottdale, PA: Herald Press, 1980. Cookbook for children which emphasizes eating one's fair share of healthful food in a world of limited resources. Includes over one hundred recipes.

Lappe', Frances Moore. Diet for a Small Planet. New York: Ballantine Books, 1984. Cookbook emphasizing conservation of earth's resources.

Longacre, Doris Janzen. More with Less Cookbook. Scottdale, PA: Herald Press, 1977. Classic cookbook which contains recipes and information promoting a more simple and healthy lifestyle.

Wezeman, Phyllis Vos. "Peacemaking Creatively...Through the Culinary Arts." Church Educator. Mar. 1990: 9-10. Ideas using foods to help children become more aware of the customs and cultures of people around the world.

Dance

Casey, Betty. International Folk Dancing U.S.A. New York: Doubleday and Company, 1981. Information on and directions for dances from twenty countries.

De Sola, Carla. Learning Through Dance. New York: Paulist Press, 1974. Information and directions for using dance in worship and education.

Ortegal, Adelaide. A Dancing People. West Lafayette, IN: The Center for Contemporary Celebration, 1976. Designed to highlight the use of dance as an expression of faith, the book includes information on the history of dance in religious contexts as well as steps and suggestions for its use in many settings.

Drama

DeFrange, Tim, and Tom DeFrange. Alice in Blunderland. Stow, OH: Legacy, Inc., 1983. A musical satire on nuclear issues which uses characters based on Alice in Wonderland.

Graczyk, Ed. Appleseed: A Play of Peace. New Orleans: Anchorage Press, 1971. An allegory of the story of Johnny Appleseed which presents the apple as a symbol of peace.

Grossman, Carlo. City at Peace. Fairfax, VA: Peace Child Foundation, 1989. A musical about bringing peace to a strife-ridden inner city community.

Hansen, Brian, and students at University of New Mexico. La Umada. Albuquerque: University of New Mexico Theatre Department, 1986. A play about a church confronted with providing sanctuary for a refugee from Guatemala.

Hubbard-Brown, Janet. The Heart of the Mountain. Moretown, VT: Parents and Teachers for Social Responsibility, Inc., 1988. The story of a group of children who determine to turn a bomb into an instrument of peace.

Hurst, Brenda, ed. Remembering: Stories of Peacemakers. Akron, PA: Mennonite Central Committee Peace Section, 1982. Sixty pages of stories, monologues and short plays compiled to commemorate the fortieth anniversary of the Mennonite Central Committee Peace Section. The collection is intended to help people remember how their forebears faithfully witnessed to the way of peace and non-resistance.

Kraus, Joanna Halpert. Kimchi Kid. Bethel, CT: New Plays, Inc., 1985. A play about an Asian child adopted into an American family and the understanding that takes place between them.

Marsh, Donald F. Live in Peace: A Musical Drama for Boys and Girls. Nashville: Graded Press, 1984. Kit containing a musical drama on living in peace, plus a record, four posters and a production guide.

Miller, Madge. OPQRS, ETC. New Orleans: Anchorage Press, 1984. Clever and non-violent resolution occurs when people see new ways of looking at themselves and the world.

Robertson, Everett, ed. Introduction to Church Drama. Nashville: Broadman Press, 1978. Basic resource on drama techniques and emphasis on application to religious use.

Rogers, Ingrid. Swords Into Plowshares: A Collection of Plays About Peace and Social Justice. Elgin IL: Brethren Press, 1983. An anthology of twenty-seven skits and one-act plays which come under the category of historical peacemakers or problems facing peacemakers today. Each play is followed by suggestions for discussion and activities related to the play's theme or focus.

Segal, Elizabeth. Peace Themes, Dreams and Schemes in Plays for Youth. Washington: Elizabeth Segal, 1989. An annotated bibliography of plays for young people with a broad range of peace themes.

Smith, Judy Gattis. Twenty Ways to Use Drama in Teaching the Bible. Nashville: Abingdon Press, 1981. Ideas for using drama techniques as tools for teaching religious education.

Surface, Mary Hall. Square Pegs, Round Holes. Washington: Mary Hall Surface, 1987. A play about two sides, the Rounds and the Squares, who believe they are right about everything and learn a new perspective.

Woollcombe, David. Earth Child. Fairfax, VA: Peace Child Foundation, 1990. One act musical to promote discussion of environmental issues and to promote the celebration of Earth Day.

Woollcombe, David. Peace Child. Fairfax, VA: Peace Child Foundation, 1981. A musical fantasy, set in the future, which recounts how children brought peace to the world.

Woollcombe, David, et al. Peace Child Study Guide. Fairfax, VA: Peace Child Foundation, 1987. Script, musical score, study guide, production and follow-up information for the musical fantasy, Peace Child.

Games

Animal Town Game Company. Animal Town Game Company Catalog. Santa Barbara, CA: Animal Town Game Co., 1989. Excellent resource for cooperative and non-competitive board games, outdoor and group playthings, games of the world, puzzles, discovery kits, children's books, books on parenting and cooperation, rubber stamp sets, tapes and more.

Fluegelman, Andrew, ed. More New Games and Playful Ideas from the New Games Foundation. San Francisco: The Headlands Press, Inc., 1981. Games for two, a dozen, two dozen and many more people.

Fluegelman, Andrew, ed. The New Games Book: Play Hard, Play Fair, Nobody Hurt. San Francisco: The Headlands Press, 1976. Sixty new games, together with many photographs, to encourage creativity and cooperation.

Grunfeld, Frederic V. Games of the World: How to Make Them, How to Play Them, How They Came to Be. Zurich, Switzerland: Swiss Committee for UNICEF, 1982. Information on one- hundred games from various parts of the world is contained in a book lavishly illustrated with photographs, drawings and diagrams. For each game there is a section on its history, directions on how to play it and instructions on how to make it.

Harbin, E. O. The New Fun Encyclopedia: 1 — Games. Ed. by Bob Sessoms. Nashville: Abingdon Press, 1983. Information for the recreational leader and a variety of games to use with groups.

Harbin, E. O. The New Fun Encyclopedia: 2 — Parties and Banquets. Ed. by Bob Sessoms. Nashville: Abingdon Press, 1984. Nearly three-hundred pages of ideas for banquets, parties, fellowships, seasonal celebrations and recipes.

Harbin, E. O. The New Fun Encyclopedia: 3 — Home and Family Fun. Ed. by Bob Sessoms. Nashville: Abingdon Press, 1984. Activities and games for family use.

Harbin, E. O. The New Fun Encyclopedia: 4 — Skits, Plays and Music. Ed. by Bob Sessoms. Nashville: Abingdon Press, 1984. Collection of dramas, stunts and skits together with musical activities, games and many songs.

Harbin, E. O. The New Fun Encyclopedia: 5 — Sports, and Outdoor Fun. Ed. by Bob Sessoms. Nashville: Abingdon Press, 1985. The book contains a section for the leader and chapters on novelty sports, camping, hiking, picnic and nature.

Harrison, Marta. For the Fun of It: Selected Cooperative Games for Children and Adults. Philadelphia: Non-violence and Children Friends Peace Committee, 1975. Ideas for using cooperative games and many suggestions from which to choose.

Orlick, Terry. The Second Cooperative Sports and Games Book: Challenge Without Competition. New York: Pantheon Books, 1978. Over two-hundred new non-competitive games for children and adults.

Orlick, Tom. The Cooperative Sports and Games Book. New York: Pantheon Books, 1978. Book with a wealth of activities emphasizing cooperative approaches to playing sports and games.

Weinstein, Matt, and Goodman, Joel. Play Fair: Everybody's Guide to Noncompetitive Play. San Luis Obispo, CA: Impact Publishers, 1980. An introduction to the area of play and chapters on cooperative games including mixers, energizers, mind games, leadership training games and endings.

Music

Bryan, Ashley, comp. <u>Walk Together Children: Black American Spirituals</u>. New York: Atheneum, 1974. Music and illustrations for traditional black spirituals.

Grammer, Red. <u>Teaching Peace</u>. Peekskill, NY: Smilin' Atcha, n.d. Cassette tape of the creative and catchy songs of Red Grammer, a folk singer who promotes peace.

Hawkes, Mary, and Paul Hamill, eds. <u>Sing to God: Songs and Hymns for Christian Education</u>. New York: United Church Press, 1984. Hymnal especially designed for children which contains sections on God's global family as well as peace and justice.

Huber, Jane Parker. <u>A Singing Faith</u>. Philadelphia: The Westminster Press, 1987. A volume of songs, based on familiar tunes, which stress inclusive language and peace and justice themes.

Huber, Jane Parker. <u>Joy In Singing</u>. Louisville, KY: The Joint Office of Worship, 1983. A booklet of hymns which center on themes of justice, liberation and peacemaking. Inclusive words are written to existing tunes.

Illinois Chapter United Church of Christ Fellowship in the Arts. <u>Songs of Hope and Peace</u>. New York: Pilgrim Press, 1988. Collection of peace and justice songs from a variety of sources.

Krehbiel, Jude, and Doug Krehbiel. <u>I Can Make Peace</u>. Scottdale, PA: Herald Press and Mennonite Central Committee, 1983. A tape of children's songs on peace themes.

Lenski, Lois, and Clyde Robert Bulla. <u>Sing for Peace</u>. Scottdale, PA: Herald Press, 1985. Ten songs in an illustrated booklet, which deal with peace from a child's perspective and encourage the theme of responsibility for self and others.

<u>National Anthems of the World</u>. New York: Sterling Publishing, 1985. One-hundred-seventy-two national anthems, with English translation and piano accompaniment.

<u>Sing of Life and Faith</u>. Philadelphia: Pilgrim Press, 1969. Children's songbook containing many selections on peace and justice themes.

<u>The United Methodist Hymnal</u>. Nashville: The United Methodist Publishing House, 1989. Revised version of the United Methodist Hymnal. It contains many songs on peace and justice themes which are listed in the topical index.

<u>Their Words, My Thoughts</u>. Oxford: Oxford University Press, 1981. Compilation of familiar and unfamiliar songs and hymns together with drawings, illustrations and poetry on the themes.

Weiss, Evelyn, ed. <u>Children's Songs for a Friendly Planet</u>. Burnsville, NC: World Around Songs, 1986. A collection of songs for children in kindergarten through sixth grade, with themes such as friendship, self-affirmation, resources, peoples, and peace heroes and heroines.

Wezeman, Phyllis Vos. "Peacemaking Creatively...Through Music." <u>Church Educator</u>. Sept. 1989: 3+. Ideas on using music to explore peacemaking themes with children.

Winter, Miriam Therese. <u>An Anthology of Scripture Songs</u>. Philadelphia: Medical Mission Sisters, 1982. A collection of biblically based songs, written by Miriam Therese Winter, which have themes of "justice and liberation, peace, compassion, mercy, healing, hope, love, longing, wholeness and an end to all the hungers of the heart."

Young, Carlton, comp. <u>Genesis Songbook</u>. Carol Stream, IL: Agape Publishers, 1973. Collection of songs with peace and justice emphasis.

Photography

Dowling, John. <u>War. Peace. Film Guide</u>. Chicago: World Without War Publications, 1980. An annotated resource of two-hundred-eighty-seven films, covering seventeen categories. The book is intended to be a guide for using media in classrooms and organizations, in film series and as a focal point in retreats and seminars. Includes detailed descriptions and ratings as well as an extensive list of distributors.

Le Baron, John, and Phillip Miller. <u>Portable Video: A Production Guide for Young People</u>. Englewood Cliffs, NJ: Prentice- Hall, 1982. Complete instructions for producing a video including information on the use of the equipment and techniques for filming.

Office of Religious Education. Create in Me: Media Resources for Peace and Justice. Ft. Wayne, IN: Diocese of Ft. Wayne/South Bend, 1984. An annotated bibliography of movies, filmstrips, slides, videos and records to help a religion teacher educate for peace. The divisions are: Foundations of Catholic Social Teaching, The Development of Catholic Social Teaching, Facing Contemporary Social Issues, Nuclear Issues, and The U.S. Bishop's Peace Pastoral.

Taylor, Neil, and Robin Richardson. Seeing and Perceiving: Films in a World of Change. Ipswich, Suffolk: Concord Films Council, 1977. Suggestions and resources for using film and video for global education.

Wezeman, Phyllis Vos. "Peacemaking Creatively...Through Photography." Church Educator. Feb. 1990: 5+. Tips on using various methods of photography to teach peacemaking.

Photography/Media

Bombs Will Make the Rainbow Break. Zahm-Hurwitz, 1983. Children's art work and narration are used to depict the confusion they feel over the issue of nuclear war. Available from: Films Incorporated, 5547 N. Ravenswood Ave., Chicago, IL 60640.

Buster and Me: Getting Active. KRON-TV, 1983. A puppet program which addresses children's fear and confusion about the threat of nuclear war. The point is made that the cost of the arms race means less money is available for education and school programs. The twenty-five minute video promotes action and discussion. Available from: Church World Service, P.O. Box 968, Elkhart, IN 46515-0968.

Charlie Cheddar's Choice. United Presbyterian Health, Education and Welfare Association, 1976. A thirteen minute filmstrip which shows Charlie the Mouse having a series of dreams which stimulate him to read, think, learn and take action on hunger issues. Available from: Church

World Service, P.O. Box 968, Elkhart, IN 46515-0968.

The Daisy. Bulgarian State Film Board, 1967. Peace in the neighborhood is disrupted when a man throws his trash over the fence and into his neighbor's yard. The neighbor retaliates. The scene is replayed with a flower being thrown over the fence instead and a totally different interaction occurs. Available from: BFA Educational Media, 2211 Michigan Ave., Santa Monica, CA 90404.

I Wonder Why. Robert Rosenthal, 1965. When a young black girl reflects on the experiences and emotions which are important to her, she includes many things common to all people. She then raises the question, "I Wonder Why Some People Don't Like Me?" This five minute film is a good tool for discussing personal peace and also for addressing the issue of prejudice. Available from: CRM/Mc Graw-Hill Films, 110- 15th St., Del Mar, CA 92014.

Once Upon a Rainy Day. Church World Service, 1981. When Wally the Water Wizard drops in, an adventure including riding on a cloud and journeying into the future begins for two children who learn the importance of water. Available from: Church World Service, P.O. Box 968, Elkhart, IN 46515-0968.

People Are Different And Alike. Coronet Films, n.d. A film to aid children in understanding that people are a family. This eleven minute film shows that people may be different races and colors and still be alike in many important ways. Available from: Mennonite Board of Congregational Ministries Audio Visual Library, Box 1245, Elkhart, IN 46515.

Remember Me. Dick Young Productions for the United Nations, 1980. Challenging portrayal of the ways in which the environment shapes the lives of several impoverished children in many countries of the world. Available from: Church World Service, P.O. Box 968, Elkhart, IN 46515-0968.

Walter Fish. Alba House Communications, 1976. The theme of the parable of the Good Samaritan is depicted in this filmstrip about a fish, stranded on the shore, who attempts to find someone to throw him back into the sea and save his life. The message suggests people's responsibility to help others help themselves. Available from: Church World Service, P.O. Box 968, Elkhart, IN 46515-0968.

Puppetry

Condon, Camy. Sticks and Stones and the Dragon. Albuquerque: Camy Condon, n.d. Script, finger puppet outlines, stick puppet patterns and ideas for a participatory puppet play about peacemaking.

Condon, Camy, and James McGinnis. Global Family Puppets. St. Louis: Institute for Peace and Justice, 1984. Skits and stories for using puppets for global education.

Condon, Camy, and James McGinnis. Helping Kids Care. St. Louis: Institute for Peace and Justice and Meyer Stone Books, 1988. Revised and combined versions of the Institute's resources, Global Family Puppets and Puppets for Peace.

Condon, Camy, and James McGinnis. Puppets for Peace. St. Louis: Institute for Peace and Justice, 1984. Plays and simple performances for puppets on various peace themes.

Condon, Camy, and Lynne Jennings. Try On My Shoe. Step Into Another Culture. Chula Vista, CA: Camy Condon and Lynne Jennings, 1981. Folktales, puppet patterns and cultural notes to introduce children to people of North America, East Africa, Mexico and Viet Nam.

Hunt, Tamara, and Nancy Renfro. Celebrate! Holidays. Puppets and Creative Drama. Austin, TX: Nancy Renfro Studios, 1987. Over two-hundred pages of ideas for making and using puppets for special days in every month of the year.

Hunt, Tamara, and Nancy Renfro. Puppetry In Early Childhood Education. Austin, TX: Nancy Renfro Studios, 1982. Wealth of information for teachers on incorporating puppetry into the classroom. Contains directions, patterns, poems and much more.

Wezeman, Phyllis Vos. "Giant Puppets." Church Educator. Aug. 1989: 9. Instructions for making giant parade puppets.

Storytelling

Austin, Mary C., and Esther C. Jenkins. Promoting World Understanding Through Literature. K-8. Littleton, CO: Libraries Unlimited, 1983. Annotated bibliographies of multi-ethnic books and suggestions for incorporating literature into the classroom.

Bauer, Caroline Feller. Handbook for Storytellers. Chicago: American Library Association, 1977. Thorough resource on storytelling techniques.

Bettelheim, Bruno. The Uses of Enchantment. New York: Alfred A. Knopf, 1975. A psychoanalytical interpretation of common fairy tales. Contains an exposition of the significance of these stories in the development of children as they struggle to find inner peace amid the existential realities of their world.

Careme, Maurice. The Peace. La Jolla, CA: Green Tiger Press, 1982. A short picture book about a child who draws a picture of war, declares he is peace and takes out an eraser to wipe away the army.

MacDonald, Margaret Read. The Storytellers' Sourcebook. A Subject. Title. and Motif Index to Folklore Collections for Children. Detroit: Newl-Schuman Publishers, 1982. Index of five-hundred-sixty-six folktale collections as well as numerous picture books, which give access by subject, ethnicity and more.

Martin, William. Enough Love to Go Around: Children's Sermons with a Peace Theme. Lansing, IL: Reformed Church Press, 1982. Ten children's sermons which illustrate the biblical values of Christian peacemaking through objects and images.

McCormick, Carol. In The Way of Peace: Stories of Vision and Action. Minneapolis: Carol McCormick, 1985. Collection of stories from various cultures compiled to provide people with new perspectives on challenges and with hope for the future.

Morrison, Dorothy, Roma Dehr, and Ronald M. Bazar. We Can Do It! A Peace Book for Kids of All Ages. Vancouver, BC: Namchi United Enterprises, 1985. A creative, informative, positive A,B,C book which helps adults talk with children about fears of war and hopes for peace. The book encourages children to believe that they are not powerless and that they can bring about change in the world.

Sawyer, Ruth. The Way of the Storyteller. 2nd ed. New York: Penguin Books, 1962. Classic book on basic storytelling techniques.

Sipson, Greta B., and Baxter Morrison. Fact, Fantasy and Folklore: Expanding Language Arts and Critical Thinking Skills. Carthage, IL: Good Apple, 1977. Lesson plans for using folk and fairy tales to expand higher level thinking skills.

White, William R. Speaking in Stories. Minneapolis: Augsburg, 1982. Storytelling information and stories with religious emphasis.

White, William R. Stories for Telling: A Treasury for Christian Storytellers. Minneapolis: Augsburg, 1986. Stories, including several on peace themes, for Christian storytellers.

Storytelling: Children's Books

Aliki. Feelings. New York: Greenwillow Books, 1984. Book to help children explore the various feelings all people experience.

Aliki. The Story of Johnny Appleseed. Englewood Cliffs, NJ: Prentice-Hall, Inc., 1963. Johnny Appleseed spread a message of peace wherever he went as he traveled around with a bag full of apple seeds on his back and a cooking pan on his head. Johnny's story serves to remind children to spread peace in many ways.

Ancona, George. I Feel. New York: E. P. Dutton, 1977. Many emotions are covered, pictures are included, and children are encouraged to talk about how they feel.

Anders, Rebecca. A Look at Prejudice and Understanding. Minneapolis: Lerner Publications Co., Inc., 1976. Photographs and text explore prejudice and its causes. The book serves to remind children that people who isolate themselves from other types of people are the "losers" since they are not open to new experiences and growth.

Anderson, LaVere. Quanah Parker: Indian Warrior for Peace. Champaign, IL: Garrard Publishing Co., 1970. A true account, based on the life of an Indian warrior who had an Indian father and a white mother. Contains the message that all people in a nation must unite for peace.

Asher, Marty. Fifty-seven Reasons Not to Have a Nuclear War. New York: Warner Books, 1984. Fifty-seven drawings that illustrate reasons for having peace rather than war.

Babbitt, N. The Search for Delicious. New York: Farrar, Straus and Giroux, 1969. When the King's messenger conducts a search to determine the most delicious food in the kingdom, the results are chaos and the possibility of war. Children will learn that wars may start for reasons that are ridiculous.

Benson, Bernard. The Peace Book. Toronto: Bantam Books, 1982. The story of a little boy who declares "I want to live" and sets out on a mission to expose the dangers of nuclear warheads. He meets with world leaders, unites children as well as adults and devises an exchange program which brings peace to the world.

Berry, Joy Wilt. Let's Talk about Fighting. Chicago: Children's Press, 1984. Conflict resolution is the theme of this book, which talks about the ways quarrels and fights begin, and explores alternatives to fighting.

Bunin, Catherine, and Sherry Bunin. Is That Your Sister? New York: Pantheon Books, 1976. Sensitive treatment of interracial adoption told by one of the adopted children. Emphasizes that parents and children do not have to be biologically related to be a genuine, caring family.

Charters, Janet, and Michael Foreman. The General. New York: E.P. Dutton and Co., Inc., 1961. While riding through the field, the general is thrown off of his horse and lands in the grass. For the first time he notices the wonders of nature. That night, he envisions his soldiers marching all over the beautiful flowers, and he puts an end to the army to save the earth and the world.

Clifton, Lucille. My Friend Jacob. New York: E. P. Dutton, 1980. Story of the friendship of Jacob and Sam serves as a reminder that although people may be different physically and mentally, everyone is special and needs acceptance.

Coerr, Eleanor. Sadako and the Thousand Paper Cranes. New York: Dell Publishing, 1977. Story of Sadako, a Japanese girl, who gets leukemia as a result of the bombing of Hiroshima, and her quest to fold a thousand paper cranes so she may make a wish to regain her health. After her death, her classmates finish folding the cranes to make a wish for world peace.

Cohen, Miriam. Liar, Liar, Pants on Fire. New York: Greenwillow Books, 1985. The new boy in first grade, Alex, was always bragging about something and his classmates continually called him a liar. A special discovery was made at the Christmas party.

Cowley, Joy. Duck in the Gun. New York: Doubleday, 1969. The army's plans to start a war were halted when they found a duck had built a nest in a gun. While waiting for the duck to leave, friendships between the opposing sides occurred and they could not fight each other.

Davis, Carl, and Dorothy Brandt Davis. The Tall Man. Elgin, IL: Brethren Press, 1963. Story of John Naas, called "the tall man," and his mission for peace.

De Paola, Tomie. Francis, the Poor Man of Assisi. New York: Holiday House, 1982. Written to celebrate the eight hundredth anniversary of St. Francis of Assisi, the book tells the story of a man who exchanged a life of wealth and luxury to serve the poor and needy for the cause of peace.

Druon, Michael. Tistou of the Green Thumbs. New York: Charles Scribner's Sons, 1958. "Look at world problems in a new light" is the message children receive from reading Tistou's story.

Freedman, Russell. Immigrant Kids. New York: E. P. Dutton, 1980. The theme of acceptance is addressed in a book about people, especially children, who have immigrated to the United States.

Fujikawa, Gyo. That's Not Fair. New York: Grosset and Dunlap, 1983. When four friends were playing together on a winter day, a snow ball fight started an argument. Although they all went home angry, they soon became lonely, and made up the next day.

Harrison, David. Children Everywhere. Chicago: Rand McNally and Co., 1973. Interesting, informative book about children around the world and the way they live.

Hill, Elizabeth. Evan's Corner. New York: Holt, Rinehart and Winston, 1967. Story of a small boy who discovers that a peacemaker cannot stay within his own room, but must help others in the world as well.

Johnson, Anna. Value of Friendship. La Jolla, CA: Value Communications, Inc., 1979. Emphasis is placed on friendship in the story of Jane Addams' work with the poor.

Kirkpatrick, Oliver. Naja, the Snake and Mangus, the Mongoose. Garden City, NY: Doubleday and Co., Inc., 1970. Jamaican folktale which parallels the biblical story of the lion lying down with the lamb. Although the snake and the mongoose thought they would like to fight each other, they discover instead that they like each other and that a special bond exists between them.

Ladd, Elizabeth. The Indians on the Bonnet. New York: William Morrow and Co., 1971. Accepting people from different races and cultures is a state-wide challenge. The story of a boy and his grandmother who befriend an Indian family, amidst opposition from the townspeople, will help children consider this theme.

Leaf, Munro. The Story of Ferdinand. New York: Ruffin, 1977. Popular story of a peace loving bull, who appears to be ferocious after being stung by a bee. Although he is chosen to fight, the story has a happy ending.

Lehn, Cornelia. The Sun and the Wind. Newton, KS: Faith and Life Press, 1983. Re-telling of an Aesop fable which exemplifies that love and non-violence are stronger than force and violence.

Lionni, Leo. The Alphabet Tree. New York: Pantheon, 1968. Words and sentences that bring hopeful messages are formed on this special tree with the help of two insect friends.

Lobel, Anita. Potatoes, Potatoes. New York: Harper and Row, 1967. Two brothers in opposing armies meet at their mother's home with their troops. They are hungry and ask her for potatoes from her field, but she will not feed them until they promise to put down their weapons and stop fighting.

McNeer, May, and Lynda Ward. Armed With Courage. Nashville: Abingdon Press, 1957. Short stories about seven people who spent their lives working for peace and justice. Biographies include: Florence Nightingale, Father Damien, George Washington Carver, Jane Addams, Wilfred Grenfell, Mahatma Gandhi and Albert Schweitzer.

Meriweather, Louise. Don't Ride the Bus on Monday. Englewood Cliffs, NJ: Prentice-Hall, 1973. Rosa Parks' courage and conviction is evident in the story of her refusal to give up her seat on the bus. Her non-violent protest sparked a campaign to end discrimination in the United States.

Moore, Joy Hofacker. Ted Studebaker: A Man Who Loved Peace. Scottdale, PA: Herald Press, 1987. Story of Ted Studebaker and how he spent his life working for peace.

Oppenheim, Joanne. On the Other Side of the River. New York: Franklin Watts, Inc., 1972. When the bridge that connected the east side and the west side of the small town of Wynlock-on-the-River collapsed, the people, who usually argued all the time, realized how much they needed each other.

Phillips, L., and P. Phillips. Two Silly Kings. Austin, TX: The Steck Co., 1964. Two kings decide to go into battle and in the process of preparing for the confrontation, forget why they are fighting. A young boy playing a flute changes the situation to a scene of joy.

Reyher, Becky. My Mother is the Most Beautiful Woman in the World. New York: Lothrop, Lee and Shepard Co., Inc., 1962. Adaptation of a Russian folktale which points out that inner beauty is more important than outer beauty.

Richards, Dorothy Fay. Marty Finds a Treasure. Chicago: The Dandelion House, 1982. Modern day story of the prejudice of a boy for the Mexican people forms an analogy to the New Testament story of the Good Samaritan.

Schindler, Regine. God's Creation - My World. Nashville: Abingdon, 1982. Book which affirms God as the Creator of the world and the one who gives us the ability to help and love others.

Seuss, Dr. The Butter Battle Book. New York: Random House, 1984. A disagreement over whether bread should be buttered on the top or on the bottom causes a war between the Yooks and the Zooks. They build bigger and bigger weapons to destroy each other and the book concludes with the question, "Who will drop their weapon first?"

Shles, Larry. Hugs and Shrugs: The Continuing Saga of a Tiny Owl Named Squib. Rolling Hills Estates, CA: Jalmar Press, 1987. Story of Squib, the owl, who feels something is missing and sets out to find it. He discovers that what is missing is found inside, inner peace, not outside in the world.

Simon, Norma. All Kinds of Families. Chicago: Albert Whitman and Co., 1976. Themes of love, trust and belonging are shown through a series of pictures on the topic of family.

Simon, Norma. Why Am I Different? Niles, IL: Albert Whitman and Co., 1976. Illustrated book covering the many ways in which children are different. Discussion suggestions are included.

Singer, Isaac Bashevis. Why Noah Chose the Dove. New York: Farrar, Straus and Giroux, 1974. Illustrations highlight this re-telling of the story of Noah and why the dove was chosen to be the bird of peace.

Smith, Robert Kimmel. The War with Grandpa. New York: Delacorte Press, 1984. Peter has to give up his room when his grandfather moves into his house, and he isn't happy about it. He declares "war" on grandfather and plays tricks on him until grandfather begins to play tricks on Peter. Peter realizes, not only that war isn't fun, but that grandfather is important to him.

Smith, Samantha. Samantha Smith: Journey to the Soviet Union. Boston: Little, Brown and Co., 1985. Samantha Smith was the schoolgirl who asked, "Why do the Russians want to blow us up?" and was then invited to visit the Soviet Union. This book, one-hundred-twenty-two pages, is filled with photographs and memories of her visit.

Spier, Peter. People. New York: Doubleday and Company, 1980. Highly illustrated book with the theme of individual uniqueness and respect for all people of the world.

Steig, William. Amos and Boris. New York: Farrar, Straus and Giroux, 1971. At first it seemed like they had nothing in common, however, Amos and Boris, a mouse and a whale, become best friends.

Testa, Fulvio. Wolf's Favor. New York: Dial Books for Young Readers, 1986. Cooperation is stressed in the story of a wolf who does a favor which is eventually returned to him.

Udry, Janice. Let's Be Enemies. Maurice Sendak, illus. New York: Harper and Row, 1961. Illustrated book about the conflict between two boys which results in them becoming "enemies," until they decide they have more fun as friends.

Walton, Darwin. What Color Are You? Chicago: Johnson Publishing Co., Inc., 1973. Despite differences in color, people are basically the same and have the same needs. This book explains this through words and pictures.

Wondriska, William. John John Twilliger. New York: Holt, Rinehart and Winston, 1966. John John Twilliger lived in Merryall, a town with a fort in the middle. The Machine Gun Man ran the town and did not want anyone to be happy or to have fun, that is, until he met John John. After that, the town was changed drastically.

Zolotow, Charlotte. <u>The Hating Book</u>. New York: Harper and Row, 1969. A little girl felt her friend hated her, and finally got up the courage to ask her the reason. They parted friends. Illustrates the importance of talking through a problem.

Zolotow, Charlotte. <u>The Quarreling Book</u>. New York: Harper and Row, 1963. The dog reverses a chain reaction of unhappiness that has been passed to each member of the family to one of happiness that is passed to everyone.

Storytelling: Folktales

Asbjornsen, Peter Christian. <u>The Three Billy Goats Gruff</u>. Retold by Paul Galdone. New York: Clarion Books, 1973. Norwegian folktale about the three goats and the troll, which can have a peaceful ending.

Brown, Marcia. <u>Stone Soup</u>. New York: MacMillan, 1947. Cooperation is the theme of this European folktale.

Grimm, Jakob Ludwig, and Wilhelm Grimm. <u>The Fisherman and His Wife</u>. Trans. Elizabeth Shub. Illus. Monika Laimgruber. New York: Greenwillow Books, 1978. Classic German tale which can help children focus on ways in which the greed of some may contribute to problems for others.

Leach, Maria. "The Blind Men and the Elephant." <u>Noodles, Nitwits and Numskulls</u>. Cleveland, OH: William Collins, 1961. A folktale from India which can help children realize that being aware of different perspectives is necessary for peacemaking.

Martignoni, Margaret E., ed. "Henny Penny." <u>The Illustrated Treasury of Children's Literature</u>. New York: Grosset and Dunlap, 1955. English folktale which stresses the importance of knowing who is leading.

McDermott, Gerald. <u>Anasi the Spider: A Tale from the Ashanti</u>. New York: Holt, Rinehart and Winston, 1972. An African tale which can help children discover that their own gifts and abilities are powerful tools for peacemaking.

Parkinson, Kathy. <u>The Turnip</u>. Niles, IL: Albert Whitman, 1986. Russian folktale which illustrates that everyone is needed when it comes to cooperating on problems.

Pratt, Davis, and Elsa Kula. "The Rabbit in the Moon." <u>Magic Animals of Japan</u>. Berkeley, CA: Parnassus Press, 1967. The sacrifice the rabbit is willing to make to feed the man in this Japanese folktale points to Christ's sacrifice for His people.

Spy, Deborah, ed. <u>Beauty and the Beast</u>. Illus. Michael Hague. New York: Holt, Rinehart and Winston, 1980. A story from France which reminds young people to look at the inner worth of a person rather than their outward appearance.

Wezeman, Phyllis Vos. "Peacemaking Creatively...Through Folk Tales." <u>Church Educator</u>. Jan. 1990: 5+. Learning activities involving folktales which will help children explore peace themes.

Visual Aids

Hug-A-Planet. XTC Products, Inc. 247 Rockingham Avenue, Larchmont, NY 10538. Soft, huggable globe of the world in various sizes.

Peter's Projection Map. Friendship Press, P.O. Box 37844, Cleveland, OH 45237. Most accurate portrayal of area, axes, position and people of the earth.

Scriptural Posters. Church World Service, P.O. Box 968, Elkhart, IN 46515-0968. Six posters, with black and white line drawings, on scripture passages related to justice themes. Study booklets are available for each poster.

The Whole Earth Ball. Pacific Drum Company, P.O. Box 4226, Bellingham, WA 98227. Large inflated replica of the earth.

Organizations

Abrams, Grace Contrino Peace Education Foundation, Inc. P.O. Box 191153, Miami Beach, FL 33119.

American Friends Service Committee. 1501 Cherry Street, Philadelphia, PA 19102. (215) 241-7177.

Bread For The World. 802 Rhode Island NE, Washington, DC 20018.

Center for Teaching International Relations (CTIR). University of Denver, Denver, CO 80208.

Children's Creative Response to Conflict. Box 271, Nyack, NY 10960.

Church World Service. P.O. Box 968, Elkhart, IN 46515. (219) 264-3102.

Clergy and Laity Concerned. 198 Broadway, Room 302, New York, NY 10038. (212) 964-6730.

Concerned Educators Allied for a Safe Environment. 17 Gerry Street, Cambridge, MA 02138.

Council on Interracial Books for Children. 1841 Broadway, New York, NY 10027.

Educators for Social Responsibility. 23 Garden Street, Cambridge, MA 02138. (617) 492-1764.

Evangelical Lutheran Church in America. 8765 W. Higgins Road, Chicago, IL 60631. (312) 380-2700.

Fellowship of Reconciliation. Box 271, Nyack, NY 10960. (914) 358-4601.

Global Education Associates. 552 Park Avenue, East Orange, NJ 07017.

Global Perspectives in Education, Inc. 218 E. 18th Street, New York, NY 10003.

Heifer Project International. P.O. Box 808, Little Rock, AK 72203.

Mennonite Central Committee. 21 South 12th Street, Akron, PA 17501.

Parenting for Peace and Justice Network. Institute for Peace and Justice, 4144 Lindell, #400, St. Louis, MO 63108.

Parents and Teachers for Social Responsibility, Inc. Box 517, Moretown, VT 05660. (802) 223-3409.

Presbyterian Church Peacemaking Program. 100 Witherspoon, Louisville, KY 40202. (502) 569-5000.

Riverside Church Disarmament Program. 490 Riverside Drive, New York, NY 10027. (212) 222-5900.

United Methodist Church Department of Peace. 777 UN Plaza, New York, NY 10017. (212) 682-3633.

United Nations U.S. Committee for UNICEF. 331 East 38th Street, New York, NY 10016.

Wilmington College Peace Resource Center. Pyle Center, Box 1183, Wilmington, OH 45177.